RESEARCH METHODS
IN PSYCHOPATHOLOGY

APPROACHES TO
BEHAVIOR PATHOLOGY SERIES
Brendan Maher—Series Editor

RESEARCH METHODS IN PSYCHOPATHOLOGY

**THEODORE MILLON
AND
HERMAN I. DIESENHAUS**

John Wiley & Sons, Inc.

New York · London · Sydney · Toronto

Library of Congress Catalogue Card Number: 75-172952

ISBN 0-471-60625-1 (cloth); ISBN 0-471-60626-X (paper)

Printed in the United States of America.

10 9 8 7 6 5 4 3 2 1

To the memory of our fathers
ABNER MILLON
JOSHUA DIESENHAUS
whose probing questions set
us on the road to research

SERIES PREFACE

Abnormal psychology may be studied in many different ways. One traditional method of approach emphasizes the description of clinical syndromes with an extensive use of case histories to illustrate the central phenomena and the psychological processes believed to underlie them. Another common position is found in the adoption of a systematic theory (such as psychodynamic or behavioral) as a framework within which important problems of abnormal psychology may be delineated and interpreted.

Whether systematic or eclectic, descriptive or interpretive, the teaching of a course in abnormal psychology faces certain difficult problems. Similar to other areas of science, abnormal psychology has exhibited a rapid increase in knowledge and in the rate at which new knowledge is being acquired. It is becoming more and more difficult for the college teacher to keep abreast of contemporary developments over as wide a range of subjects as abnormal psychology encompasses. Even in the areas of his personal interest and special competence the instructor may be hard pressed to cover significant concepts and findings with real comprehensiveness.

Adding to this spate of new knowledge is the fact that, in the field of abnormal psychology, we are witnessing a resurgence of enthusiasm for empirical research of an experimental kind together with a growth of interest in deviant behavior on the part of other scientists, notably the geneticists, neurobiologists, biochemists on the one hand and epidemiologists, anthropologists and social scientists on the other. It is less and less possible to claim mastery of a topic area in abnormal psychology when approaching it purely from the standpoint of a single psychological theory. An adequate understanding of any central topic now depends on familiarity with literature coming from many quarters of the scientific community.

Knowledge multiplies but time does not. Working within the limits of forty to fifty lecture hours available for the usual course in general abnormal psychology, it has become necessary for the student to turn more and more often to specialized outside reading to acquire the depth that cannot be given by any one textbook or by any one instructor. Although much can be gained by reading a range of selected reprints, these are often written originally for audiences other than the undergraduates and for purposes too narrowly technical to be entirely suited to instruction.

The present volume is one of a series developed to meet the need for depth of coverage in the central topic areas of abnormal psychology. The series is prepared with certain criteria in mind. Each volume has been planned to be scientifically authoritative, to be written with the clarity and directness necessary for the introductory student, but with a sophistication and timeliness of treatment that should render it of value to the advanced student and the fellow-specialist. Selection of the topics to be included in the series has been guided by a decision to concentrate on problem areas that are systematically and empirically important: in each case there are significant theoretical problems to be examined and a body of research literature to cast light on the several solutions that are adduced. Although it is anticipated that the student may read one or more of these volumes in addition to a standard text, the total series will cover the major part of a typical course in abnormal psychology and could well be used in place of a single text.

We are in a period of exciting growth and change in abnormal psychology. Concepts and hypotheses that have dominated the field for over half a century are giving place to new and provocative viewpoints. Much of this has been accomplished in one short decade: it is clear that the character of the field will be changed even more radically in the decades to come. It is the hope of the editor and the contributors to this series that they will play a useful part in preparing the coming generation of psychopathologists for the challenge of the years that lie ahead.

BRENDAN MAHER

PREFACE

When writing the preface for an earlier textbook, the senior author asked himself this question: Why, in view of the surfeit of publications in the field, do we need another volume? What contribution does this book offer that has not already been presented. An embarrassingly simple answer came to mind then; it again seems appropriate. In the vast and ever-burgeoning library of psychology, no textbook fills the need we set out to meet; specifically, no other book presents the logic, steps, and methods of research in psychopathology for the undergraduate and beginning graduate student.

The fact that the data of empirical clinical research are entering the undergraduate curriculum is most heartening; other volumes of this Wiley series illustrate the fruits of this direction. The present volume adds to this growing empirical orientation because it does not focus on the results of research but on the methods by which research can produce valid results. Of course, excellent works have been written on research methodology for the undergraduate, but invariably these focus on content areas such as learning, perception, and sensory processes; rarely are procedures, discussions, and illustrations presented in terms relevant to *abnormal* behavior. In no other field of undergraduate psychology are the techniques of research methodology and substantive content so isolated from one another. In this respect, an inexplicable and unfortunate schism has appeared in the literature; several books on clinical research methods have been written, but only with the professional or advanced graduate student in mind. As a result, the unparalleled growth of experimental psychopathology continues to be isolated from undergraduate programs. The beginning student, who is interested in abnormal behavior, is subjected to the fate of learning the logic and procedures of research on topics of only tangential or minimal relevance to clinical matters. Obviously, this state of affairs is lamentable. It is equally obvious that there is a need to provide a remedy; hence, this book has been written.

It is imperative that undergraduates and beginning graduate students be shown (before their interest in clinical research is extinguished) that effective studies on issues of genuine psychopathological significance is not only possible but that it may be the most challenging and exciting direction for a psychological career. We recognize that this brief volume only begins to acquaint the young student with these rich opportunities. Hopefully, however, it will inspire him to continue his studies.

When a book is the product of joint authorship, it is only proper to record, as clearly as possible, the particular responsibilities of each contributor. The first draft of the text was written by Theodore Millon as an extension of ideas first formulated in two other books, *Theories of Psychopathology* and *Modern Psychopathology*. Herman Diesenhaus assumed the task of strengthening and revising the initial draft so as to bring it more in line with the Wiley Series of which it is a part. The final product reflects a synthesis of our views, both substantive and stylistic.

Theodore Millon

Herman I. Diesenhaus

ACKNOWLEDGMENTS

Numerous improvements in the manuscript were suggested by Joseph Zubin, Brendan Maher, and Richard Suinn. We thank Luberta Shirley and Gwendolyn Spicer for their skill in decoding our tortuous and obscure scribblings. As ever, we are indebted to our wives, Renée and Judith, for facilitating our work. Our deep affection for our fathers is only partially conveyed by dedicating this book to their memory.

T. M.

H. I. D.

CONTENTS

CHAPTER ONE

INTRODUCTION

The primary objective of research in psychopathology is the discovery of new and verifiable data about maladaptive behavior. No less significant is its role in disproving erroneous past findings or refining and elaborating already established relationships. The ease with which so many promising theoretical ideas in psychopathology have been proved wrong is most disheartening. Even more distressing is the frequency with which trivial or false findings have been gathered by unimaginative or naive experimenters. All too many investigators fail to clarify their concepts and research hypotheses, collecting reams of data in futile hope that significant results will emerge spontaneously. Others select measures that are so imprecise as to detect only the grossest of differences among patients. Often, appropriate statistical designs and controls have been overlooked. Although fruitful research depends on the ingenuity of the investigator, his intuition must eventually be tested by rigors of proper scientific methodologies. It is our aim to bring together the substance of psychopathology with the rules of research so that these past errors need not be repeated.

This brief text will not present an uncompromising set of rules to which the student must adhere in doing research in psychopathology. Not only do space considerations preclude a presentation of such magnitude and detail but also no manual can provide a true picture of the informal and creative elements that comprise the research endeavor. Instead, an attempt will be made to outline some of the prime considerations in the planning, design, and analysis of psychopathology research so that the student can begin to temper his intuition with scientific rigor. Our chief objectives are to review alternative methods of productive investigation, describe the steps involved and their accomplishment, highlight a number of factors to increase their effectiveness, and present a sampling of data collection methods currently used in psychopathology research.

In this introductory chapter, we shall briefly define the terms "psychopathology" and "research," specify the aims of research, review the historical background and current status of research in psychopathology, and outline a number of problems that continue to face investigators in the field.

Psychopathology—An Attempt at Definition

Elsewhere (Millon, 1969), psychopathology has been defined succinctly as that "field of medicine and psychology concerned with the study of maladaptive behavior, its etiology, development, diagnosis, and therapy." The range of behaviors subsumed under this term is wide—from the undramatic, ordinary, yet immobilizing anxieties and conflicts, through the longer lasting, more pervasive, self-defeating behaviors, to the markedly disturbed, obviously incapacitating disorders.

The question, "What is psychopathology?" is answered quite differently by those who subscribe to different theories. These theories have not only grown out of different historical traditions and professional orientations but, more importantly, have also typically looked at different types of data for their concepts and research. Four *data levels* may be usefully differentiated; they are; (1) *biophysical* data, such as neurophysiological processes and anatomical defects, most frequently gathered in physical examinations and laboratory tests; (2) *intrapsychic* data, such as unconscious conflicts and defensive processes, usually inferred from therapy verbalizations, dream recollections, and projective tests; (3) *phenomenological* data, such as self-perceptions, feelings, and attitudes, expressed in and inferred from conversations, formal interviews, and personality inventories; and (4) *behavioral* data, such as the frequency of various forms of overt activity, typically recorded in systematic fashion by observers.

These four data levels allow investigators to analyze psychopathology from different frames of reference. Man facilitates his understanding of an intrinsically indivisible natural world by differentiating it, more or less arbitrarily, into conceptually discrete units; this enables him to focus his observations more sharply and to make his study of nature less unwieldy than it would be otherwise. Although one class of data may prove more useful for particular purposes than another, knowledge gained at each level should ultimately be translated into or coordinated with the others.

Since most theories of psychopathology have been framed within the conceptual boundaries of one or another class of data, we have no choice for the present but to pursue knowledge in a segmented fashion. However, as has been shown elsewhere (Millon 1967, 1969), approaching the field of psychopathology in terms of biophysical, intrapsychic, phenomenological, and behavioral data levels should facilitate the integration of research findings with comparably categorized theoretical and clinical materials; hence, the reason for organizing our discussion of data collection techniques in accord with these four data levels. Table 1.1 briefly summarizes not only the type of data collection techniques associated with each data level but also the theoretical orientation and major concepts associated with each.

TABLE 1.1: Relation of Four Data Levels to Theoretical Approaches

	Biophysical	*Intrapsychic*	*Phenomenological*	*Behavioral*
Basic Model	*Disease*	*Adaptation*	*Dissonance*	*Learning*
Definition of Pathology	Biological dysfunctions and dispositions	Unresolved conflicts, repressed anxieties	Self-discomfort	Maladaptive behavior
Types of Pathology	Traditional psychiatric disorders	Symptom disorders, character patterns	Impoverishment, disorganization	Numerable specific behavioral symptoms
Causes of Pathology	Heredity, constitution, defects	Instinct deprivation, childhood anxieties	Denied self-actualization	Deficient learning, maladaptive learning
Types of Concepts	Operational definitions, intervening variables	Hypothetical constructs, intervening variables	Hypothetical constructs, intervening variables	Intervening variables, operational definitions
Major Concepts	Genes, temperament constitution, defects	Instincts, ego, unconscious defense mechanisms	Self, self-regard, Eigenwelt	Conditioning, reinforcement, generalization
Data	Heredity, anatomy, physiology, biochemistry	Free association, memories, dreams, projective tests	Interviews, self-reports of conscious attitudes and feelings	Overt behavior observed and recorded objectively

Modified from Millon (1969)

Research—An Attempt at Definition

There are no simple or durable definitions of "research." The methods and tools of which it is composed are neither fixed nor immutable, but everchanging and fluid; as knowledge and technology evolves, so has the meaning and scope of research. Essentially, research is a process of inquiry that employs both informal and systematic methods of observation; its goal, broadly speaking, is to explore, describe, and confirm empirical relationships and scientific hypotheses. Not all inquiry is research. What distinguishes research from "common-sense" inquiry is that it is systematically related to an orderly body of knowledge, derives its impetus from that knowledge, and is executed in accord with certain "scientific" principles and procedures.

Scientific research need be neither quantitative nor restricted to the "classical" methods of experimental control and manipulation; the research of Charles Darwin was both qualitative and noncontrolled, yet produced the most important of scientific laws. Much of the work of scientific investigators may deal, then, with naturalistic phenomena that do not lend themselves to measurement and manipulation. Exploring "hunches," or merely describing ongoing natural processes and relationships, characterizes in large part the activities of scientific researchers. However, in contrast to the casual and unplanned inquiries of the "common man," the scientist has an established body of data and a methodological expertise to guide his observations.

DEVELOPMENT AND STATUS OF PSYCHOPATHOLOGY RESEARCH

Common use of research models, philosophies, and techniques took hold only slowly in psychopathology. The German psychiatrist Emil Kraepelin, known best for his signal achievement in designing an integrative system of psychiatric classification (nosology) based on regularities in onset, course, and outcome, was a strong early exponent of laboratory experimentation; as a former student of Wundt, the father of academic psychology, Kraepelin not only insisted that psychiatric theories be founded on careful observation and research but also invested much of his own energy testing his ideas in the laboratory. In 1892, the first facilities in this country for the experimental study of psychopathology were set up at McLean Hospital in Massachusetts. Although most of the work at the turn of the century could be faulted on numerous methodological grounds, the foundations of psychopathologic research had at least begun.

In 1910, the first systematic treatise in the field, *Leitfaden der Experimentellen Psychopathologie,* was published by the German psychiatrist, Gregor. Some years thereafter, comparable volumes were written in this country by Hamilton (1925) and Cameron (1935). By the beginning of World War II, research laboratories had been established throughout the world, albeit slowly and sparsely; the most notable of these were at the Boston Psychopathic Hospital, the New York State Psychiatric Institute, and the Worcester State Hospital in Massachusetts. Following the war, interest surged and well-endowed research facilities were founded at many clinics, hospitals, and medical schools; most important of these developments was the organization of the federally supported National Institute of Mental Health. The number of active research centers, books, and periodicals in the field has mushroomed in the past 15 years far beyond the expectation of even the most optimistic of forecasters. Much remains to be done, however, although the encouraging trend of recent years augurs well for the continued growth of empirically sound psychopathologic knowledge.

Although the history of research in psychopathology covers a period of no more than half a century, the advances in technical instrumental devices during this brief span has been most impressive. Complex data can be recorded, synchronized, and analyzed with amazing speed and accuracy with the new digital computers; relationships among thought, behavior, physiology, and biochemistry can be obtained through simultaneous measures; cerebral self-stimulation, programmed conditioning-therapy, multiple-site electronic recording, quantitative analyses of therapeutic protocols, electron microscopic detection, and computer diagnoses of clinical syndromes, all illustrate the increasing array of technical procedures available to the researcher in the last two decades. Technology has become an integral part of every science, and the future of psychopathology cannot be gauged without considering the role that continued technical advance will play.

Despite a growing sophistication in instrumentation, scientific and theoretical knowledge in psychopathology is still inchoate and many investigators are unable to pursue their research goals in as clearly articulated a manner as they would like. The published literature in psychopathology gives the appearance that research has been executed in a neat and precise manner; this impression is frequently misleading. Clothed in the exacting format of journal articles, the rather feeble logic and coarse procedures of many studies are made to look elegant and refined.

Not only is the present state of methodological technique and substantive knowledge far short of ideal, but the implications of most research are far from clear. We have scattered "islands" of hard data based on exquisite research procedures (e.g., operant conditioning studies, neurophysiological correlates of anxiety), but these data fragments have not been coordinated, and their significance to the larger body of psychopathological knowledge remains obscure.

Unfortunately, too many investigators are absorbed in but one facet of psychopathology, or pursue their work with but one or two research instruments; as a consequence, they lose sight of the broader perspective and begin to confuse their "specialty" with the whole of the field. Students, however, must not have their perspective narrowed too soon; they should be exposed to the many alternatives of research endeavor, learn the comparative merits and limits of each of the various tools and instruments of the science, and view this multiplicity as a healthy diversity that leads to the discovery of knowledge in each facet of the wider subjects. Thus, as with the practice of psychotherapy, the research novice should be broadly skilled and open-minded, capable of selecting methods that are suited to the solution of significant problems, rather than limiting himself to problems that fit the narrow-band of his research competencies.

AIMS OF RESEARCH IN PSYCHOPATHOLOGY

No two investigators begin their studies of psychopathology with exactly the same goals in mind. Some start with a vague hunch, intending to probe in a rather cursory way a previously unexplored region; others have a clear objective in mind, but lack adequately developed instruments to answer the questions they pose; in other cases, the state of theory, accumulated empirical data, and methodological tools are such as to demand an investigation of the highest level of abstraction and executed under the most rigorously controlled of procedures.

Because of these wide differences in established theory, data, and instrumentation, researchers approach their studies with different aims or objectives in mind. Three such objectives will be outlined in the following paragraphs: *exploration, description,* and *confirmation.* These three aims will be more sharply distinguished in this discussion than they are in reality; most studies have mixed goals, rather than one. It is impossible to review the many combinations of research aims in so brief a survey as this; thus, the three-way breakdown to be presented will serve as an introduction.

Exploration

Among the major objectives of many studies is the discovery of new ideas and promising leads in a subject that has few well-trodden paths or directions for definitive research. Under these conditions, the investigator must proceed in an open and flexible manner, examining this or that variable before deciding which ones are most relevant to his problem. Selltiz et al. have summarized the goals of exploratory research as follows (1959):

> Many exploratory studies have the purpose of formulating a problem for more precise investigation or of developing hypotheses. An exploratory study may, however, have other functions; increasing the investigator's familiarity with the phenomenon he wished to investigate in the subsequent, more highly structured, study, or with the setting in which he plans to carry out such a study; clarifying concepts; establishing priorities for further research; gathering information about practical possibilities for carrying out research in real-life settings; providing a census of problems regarded as urgent by people working in a given field. . . .

In contrast to most research, where facts are sought, exploratory work is largely an unstructured excursion into the unknown, a scouting expedition to uncover relevant variables and to formulate significant hypotheses for subsequent study. If successful, it should also help the investigator to decide his future research strategy by exposing the methodological complications that must be solved before pursuing his project further.

Exploratory research often progresses from a preliminary "impressionistic" phase to one that is more systematic and goal-directed. For example, on the basis of incidental observations made in the course of everyday treatment, a therapist may gain the impression that a particular form of early experience appeared with regular frequency among his schizophrenic patients. Wondering whether this occurrence was a matter of chance or interpretive bias on his part, he may discuss his observations with other therapists with the thought of checking whether their impressions correspond with his. If enough consistency is obtained to justify further investigation, the study may progress into a goal-directed phase during which more extensive documentation is gathered. Using the first therapist's impressions as a starting place, a group of therapist-researchers may begin to examine their ongoing cases in a systematic fashion, probing more and more carefully in the hope of illuminating further their hypothesis about the presence of these early experiences in the life history of schizophrenics.

Some investigators consider exploratory work to be "beneath the dignity" of the honorific label of research. Matters of scientific status and semantics aside, there can be no question as to the importance of these pioneering excursions, not only as forerunners of more systematic studies but also as vehicles for discovering and elucidating the "hunches" of creative men.

Description

Many investigators direct their attention to establishing the natural distribution and interrelationships of well-defined variables. Prominent among studies of this kind are those that seek to establish the incidence or prevalence of various types of psychopathology, as in a particular geographic region or socioeconomic class (i.e., epidemiological surveys). Other descriptive studies may seek to trace the developmental "outcome" of children with different patterns of early experience. And, in addition to these aims, many investigations seek to measure intercorrelations among pathological traits or their covariation with particular sociologic indices.

A classical example of a descriptive study is Faris and Dunham's (1939) examination of the ecological or spatial distribution of mental illness within a large urban area. They found that mental illness, as measured by rates of hospitalization for psychiatric disorders, varied with social disorganization indices (e.g., type of housing, economic level). Although the highest rates of hospitalization were found in the most disorganized regions, specific diagnoses were distributed unequally throughout the area: schizophrenia, which accounted for the majority of cases, correlated closely with social disorganization, while the distribution of manic-depressive diagnoses did not. This variation in the locale of different disorders led to speculations about differences in etiology (environmental influences versus biophysical causes) and generated further research on the covariation of social factors and psychopathology.

In contrast to exploratory studies, descriptive research usually entails a clear specification and quantification of known variables. Great care is taken with regard to sampling procedures, research designs, validity of measures, and the statistical analysis of data. In discussing distinctions between exploratory and descriptive studies, Selltiz et al. note the following (1959):

> The research questions presuppose much prior knowledge of the problem to be investigated as contrasted with the questions that form the basis for exploratory studies. The investigator must be able to define clearly what it is he wants to measure and must find adequate methods for measuring it. In addition, he must be able to specify who is to be included in the definition of a "given community" or a "given population." In collecting evidence for a study of this sort, what is needed is not so much flexibility as a clear formulation of what and who is to be measured, and techniques for valid and reliable measurements.
>
> Although descriptive studies may use a wide range of techniques, this does not mean that they are characterized by the flexibility that marks exploratory studies. The procedures to be used in a descriptive study must be care-

fully planned. Because the aim is to obtain complete and accurate information, the research design must make much more provision for protection against bias than is required in exploratory studies. Because of the amount of work frequently involved in descriptive studies, concern with economy of research effort is extremely important. These considerations of economy and protection against bias enter at every stage; formulating the objectives of the study; designing the methods of data collection; selecting the sample; collecting, processing, and analyzing the data; and reporting the findings.

Confirmation

Exploratory and descriptive studies are neither designed for nor capable of answering questions concerning "causal" relationships; that is, they are not arranged to determine the effect of one set of variables upon another, or do not control confounding influences sufficiently to establish such relationships with confidence.

There is, of course, no sure way, either methodologically or philosophically, to "prove" the existence of a cause-effect relationship. Confirmation of causality is gauged largely by scientific convention, and confidence in such conclusions is largely a product of the utilization of proper research design procedures and theoretic logic. Systematic experimental control and logical causal analysis are the two essential features of confirmatory research.

Control procedures are designed to assure that variables which appear related to one another are, in fact, so related. One may control the operation of potentially intruding factors by preventing their effects experimentally. The other method of control is accomplished by measuring the effects of intruding factors through statistical means. Without these procedures, valid conclusions about hypothesized relationships cannot be established.

The second feature of confirmatory research, the analysis of causality, is not only methodologically difficult, but philosophically impossible. Instead of seeking "causality," one attempts to specify the antecedent of the concomitant conditions associated with an event to be studied. Thus, the question posed for analysis becomes "Does x precede or covary with y?" and not, "Does x cause y?"

Let us note briefly that inferences of causality depend on satisfying three conditions: (a) that cause and effect variables change concomitantly; (b) that causal variables either precede or occur simultaneously with effect variables; and (c) that alternative variables which might account for the observed effects are removed or under tight control (Selltiz et al., 1959).

Most of what will be presented in the following chapters is more relevant to research whose aims are descriptive and confirmatory rather than

TABLE 1.2: Research Aims and Their Distinguishing Characteristics

	Exploration	*Description*	*Confirmation*
1. Primary Aim	Probe hunches; generate new hypotheses and strategies for later research	Establish natural quantitative distribution and (degree and kind of) relationships among variables	Test causal hypotheses and calculate functional relationships
2. Dependence on:			
a. Prior theory	Conceptualization minimally developed	Conceptual role of variables well understood	Conceptualization of variables and relationships well developed
b. Prior data	Impressionistic	Scattered	Substantial
c. Nature of hypotheses	Loosely formulated or unformulated, though tentative, vague lines of speculation used to guide study	Loosely formulated or unformulated (for incidence studies), well formulated (for relationship studies) as quantitative statements about relationship among clearly identified variables	Explicitly formulated as deductive or predictive cause effect statements about operationally defined variables
3. Design Features			
a. Sampling	Little concern with representative sampling	Careful consideration of sampling representativeness	Random sampling often employed
b. Controls	Minimal	Often employed	Rigorous
c. Design	Informal, naturalistic and/or experimental	Formal, statistical naturalistic	Formal, experimental
4. Data Collection Methods	Flexible, guided by nature of findings	Predetermined valid and reliable techniques	Predetermined valid and reliable techniques

exploratory. Whatever the aim, the issues to be discussed should prove a useful introduction to the design of scientifically sound investigations. The relationship of the aims of research to features of prior knowledge and of research design are summarized in Table 1.2.

SPECIAL PROBLEMS OF RESEARCH IN PSYCHOPATHOLOGY

Research in psychopathology has more than its share of complications, so many that sometimes it seems as if successful investigations are almost impossible. There is some cogency to this pessimistic view but, for the most part, the problems that beset psychopathological research are neither unique to the field nor insurmountable; the greater number can be dealt with if they are fully recognized and if proper procedures of design and control are instituted to minimize their effects. Let us review a few of the difficulties that resist simple solution.

The Presence of Obscure and Unreliable Data. Psychopathologists envy researchers in the physical sciences who employ precise instruments and deal exclusively with objective phenomena. Much of the important data of psychopathology are difficult to define and measure, or are highly subjective and unreliable. Not only are phenomenological feelings and unconscious processes difficult to capture but also the methods by which they are gathered often corrupt and distort them further; for example, data can be contaminated by motivational and memory distortions on the part of the patient and also by the subjectively biased and insensitive measuring instruments of the researcher.

Choosing Between Scientifically "Safe" and Clinically Significant Problems. In contrast to many of his colleagues in general psychology research, whose interests center on "abstract" or "basic" scientific problems, the researcher in psychopathology must always keep in mind the clinical significance of his work. This presents him with dilemmas concerning the types of problems he can and should investigate; in effect, he must ask himself: "How can I fulfill the demands required for methodological precision and control without losing perspective or abandoning my commitment to pursue truly significant clinical problems?"

There is no question that "exact" methodologies, employing well-honed instruments and efficient research designs, have curbed the flow of sloppy studies that have burdened the field with unverifiable or invalid data. However, many clinicians assert that scientists who are preoccupied with precise tools and mathematical niceties and who insist on rigid standards of procedure often limit their endeavors to rather trivial topics at the expense of very important ones (see Loevinger, 1963, for a thoughtful discussion of this issue). It is no easy task to maintain a high level of methodological control without succumbing to the pursuit of sterile or petty research problems.

Issues of Clinical Responsibility and Ethics. It is natural and laudable that clinicians should be concerned with the welfare of their patients, seeking to guard them from research that may prove detrimental to their well-being. Commendable though this motive may be, it does create problems for investigators, especially if compounded by a resistance to changes in administrative routine, or by a basic antipathy to the methods and goals of research.

Questions of ethics should be raised where studies call for deception, the invasion of delicate therapist-patient relationships, or the necessity for depriving certain patients of needed treatment in order to compare them with a treated group of patients. Less valid, though still reasonable, are objections which contend that mental patients are particularly vulnerable to the stress of laboratory procedures and may suffer longstanding discomforts as a consequence.

In many studies, patients are given no option to volunteer or refuse participation; and even if they had the option, one may ask whether they are capable in their disturbed state of making the same choice they would if they were well. Moreover, since many of the data of research pertain to highly personal life experiences, is it ethically right, even in the cause of science, to probe and expose these private thoughts and feelings, some of which patients may be ashamed and perhaps unaware?

Complications of Execution. Many researchers who start their projects with clear-cut hypotheses, excellent research designs, and procedures that maximize control still run into difficulties in carrying them out since unforeseen complications often intrude to upset the plan and smooth running of the investigation. Any study dealing with human subjects, especially those who suffer cognitive disorders and emotional upsets, invites a host of problems that are difficult to anticipate and control, for example, patients resist following or misinterpret instructions, are susceptible to incidental and normally trivial influences, etc.

The following chapters will survey the essential procedures and tools of research inquiry. Because the scope of these topics is so wide and grows so rapidly, we can, at best, merely acquaint the student with them, and perhaps whet his appetite for more.

Let us note at the outset that the conduct of "real" research does not proceed in accord with rigid rules, and that the guidelines provided in the following chapters are not immutable regulations inevitably followed by creative scientists. In fact, the converse is likely to be true, as indicated in this statement prepared by a committee on education for research in psychology (Taylor et al., 1959):

> Over the years a stereotype has developed in the scientific as well as in the public mind as to what constitutes serious psychological research and scientific proof. Crucial experiments growing out of previous findings, elaborated by self-conscious and prescient genius, are performed with great precision. The results are subjected to the closest scrutiny, with all alternative interpretations judiciously considered and accepted or rejected in accordance with the most explicit canons of scientific rigor. Finally, the now confirmed discovery is inserted in a systematized lattice of already available knowledge to complete for posterity a forward step, however small, toward man's mastery of the unknown. Commonly, these developments are seen as accomplished only with the aid of extensive intellectual paraphernalia of confirmation that include logic, theory, broad and scholarly knowledge, technical proficiency in mathematics and statistics, and a self-conscious awareness of one's place and role in the larger scheme of things, as given by the history and philosophy of science.
>
> Make no mistake about it, however, this stereotype in name is a stereotype in fact, with all the oversimplification, misemphasis, and error which stereotypes involve.
>
> . . . the confirmatory activities described by the stereotype constitute but a small part of the process of active research and that mostly in the terminal phases. While indeed this model may be reasonably accurate in describing such terminal phases and also useful in communicating clearly the results of research to others, it does not represent well the activities of the individual scientist.
>
> Actually, the process of doing research—that is, of creating and building a science of psychology—is a rather informal, often illogical and sometimes messy-looking affair. It includes a great deal of floundering around in the empirical world, sometimes dignified by names like "pilot studies" and "exploratory research." Somewhere and somehow in the process of floundering, the research worker will get an idea. In fact, he will get many ideas. On largely intuitive grounds he will reject most of his ideas and will accept others as the basis for extended work.
>
> If an idea he chooses to accept happens to be a poor one, the researcher will perhaps waste a lot of time. But there is no way of knowing this beforehand. If the idea happens to be a good one, he may make a significant positive contribution to his science—"may" because between the idea and the contribution lies a lot of persistence, originality, intuition, and hard work. It is in this sort of activity rather far removed from the public, more orderly and systematic phases of scientific work, that the productive researcher spends much of his time and effort.

CHAPTER TWO

SPECIFYING THE PROBLEM

The range and diversity of potential topics for psychopathology research is limitless; no matter which facet of the field one may study—etiologic influences, syndrome clusters, therapeutic efficacy—problems and issues mushroom forth, expanding and proliferating in novel and potentially fruitful directions. In this chapter, we shall attempt to outline the sources from which such ideas are generated and describe some of the steps by which these ideas are transformed into researchable projects. Starting with a rather vague notion about a problem, the investigator focuses and delimits his study by clarifying his hypotheses and assumptions and by examining alternative methodological strategies for collecting and analyzing the data required to answer his questions.

SOURCE OF RESEARCHABLE PROBLEMS

The genesis of most research can be traced to four, often overlapping, sources: *curiosity, expediency, practicality,* and *theoretic logic.*

1. Personal *curiosity* is a major wellspring of ideas for investigators. For both conscious and unconscious reasons, students "drift" into subjects that satisfy their intrinsic intellectual and emotional needs.

Being personally intrigued by an idea will spur the investigator to pursue them despite the obstacles that inevitably arise in research. Of course, curiosity is an unreliable guide; researchers may be stirred by notions that prove trivial, unfeasible, and even absurd. Moreover, personal "whimsey" rarely is a sufficient basis for gaining the support needed to initiate and carry out a project.

2. Research problems are sometimes generated by *expediency;* in this category, we include the practice of following a particular line of inquiry because of its current popularity or because of the ready availability of research funds.

Few scientists would turn their backs on sources of financial support, or the quick "pay-off" in professional recognition gained by contributing to a "hot" research topic. It is all too easy to be seduced by these reinforcements, but it may be at the price of losing one's intellectual integrity and independence. Unfortunately, because of the substantial costs entailed in so much of modern research, expediency has become a too important factor in selecting study projects.

3. Much research is "needed" rather than selected. The solution of *practical* problems has been a strong impetus for many investigators. Questions such as the following, though of interest to theory, are guided primarily by practical needs: What is the best form of treatment for neurotic disorders? Is there a classification schema that will predict responses to therapy? Can we devise a diagnostic instrument that is more valid than those in current use?

Studies prompted by practical considerations often contribute to the storehouse of "basic" knowledge. To illustrate, investigations into methods of land surveying led the way to the discovery of geometric principles, and considerations of economy in agriculture spurred the development of both statistical theory and novel research designs; similarly, in psychopathology, the search for new psychopharmacologic agents has hastened progress in basic neurochemistry.

Despite the necessity of tackling practical problems in a direct fashion, questions arise as to whether this head-on approach is the most expeditious and effective way of solving them; for example, behavior therapists point out that their treatment technique, derived as an incidental by-product of "basic" learning research, has proved more effective than therapies arising out of clinical experience and the need to treat pathologic conditions.

4. From the viewpoint of science, one of the most valuable sources of research topics derives from *theoretic logic.* Theoretically based investigations are set within a coordinated set of principles; these principles suggest a specific and clearly defined sequence of studies that assure each contributing investigator that his results will be linked to an established and coherent body of knowledge. The advantage to scientific progress of

theoretical data consolidation contrasts sharply with the helter-skelter character of data that have been generated by theoretically unanchored research. Not only are the findings of these studies interrelated with previous work, but together they often furnish new insights and directions for further research. Of course, should the theoretical schema to which the researcher subscribes fail to be sound, he will have devoted his labors to a fruitless task.

CLARIFYING THE FOCUS AND LIMITS OF A PROBLEM

Except in exploratory studies, where investigators often delve immediately into their subject, most researchers do not collect data until they have outlined their hypotheses and assumptions, and have examined a number of alternative methodologies for designing and executing their study. This process of sharpening the research focus rarely proceeds in a smooth and systematic fashion; more typically, it progresses through a series of overlapping and somewhat haphazard steps. Clarity is gained slowly as the investigator reviews the existing literature, reflects on some of his own earlier work, and discusses matters with others who are conversant with the issues and techniques involved in the project. Despite this disjointed, real life, back-and-forth progression, we shall separate and present the components in an orderly manner.

Choosing Among Alternative Hypotheses. The nature and role of hypotheses were formulated as follows by Cohen and Nagel (1934):

> We cannot take a single step forward in any inquiry unless we begin with a suggested explanation or solution of the difficulty which originated it. Such tentative explanations are suggested to us by something in the subject matter and by our previous knowledge. When they are formulated as propositions, they are called *hypotheses.*
>
> The function of a hypothesis is to *direct* our search for the order among the facts. The suggestions formulated in the hypotheses *may* be solutions to the problem. Whether they are, is the task of the inquiry. No one of the suggestions need necessarily lead to our goal. And frequently some of the suggestions are incompatible with one another, so that they cannot all be solutions to the same problem.

Hypotheses differ in their scope and precision depending on the state of theory and research in the field from which they issue. In exploratory work, hypotheses are likely to be loosely formulated, representing a vague "feeling" about the character and relationship of certain ill-defined variables.

As Cohen and Nagel note above, several incompatible hypotheses may be proposed for the same problem. Not only are rival explanations possible for a single class of events but also the existence of alternative hypotheses is the primary reason for undertaking research. Unless the investigator is *uncertain* as to the outcome of his study, there is no reason why he should bother contemplating, designing, and carrying out the project.

Given the task of choosing among rival hypotheses, on what basis should the investigator select among them? Invariably, the choice is guided by previous empirical findings and by the merit of the theoretical system to which they are coordinated. Should prior data be contradictory or equivocal, however, and competing theoretical propositions equally plausible, the researcher must work out for himself a logical rationale for his preferred hypothesis. Several criteria may aid him in his task. Among them are the number of assumptions that must be made in conjunction with each of these hypotheses and the range of events that each of them will subsume. Other things being equal, then, a hypothesis that depends on few unsubstantiated assumptions and is applicable to a wider range of events is usually to be preferred. Let us comment further on these two ancillary aspects of problem formulation, *specifying the assumptions* and *recognizing the limitations on generalizability*.

Specifying Assumptions. Hypotheses and assumptions are propositional statements, but they are the antithesis of one another. Assumptions are statements that the investigator accepts as true, whereas hypotheses are statements whose "truth" is in doubt and is, therefore, the subject of research affirmation or refutation.

Assumptions often refer to characteristics of variables that are associated with the problem under study, but are not investigated because the researcher: (a) believes them to be of minor importance; (b) contends that they operate as constants, and, therefore, will have uniform effects upon the results; or (c) is unable, for various reasons, to include them within the project design and *hopes* that their omission will not obscure an evaluation of the central hypothesis.

The assumption an investigator makes may prove unwarranted, seriously limiting the validity or generalizability of his research findings. Keisler (1966), in what he has termed "uniformity assumption myths," notes that many studies of treatment efficacy have spuriously assumed homogeneity in both patient and therapist characteristics; not only does he contend that these homogeneity assumptions are unjustified but also in making them, investigators have markedly restricted the clarity and generalizability of their data. For example, in a study of "psychotherapy" with "schizophrenics," an investigator might assume: (a) that all forms of psychotherapy are equally efficacious; (b) that there are no differences in therapist variables that can influence therapeutic efficacy; and (c) that schizophrenics are homogeneous with regard to all characteristics predictive of response to psychotherapy. None of these assumptions can be substantiated, and Keisler suggests that such investigations be deferred until the assumptions themselves are fully researched.

As just noted, researchers may take a few steps "backward," and study those variables they initially conceived as assumptions. Thus, to avoid later complications and limitations, the investigator should think through his assumptions at the start, and examine their consequences upon his results. Although this is done all too infrequently, the identification of assumptions is not a difficult chore for researchers who have a thorough familiarity with their subject and with the interpretations likely to be given to their results.

Recognizing Limitations. By specifying the assumptions he has made, the investigator has acknowledged certain limitations that must be imposed upon the conclusions of his study. However, there are additional factors that will restrict the generalizability of his findings if not recognized and dealt with.

Paramount among these is the character of the subjects, procedures, and settings he has employed in his research. What he has included in his study is only a sample of the larger class of events and populations to which his findings will ostensibly apply. Whether these extrapolations will in fact be valid can never be proved; however, the investigator must specify the particular conditions and persons represented in his study, and acknowledge the restrictions these may impose on the conclusions he should like to draw. Unless he recognizes at the start of his study the boundaries within which his results can safely be generalized, he may find himself expending energies in a task far more limited in value than he initially thought.

PRELIMINARY PLANNING

Once the contours of the study have been clarified in the form of hypotheses, assumptions, and limitations, the investigator is ready to translate his ideas into researchable form. This phase of study formulation may be divided into three stages: *defining concepts, examining alternate methodological strategies,* and *considering matters of practicality.*

Defining Concepts

One of the first steps by which a general hypothesis is transformed into an empirically researchable procedure entails the translation of theoretical concepts into their empirical coordinates. Concepts are linguistic abstractions that represent a general class of events or objects. Some concepts are anchored in a relatively precise way to observable phenomena (have operational definitions), while others represent mediating processes that cannot be observed directly, but which may be defined in whole or in part by observable events (intervening variables and hypothetical constructs).

For a concept to have an *operational definition* means it can be fairly easily and unambiguously measured by a given procedure; however, in the most strict interpretation of operationism, there is a different concept for each procedure—anxiety as measured by the Taylor Manifest Anxiety Scale (a set of self-report items originally taken from the Minnesota Multiphasic Personality Inventory) is different from anxiety as measured by the galvanic skin reflex (GSR—sweating increasing the skin's electrical conductivity). For a concept to be classed as an *intervening variable* is to suggest that it represents an inferred, unobserved event that cannot yet be measured by current procedures, but which is closely tied to observable events and may be observed and measured in the future; pathological symptoms viewed as *habits* represent intervening variables, which have yet to be satisfactorily measured, although approximations have been tried. Still other concepts are even more speculative and are not as easily tied to observable, measurable events; many psychoanalytic concepts such as ego, superego, and libido represent such *hypothetical constructs*.

Hypotheses are formulated in conceptual terms. To make them amenable to empirical research, they must be redefined in terms of the specific procedures and measures used to represent them in the study. In other words, conceptual abstractions, and the hypotheses that contain them, must be translated into their observable counterparts or empirical coordinates. These coordinates are referred to in the context of an investigation as *research variables;* they are the concrete operations, events, or objects of the study, the tangible phenomena that represent the abstract language of the theoretical concepts. The object of research is to investigate any of several combinations of these variables, operationally defined yet theory-linked.

Each empirical variable of the study must be an accurate index of the abstract concept it defines. This need is an issue of no small importance since data obtained with these highly specific indices will be assumed to hold for the entire class of events subsumed by the more nebulous theoretic concepts they ostensibly represent. Holt (1965) comments on the complications of faulty empirical definitions as follows:

> It sometimes happens, for example, that an experimenter gives an excellent treatment of the concept of anxiety in theory and then adopts a conventional, available measure like GSR without making any linkage between the two types of definition, which leaves it an open question whether his work has any relevance to theory or not. For it is a serious but common error to think

that the problems of definition are solved simply by the declaration that a specified measure is the operational definition of a term from some theory, which the experimenter then proceeds to bandy about, taking advantage of all of its surplus meaning in the theory and in common usage, little of which may have any relation to the operation in question.

In this section we shall discuss in greater detail the criteria by which the concepts that comprise the body of the hypothesis are translated into their coordinates in the empirical world.

Variables in psychology have traditionally been divided into three classes: stimulus (S), response (R), and organismic (O). Edwards (1954) describes and illustrates several of their distinguishing features in the following:

> The variables which psychologists observe in research may be represented as response variables, stimulus variables, and organismic variables. These three terms are used in a broad sense. Response, for example, is used to designate any kind of behavior or action of the organism. Some responses may be very simple in nature, such as a finger flexion, and others may be highly complex, such as the behavior we call aggression. Stimulus variables also range in complexity. In some experiments the stimulus may be of a relatively simple kind, such as a flash of light. In other experiments the stimulus may represent a complex social situation.
>
> Any property or characteristic of the organism may, in a given experiment, be called an organismic variable. A clear-cut example of an organismic variable would be height or weight, neither of which seems properly to fit within the class of stimulus or response variables. Other organismic variables may be designated upon the basis of prior experience of the individuals. Subjects in an experiment, for example, may be classified into groups in terms of their degree of prior education. Sometimes an experiment may incorporate into its design an organismic variable based upon some previous observation of behavior of the subjects. For example, it may be useful in some experiments to classify subjects upon the basis of their present attitudes toward some issue, or on personality traits. This classification, in turn, might be based upon prior observation of a response variable, i.e., scores upon an attitude scale or a personality inventory.

Stimulus Variables. Stimulus variables take innumerable forms, and may be contemporaneous with the study or antecedent to it. In most experimental designs, the stimulus is a current event that is subject to the investigator's observation and manipulation. For example, he may arrange a laboratory setting in which "frustrating" events are produced to influence the responses of subjects; in this design, the stimulus conditions are available to the researcher for purposes of control and systematic variation. Other research designs include stimulus variables that are part of the distant past (e.g., early parent-child relationships), and are not available for present-day manipulative purposes. In case studies, for example, the researcher has no control of many of the stimulus conditions that may be crucial to his hypothesis. He must infer these stimulus experiences retrospectively; and, on the basis of rather scattered and unreliable evidence, he will attempt to gauge their determinant role in shaping the effects his hypothesis attributes to them. Problems of this latter kind limit the degree of confidence one can place in the results and conclusions of studies.

Whatever the character of the stimulus variables, it is not sufficient for an investigator to simply "operationally define" them; to be meaningful, operational definitions should be selected in accord with certain criteria, which we will outline in the following paragraphs. None of those to be described is crucial, especially in exploratory research; however, each is likely to be related to the validity of a study's findings.

Theory Embeddedness. In an earlier discussion, we indicated the importance of translating theoretical concepts into concrete or observable events that serve to represent them in the context of empirical research. Numerous situational arrangements and procedures may be employed to designate a stimulus concept, but not all of them "capture the flavor," or "get at the essence" of the more subtle or complex intent of that concept. Thus, a "stress condition," such as periodic interruptions while attempting to complete an arithmetic task, may possess the merits of a "clean" operational definition of stress that can be manipulated in a neat experimental fashion, but have no relevance to the concept of stress as intended by the theory that prompted the study. Thus, despite difficulties in controlling and measuring its impact with precision, a "stress" event, such as the simulation of an unanticipated severe argument between two members of a problem-solving group, would approximate the notion of stress for a theory of social interaction far better than would arithmetic task interruptions. Stimulus variables that are embedded in a broadly based theory will connect the obtained research data to a coherent body of knowledge, thereby enriching the results with a significance greater than if they were only tangentially relevant.

Generalizability. Stimulus variables that simulate or correlate with a wide range of situational events are preferable to those with highly distinctive or unique features. As noted in the previous section, the value of research findings are increased when they are coordinated with an established theory. Theoretical embeddedness permits the data to be related in a logical manner to *different* classes of variables; for example, the effects wrought by a particular stress stimulus may be linked to clinical symptoms, biophysical traits, features of early experience, as well as other variables that are interwoven in the theoretical system. Generalizability, as employed here, provides similar gains, but relates to extrapolations made to the *same* class of events as those represented by the stimulus variable; for example, the effects produced by a stress stimulus, defined operationally by repeated task interruptions, can be safely assumed to apply to other forms of stress induction that may be employed to operationally define the concept of stress, such as threats of an electric shock or hearing critical comments from the experimenter.

The criterion of generalizability can best be met in one of two ways: representative content and empirical correspondence.

By *representative content,* we mean that the stimulus variables chosen are a sample of the actual situational events represented by the concept; for example, the experimenter actually creates interpersonal hostility as the stimulus variable in a hypothesis that states that "interpersonal hostility leads to withdrawal behavior in schizoid patients." In achieving this form of generalizability, the settings and arrangements of the research study are chosen to simulate or exemplify as much as possible the "real-life" situations represented by the hypothesis.

There are occasions when the "reality" conditions cannot be reproduced or sampled; thus, the stimulus concept of "family conflict," included in a hypothesis that states that "schizophrenic-prone persons evidence cognitive disorganization in response to situations of unresolvable family conflict," may not be possible to duplicate or effectively simulate in the laboratory. Rather than arrange a set of stimulus conditions that tap the essential dimensions of family conflict in a feeble or dubious manner, the investigator may seek to find a stimulus condition, such as a simple perceptual task, that has been demonstrated to *empirically correspond* with the conditions of "real" family conflict. Unfortunately, there are very few empirical correlates of difficult-to-reproduce "real" stimuli.

In the main, generalizability of stimulus variables in psychopathologic research rests on assumptions that events which *appear* similar in content to their "real" counterparts do, in fact, represent them fully and accurately. These assumptions are among the weakest links in psychological studies.

Separability and Manipulability. Another criterion to be considered is whether the several ingredients that comprise most stimulus variables can be separated from each other and be controlled or modified systematically. For example, the stimulus complex of "family conflict" is a gross variable comprising many elements such as physical contact, cognitive interchanges, affective expressions, etc. The criterion of "separability" reflects the extent to which these ingredients can be both empirically disconnected and isolated; "manipulability" reflects the extent to which each of them can be regulated or subjected to experimental control. Thus the stimulus complex of "desensitization therapy" consists of several subvariables, for example, the style of the therapist's behavior, the sequence of inducing the relaxed state, the procedure for facilitating cognitive imagery, and the like. Can each of these distinct ingredients be separated empirically, isolated experimentally, controlled, manipulated, etc.? Stimulus variables that can be divided into their component parts, with each of their elements discerned clearly and modified quantitatively, are generally preferable to variables that cannot be so partitioned and regulated.

Replicability. If the constituent elements of a stimulus variable can be clearly identified, then it should be possible for investigators to replicate studies that include them, and compare the results they obtain. It is not unusual for researchers to report conflicting findings because the exact stimulus conditions employed in their respective studies were not or could not be duplicated, having been formulated in an obscure fashion or muddled by extraneous factors. The criterion of replicability is achieved, therefore, when the ingredients of the stimulus variable can be specified with sufficient clarity and detail to assure that they can be repeated by later investigators with ease and accuracy.

Response Variables. Serious efforts have been made to define response variables operationally and to select instruments that measure them on the basis of well-established criteria. Difficulties are still faced, however, since there are very few techniques that satisfy these standards adequately. In this section, we shall briefly survey some of the considerations and major criteria by which response variables should be selected.

Data Levels. Responses comprise the main body of both clinical and research data; one need only scan a small segment of the professional literature to see the tremendous range and variety of responses studied by investigators. It is impossible to catalogue the proliferating list of psychopathologic responses. Judgments cannot be made a priori as to which categories are likely to be fruitful or significant; evaluations of this kind are determined by the focus and purpose of a particular study, and the extent to which specific response measures fulfill the several criteria to be noted in later paragraphs.

Despite these restrictions, we believe it useful to allocate response data sources among the four broad levels to be elaborated fully in Chapter Four: biophysical, intrapsychic, phenomenological, and behavioral (Millon, 1967, 1969). Of course, these categories are not mutually exclusive; many responses are complex and can be analyzed concurrently at several levels; for example, "anxiety" may be gauged in terms of its subjective expressions, its autonomic symptoms, its motoric manifestations, its connection to measures of defense mechanisms, and so on.

Discriminability. If the chosen response variable cannot be detected, then the investigator might as well close up shop and start anew. Similarly, if differences among types and magnitudes of response variables cannot be discriminated, the investigator will be seriously hampered in his efforts to test his hypotheses. For example, phenomenological feelings tend to be vague and difficult to describe, no less to measure and quantify; studies that depend on them often produce ambiguous and uninterpretable data.

The criterion of discriminability refers to the ease with which response variables can be registered, differentiated, and quantified. Thus, muscle reactions can be detected, and their magnitudes quantitatively discriminated by a variety of electrical recording devices; similarly, attitudes toward self and others may be differentiated by the use of questionnaires, although the best of these still lack the precision of refined quantitative measures.

Instruments designed to record, distinguish, and measure response variables differ in their discriminating power. Stevens (1951) and Torgerson (1958) have provided illuminating discussions of the discriminating power of several types of "measurement scales," notably those labeled by Stevens as *nominal, ordinal, interval,* and *ratio* scales.

Briefly, *nominal* scales represent the crudest form of discrimination, signifying nothng more than the existence of mutually exclusive categories, without reference to magnitude. In psychopathology research the most important example of nominal scales are diagnostic classifications where individuals are placed into one or another of several mutually exclusive categories on the basis of the presence or absence of specific symptoms. The distinction between "normal" and "mentally ill" would represent a two-class nominal system; "normal," "neurotic," "character disorder," "manic-depressive," and "schizophrenic" would represent a five-class nominal scale. The only information conveyed in these scales is that those in the same category are equal with regard to the response (or organismic) variable, and those in different classes are not. Other examples of nominal scales often encountered in sociological studies of psychopathology are "religion," "residence" (urban versus rural), "race," and "marital status."

An instrument based on an *ordinal* scale possesses an additional degree of discriminability in that it allows for the determination of "greater or less," that is, the relative intensity or ranking of response magnitude. Thus, not only are differences recorded but also the direction of the differences can be established. For example, some clinicians assume that the psychotic is "more ill" than the neurotic who, in turn, is "more ill" than the normal; in this three-step ordinal scale, classes are ordered along a unitary dimension of "degree of psychopathology." What is left unspecified, as in any ordinal scale, is *how much more* ill is the neurotic than the normal, or the psychotic than the neurotic. Another example of an important ordinal scale often encountered in psychopathology research is social class (e.g., lower, middle, upper); the most commonly used scheme is a modification of that originally presented in Hollingshead and Redlich (1958) where education and occupation (plus area of residence in the original) are used to classify persons in a five-step Index of Social Position.

The next advance in discriminability is achieved by instruments that meet the criteria of an *interval* scale. Here, the measuring device enables the investigator not only to rank order, but to specify the extent or magnitude of difference between ranks. This is achieved by the fact that the instrument possesses units of discriminability that are equal or consistent throughout its recording range. Scores on most tests used in psychopathology research are assumed to be interval scales, for example, IQ scores on the Wechsler Adult Intelligence Scale and the form-level rating $(F+)$ on the Rorschach Ink Blot Test. "Degree" of pathology ratings on clinical depression or anxiety instruments made by an observer would also be considered to reflect interval scale scores.

The recording range of an interval scale does not extend to a true or absolute zero point, which is what distinguishes it from a *ratio* scale. Recording instruments of this latter type possess the ultimate of discriminatory powers, for example, measures of weight, height, time. To all intents and purposes, no instrument of significance in psychopathological research has achieved the characteristics of a ratio scale, although many of the measures of biophysical phenomena (e.g., body temperature, skin conductivity), would formally qualify.

The greater the discriminability possible among response variables, for example, metrical order (ordinal scales) or equal units of measurement (interval scales), the more amenable are the resulting data to certain types of statistical analysis. Specific statistics have been developed or judged appropriate for use with each scale. It should be noted, however, that compelling arguments have been advanced, both pro and con, as to whether scaling properties should be considered in the choice of statistical techniques (Burke, 1953; Senders, 1953; Cohen, 1965). Cohen, for example, does not feel that the distinction between interval and ratio scales is as important as we once thought and suggests that having achieved an interval scale is more than sufficient for the types of studies that clinical psychologists do.

Norms and Variability Estimates. The more that is known from the past literature about the attributes and characteristics of a response variable, the greater clarity the investigator will have in planning its use, and the greater the confidence he can expect in the results it will provide. Foremost in these regards is the availability of well-established normative and variability data.

Norms serve as reference points that outline the distribution of scores exhibited by subjects who have previously performed the response under study, for example, what "schizophrenics" have actually done on a measure of cognitive speed, or on a frequency scale of ward activity. In effect, norms provide baselines for the respónse variable. If these data are available for subjects who are comparable to those to be included in a study, the investigator can determine whether the measure he is considering will prove suitable or not for his purpose.

Of particular value is information on the dispersion or variability of response measures. If previous studies have shown great variability in subject performance (i.e., a wide range of performances on the measure under standard conditions), then the experimental manipulations the investigator plans may not be sufficiently powerful to produce statistically discernible effects. Mosteller and Bush (1954) point up this problem as follows:

> A question of general interest to an investigator planning an experiment is whether his design, including sample size, has a good chance of detecting differences among conditions, methods, or ethnic, age, or other population groups. The primary value of a study of group differences is lost if the investigation is so insensitive that important differences are obscured by sampling variation. We seldom enter an investigation completely in the dark about the magnitudes of differences we expect to observe (although there seems to be great cultural value in pretending no one has ever done anything like our experiment before). This general information about magnitudes of effects and the variation ordinarily observed can be very useful in planning a study. Of course, one does not know exactly what to expect, but it is obvious, for example, that a person comparing groups on a 6-point rating scale is unlikely to find average group differences as large as 4 points. Many paper and pencil tests have been standardized on known populations, so some notion of the means and standard deviations is available for them. Similarly, various experimental devices have been used in many different situations and for them various kinds of baseline data are available to the investigator willing to take the trouble to look. These data can be used in a formal way in the design of an experiment to see what size of difference the experiment is likely to detect, or to help in revising the experiment if it is too insensitive to possible differences.

The reciprocal relationship between response variability and the number of subjects needed to obtain statistically significant results has been examined carefully by Kramer and Greenhouse (1959) and Cohen (1969); the larger the sample size, the more likely an effect may be found. Although enlargement of the sample size may compensate for measures characterized by high variability, it should be noted that one of the greatest problems in psychopathological research is the small number of patients usually available for a particular project. Thus the investigator should select measures with lower levels of response variability that will facilitate detecting, rather than obscuring, the differences proposed by the research hypothesis.

Reliability. Data obtained on all measuring instruments are subject to numerous random influences that cause scores to vary unpredictably from one occasion to the next. To the extent that these errors occur, the findings may be considered to be unreliable; that is, they are not consistent and predictable, and therefore cannot be depended on for interpretive purposes. Reliability reflects the operation of errors that distort measurement scores in a random rather than a systematic way. A reliable instrument is one that is resistant to these unsystematic errors.

Reliability is a necessary but insufficient condition for assuring that the results of a study will be of scientific value. Without reliability, the investigator can have no confidence in his findings; reliability alone, however, provides no guarantee of significance.

Replication and confirmation of empirical findings are essential features of the scientific enterprise; unreliable measures mean that the results of a study will be difficult to reproduce. No matter how elegant the apparatus involved, unless there is prior evidence of its reliability, an investigator cannot take the dependability of his instrument for granted.

Which measure of reliability is needed depends on the purpose and type of instrument used. Where clinical judgments are made with more than one rater, it is important to establish the amount of *interjudge agreement*. When one employs a personality inventory composed of numerous items that are summed to yield a single score, it is important to establish the degree of *internal consistency* of the instrument. Since much research in psychopathology involves measurement of change following an experimental intervention, the *stability* over time of an instrument must be determined. The reader should refer to any of several texts that detail the procedures for choosing and calculating the appropriate reliability coefficient.

Validity. Reliability does not assure accuracy. A measuring instrument may produce highly dependable and predictable readings, but be consistently wrong, that is, be systematically and uniformly distorted, or measure some concept or event other than it is supposed to represent.

Accurate representation is what is meant by *validity;* more specifically, a research measure is valid when it has been shown, *in fact,* to correlate with (*concurrent validity*) or predict criterion behaviors (*predictive validity*) that signify the concept under study. (The topic of validity is far too important and complex to be treated in passing; the student should make reference to Cronbach and Meehl, 1955, Megargee, 1966, Jackson and Messick, 1967, Edwards, 1970, or Fiske, 1971, for a full discussion of the logic, problems, and different methods of determining the validity of relevant measuring instruments.)

Prediction and generalization, though not mutually exclusive, are the two primary aims of employing valid measures. Scores obtained on valid instruments enable the investigator to make predictive statements about the future performance of his subjects, for example, ward behavior, job performance, response to therapy, etc. Generalization rests on the assumption that the instrument utilized in the study is but one manifestation of a broader class of responses subsumed by the theoretical concept it represents. Thus the concept should be operationally definable by several response measures, and the results obtained with one of these measures should be applicable, that is, generalize to each of its several conceptual correlates; such generalizability is termed *construct validity*. Unfortunately, little empirical research has been done to establish the network of measurement intercorrelations for psychopathological concepts.

Not only are there different ways of gauging validity but also the degree of validity established for a measure under one set of conditions, or for one group of subjects, may not hold for other conditions or subjects. Thus, researchers must examine the settings and persons for whom published validity coefficients (e.g., the correlation between the test and a criterion) are based before deciding whether or not they apply to the arrangements of his own study.

Utility. Crucial though the criterion of validity may be in selecting a response measure, the final choice of an instrument must take into account several additional, more mundane, considerations. Kogan (1960) summarizes several of these criteria in the following:

> Practicality and feasibility have to do with such things as cost in time, money, and effort in using the instrument or procedure, the need for special training, and the ease of scoring and interpretation of results, and may include attention to matters of ethics in collecting information or seeing that a research procedure does not interfere with practice objectives of administrative policies with respect to the group of clients or institutions being studied. It can readily be seen that a whole volume could be devoted to discussion of practicality and feasibility in the development and application of measurement procedures. We shall not elaborate further on these matters . . . except to emphasize that the research worker's technical competence flounders all too often on the twin reefs of practicality and feasibility.

Once matters of practicality have been weighed, the investigator can reevaluate his choice of alternate response measures. Primary in these considerations is whether the degree of predictability or generalizability gained by a particular measure is sufficiently greater than that provided by other measures which can be administered more feasibly and economically. In other words, he must base his decision on whether the *increment in validity* achieved by any one measure, or combination of measures, is worth the added effort and cost when compared to alternative methods (Meehl and Rosen, 1955; Sechrest, 1963; Mischel, 1968). Unfortunately, comparative validity levels obtained with similar subject populations are almost nonexistent in the psychopathologic literature, leaving researchers without an empirical basis for making this important utilitarian decision.

Organismic Variables. Organismic variables are relatively stable characteristics of subjects. Included among them are enduring physical traits such as sex, height, and weight, and a host of experiential and social factors such as age upon hospital admission, educational level, and socioeconomic class. Also in this grouping are response variables that the researcher considers for the purposes of his investigation to be intrinsic features of his subjects' psychological makeup; for example, intelligence, though measured previously by response to a set of test stimuli, may be classed now as an organismic variable if the researcher decides to employ it as a stable characteristic of his subjects. Psychological traits, then, such as syndrome status (judged by clinical diagnostic ratings), or social attitudes and intelligence (as gauged by questionnaires and tests), may be viewed as organismic variables, despite the fact that they were based on prior observations of response variables. This latter group of organismic variables should be selected in accord with the same criteria as were outlined above in discussing response variables; evaluations of discriminability, norms, validity, etc., are equally applicable to these variables, whether they are to be employed as response or organismic characteristics.

Representativeness. In addition to the several "response variable" criteria, special note should be made of the importance of the representativeness of organismic variables. This means that the organismic attributes of the sample of subjects chosen for study correspond to the larger population to which the findings will be extrapolated. The idea underlying this criterion is essentially the same as that conveyed in the criterion of "generalizability" for stimulus variables, and "validity" for response variables. All of these terms refer to whether or not data gathered with the particular conditions, measures, and subjects of the research study can be extrapolated to the broader class of events and persons they ostensibly represent.

Of course, not all of the organismic attributes of the research sample need match all of the attributes of the to-be-generalized population. Instead, through various selection and sampling procedures, efforts should be made to assure that the research subjects possess no characteristics that differ from those of the larger population which might systematically bias the results. We shall elaborate on several of the complications that may arise in this regard in later chapters.

Examining Alternative Methodologies

Several different approaches are likely to come to mind as ways in which the research aims can be achieved; the investigator must choose which of these approaches will prove most efficient in achieving the intent with accuracy. The investigator's plan for his approach is termed the research design. As Selltiz et al. have phrased it: "A research design is the arrangement of conditions for collection and analysis of data in a manner that aims to combine relevance to the research purpose with economy in procedure." Different research designs are appropriate for the different aims of exploration, description, and confirmation; in each case, however, the design should enable the investigator to achieve his aim as accurately, objectively, and economically as possible.

Two questions may be posed concerning the scientific status and significance of a research study: (1) Can we be confident that *no* sources of influence, other than those variables the investigator believes to be operative, account for the results he obtained? (2) To what larger class of populations, conditions, and measures can the results be generalized? Thus, there are two sets of conditions that should be considered in selecting among rival research designs; Campbell and Stanley (1966) have referred to the two conditions as "internal" and "external" validity. Designs that possess *internal validity* succeed in controlling extraneous variables that might confound the results; unless the effects of these contaminating factors are kept in check, the investigator is unable to assert with confidence that his findings can be ascribed to the variables of his hypothesis. *External validity* refers to the extent to which the data can be generalized to situations and persons other than those specifically employed in the study. Among rival designs, those that maximize both the internal and external validity of the hypothesis are to be preferred. Although the ideal research design is strong in both internal and external validity, these criteria are often difficult to satisfy simultaneously. Thus, in an effort to control extraneous factors that will confound a study's internal validity, the investigator may take precautions that decrease its external validity, that is, restrict the representativeness or wider applicability of the findings. We shall return to this troublesome incompatibility in later paragraphs. For the moment, let us note that considerations of internal validity must take precedence where the aims of the study are that of confirming causal hypotheses or describing relationships among research variables; in exploratory studies or where survey descriptions are the primary focus, considerations of external validity should be given equal, if not greater, weight.

To achieve internal validity, the investigator must employ procedures that remove the obscuring and biasing effects of various extraneous factors; unless these influences are minimized, the results of the study may be of dubious quality, or be uninterpretable, that is, fail to eliminate plausible rival hypotheses from consideration. For external validity, the investigator must select and arrange his variables in a design that enhances the generalizability of the results he obtains. Achieving *internal validity* requires: (1) instituting all necessary controls for minimizing the impact of potentially misleading and confounding variables; and (2) choosing statistical designs of maximum power and efficiency so as to decrease the probability of overlooking significant findings.

To increase the probability of *external validity,* the researcher should carefully select: (1) reliable, valid, and precise measures that are reasonably accurate counterparts of the conceptual variables under study; (2) a subject sample that is representative of the larger population to which the results are to be extrapolated; and (3) procedures and settings that closely approximate the "reality" conditions for which the hypothesis is relevant.

It is wise to anticipate and plan the manner in which the final research data will be organized for descriptive and interpretive analysis. Unless the investigator has a clear, prior notion as to how he will collate and decipher these data, he may find himself at the conclusion of his study with a muddle of irrelevant and obscure information that is neither usable nor interpretable. It will be useful to group the sources of influence in an investigation, that is, the elements that account for variations in results, into four categories:

1. The first category consists of the *research variables.* These include the stimulus, response, or organismic variables that are the primary focus of research interest, and which comprise the essential ingredients of the study's hypothesis.

2. The second category includes *confounding and limiting factors.* Confounding factors are sources of unwanted influence that obscure relationships among the research variables, or bias the results in ways that prevent an accurate interpretation of the relationships found, for example, choosing patients for a study on the effectiveness of drug treatment from a research ward with unusually well-trained and motivated personnel, hence "contaminating" the drug results with the beneficial effects of the therapeutic milieu. Limiting factors are features of the stimulus, response, and organismic variables selected for study that decrease the representativeness or generalizability of the findings, for example, using subjects of only one sex, socioeconomic status, or degree of chronicity of illness.

3. *Manipulated variables* are the third category of research components. They consist of potentially confounding or limiting factors that have been controlled or systematically varied by the investigator in order to enhance the study's internal and external validity. For example, including in the study and analyzing the data separately for males and females or acute and chronic patients are ways of avoiding confounding, broadening generalizability, and assessing the specific contribution of each of these vari-

ables. It should be noted that manipulated variables differ from research variables only in that they are *not central* elements of the study's hypothesis; though subsidiary, they are important in obtaining clear answers to questions about the main research variables (i.e., the effect of drug treatment).

4. Potentially confounding or limiting factors that are not manipulated, but are subjected to procedures of *randomization,* that is, chance assignment, comprise the fourth source of variation. By randomization procedures (e.g., ensuring by chance assignment that as many females as males are likely to be placed in one experimental condition as in any other), confounding biases are neutralized, and constraints on the representativeness of the study are loosened. In contrast to procedures of "manipulation," however, the specific contribution of the "randomized" variables cannot be separately assessed.

The aim of an efficient research design is to place or arrange as many of the sources of the second category of variation (confounding and limiting factors) into the third (manipulated) or fourth (randomized) categories.

TABLE 2.1: Checklist of Questions to be Asked About a Research Proposal

---

1. What is the problem?
   a. Is it clearly stated?
   b. Is it focused enough to facilitate efficient work (i.e., are hypotheses directly testable)?
2. What are the underlying objectives?
   a. Is the problem clearly related to the objectives?
3. What is the significance of the proposed research?
   a. How does it tie in with theory?
   b. What are its implications for application?
4. Has the relevant literature been adequately surveyed?
   a. Is the research adequately related to other people's work on the same or similar topics?
5. Are the concepts and variables adequately defined (theoretically and operationally)?
6. Is the design adequate?
   a. Does it meet formal standards for consistency, power, and efficiency?
   b. Is it appropriate to the problem and the objectives?
   c. Will negative results be meaningful?
   d. Are possibly misleading and confounding variables controlled?
   e. How are the independent and dependent variables measured or specified?

7. What instruments or techniques will be used to gather data?
   a. Are the reliabilities and validities of these techniques well established?
8. Is the sampling of subjects adequately planned for?
   a. Is the population (to which generalizations are to be aimed) specified?
   b. Is there a specific and acceptable method of drawing a sample from this population?
9. Is the sampling of objects (or situations) adequately planned for?
   a. To what population of objects (situations) will generalizations be aimed?
   b. Is there a specific and acceptable method of drawing a sample from this population?
10. What is the setting in which data will be gathered?
    a. Is it feasible and practical to carry out the research plan in this setting?
    b. Is the cooperation of the necessary persons obtainable?
11. How are the data to be analyzed?
    a. What techniques of "data reduction" are contemplated?
    b. Are methods specified for analyzing data qualitatively?
    c. Are methods specified for analyzing data quantitatively?
12. In the light of available resources, how feasible is the design?
    a. What compromises must be made in translating an idealized research design into a practical research design?
    b. What limitations or generalizations will result?
    c. What will be needed in terms of time, money, personnel, and facilities?

From Holt (1965).

This placement will increase the probability that unequivocal interpretations can be drawn with regard to the first source of influence, the research variables themselves, and increase the generalizability of the findings to a wider set of events and persons than would otherwise be the case.

Practical Considerations

Investigators should begin their planning with what Ackoff (1962) refers to as an *idealized research design,* that is, one that meets all of the essential criteria of internal and external validity. Too frequently, the larger possibilities of a research study are restricted by an initial cautious concern with economic resources, available facilities, etc.

Once an idealized design has been formulated, compromises may be gradually introduced. Budgetary matters, space requirements, approval from administrative personnel, support from funding sources and needed collaborators, time scheduling, availability of representative subjects, etc., are among the many "reality" factors that are brought to bear in scaling down the scope of the original plans. These considerations may necessitate shrinking the size of the ideal subject sample, selecting measures other than those initially scheduled, abbreviating the period of follow-up studies, changing the setting within which the study will be executed, deciding to subdivide the project into a series of less ambitious studies, or realizing that the investigation is simply not feasible at all. As practical concerns come into play, then, the researcher must refashion his ideal plans so that he can reasonably expect to carry the project to completion.

Especially in large-scale studies involving costly or untried procedures, it is often wise to undertake a "pilot" investigation, that is, a small-scale replica of the larger study. The major purpose of these preliminary excursions is to uncover flaws and complications before they create troublesome and expensive problems that cannot be remedied in the final project without serious consequences. These dry-runs are of value also as means of comparing and selecting among alternative procedures that may be employed in the final study, for example, trying out different versions in the instructions to be given subjects, checking several coding systems to assure rater-reliability (agreement) and objectivity, examining the feasibility and discriminating power of two or three otherwise comparable test instruments, etc.

CHAPTER THREE

SELECTING A
RESEARCH DESIGN

It should be evident that the task of planning and executing a research study in psychopathology is often more complicated than first meets the eye. Not only must the hypothesis be formulated in terms subject to empirical test but also the research must be designed to provide interpretable data that can be generalized to events and patients other than those specifically included in the study itself. In other words, the methods by which the research is carried out should enable the investigator to draw unequivocal answers to the questions he posed (internal validity) and his conclusions should have reasonably broad theoretical or practical implications (external validity). Unless the design strategy is appropriately selected and carefully planned, the study may produce an undecipherable hodgepodge of data or technically precise findings that are rendered useless by their triviality.

In this chapter, we shall survey several of the "standard" research designs employed by investigators in psychopathology. We shall describe in some detail two major varieties of research design, *experimental* and *naturalistic,* and briefly outline the logic and procedures by which manipulation and randomization minimize the effects of extraneous factors and maximize the representativeness of the research variables. With this presentation as a background, we shall be in a better position to understand the distinguishing features and relative merits of the various research designs for studying psychopathology.

It is necessary to simplify our discussion of the procedures involved in achieving these aims; a text such as this cannot provide details of either logic or method. Although the serious student would do well to read more elaborately developed presentations (e.g., Underwood, 1957, 1966; Kerlinger, 1964; Campbell and Stanley, 1966; Chassan, 1967; Edwards, 1968; Sjoberg and Nett, 1968; Lindzey and Aronson, 1968; Roff and Ricks, 1970), the following condensed and somewhat superficial presentation should furnish a general picture of the rationales and techniques that comprise the essentials of selecting a research design.

Varieties of Research Design

Researchers can be differentiated in terms of whether they gathered their data in rigorously controlled "experimental" settings, or in the "natural" context within which events occur. Researchers of each persuasion often contend that their methodological approach will prove most productive in advancing our knowledge of psychopathological processes. Neither side can be judged "best" since they tend to concern themselves with different research questions, focus on different levels of data, and frequently seek to achieve different scientific goals. Fortunately, there are signs that the rigid-mindedness that has long separated these "two disciplines of scientific psychology" is beginning to soften (Cronbach, 1957). Gratifying though this change may be, it should not be concluded that these approaches are indistinguishable, nor equally suited for all types of research endeavor; that is hardly the case, as will be evident in later paragraphs.

The experimental-naturalistic distinction is a broad and somewhat arbitrary one, with innumerable variants within each category. The sub-classification scheme we shall employ in this section highlights several of these more distinctive features; it is likewise arbitrary, as are all such schemas. We present these designs as discrete methods for expository purposes; that is, the schema will serve as a useful format to point out to the student certain logical and procedural commonalities among research designs. "Real" investigations often include elements of several of the "pure" designs to be discussed; in fact, methodological mixtures are typical of the work of inventive and productive scientists. For our purposes, however, it will suffice to furnish a summary review of the basic design variants. After these elementary types are thoroughly mastered (an achievement hardly attained by reading the rudimentary sketches provided here), the student may try his hand in devising more complex design arrangements.

What characteristics distinguish *experimental* and *naturalistic* methods?

Those employing the *experimental* approach stress the manipulation and control variables and seek to establish the precise sequence of cause-effect relationships. In the ideal "laboratory experiment," as borrowed from classical physics, the researcher selects certain variables that he considers basic, and then manipulates them in a specially arranged setting that is less complex than the one in which they naturally function; the virtue of this approach is that the potentially contaminating or obscuring effects of extraneous variables are removed or under tight control. Of course, not all experimental designs are executed under artificial or contrived laboratory conditions; naturally occurring events that are subjected to manipulative modifications, or arranged under conditions of systematic control, also fall within the province of the experimental approach.

For the most part, experimental designs in psychopathology are of two types: $S \rightarrow R$ (signifying the influence of an antecedent stimulus variable upon a response variable, e.g., the influence of a stressful interruption on level of anxiety) or $S \rightarrow O \rightarrow R$ (signifying the influence of antecedent stimulus and organismic variables upon response variables, e.g., psychiatric status as a mediating factor in determining the impact of stress on anxiety). The aim of these studies is to gather data that will confirm causal hypotheses. Three types of experimental designs will be described in a later section: own-control studies, pre-post control-group procedures, and factorial designs.

Naturalistic methods attempt to extract the elements of a naturally occurring complex of variables *without* the intrusion of direct manipulations or constraining controls. These approaches are suitable for generating new hypotheses, describing existing relationships, or classifying patterns among clearly defined variables. Although the data gathered in naturalistic studies may be suggestive of causal relationships, they lack the controls requisite for ruling out rival hypotheses. Nevertheless, where complex interactions exist, and where crucial variables cannot feasibly or ethically be manipulated, naturalistic designs may provide the only systematic data for causal hypotheses.

Naturalistic designs will be divided into five basic types. "Correlational techniques" are either of a $O \leftrightarrow O$, $O \leftrightarrow O \rightarrow R$; $O \leftrightarrow R$, or $R \leftrightarrow R$ type (signifying the pattern and magnitude of covariation among these organismic and/or response variables). As an example, Wittenborn (1950) attempted to uncover groups of symptomatic behaviors (responses, $R \leftrightarrow R$) that covary or occur together in the same patient. To achieve this, he asked psychiatrists to rate samples of patients' behavior on 55 symptom scales, then intercorrelated these ratings, and factor analyzed the correlation matrix to extract the major areas in which symptoms clustered together. "Survey procedures," the next of the principal naturalistic designs, are typically $O \leftrightarrow O$ studies, with description of incidence and relationships as their primary goal. The federal government's annual reports of patients in mental hospitals, classified by sex, age, diagnosis, etc., would be an example of an O↔O survey. In "field observations," S→R causal sequences are usually investigated in a descriptive or exploratory fashion. A typical example here would be a study in which patients' behaviors are recorded both before and after a planned, but rather loosely controlled, change in hospital routine. "Ex post facto methods" are of the S←O variety, and aim to infer certain causal influences on organismic variables through retrospective analyses. This method is illustrated in a study by Lindeman et al. (1959) in which 21 life history variables, obtained from clinical records, were related to the criterion of length of psychiatric hospitalization among a group of male veterans; the life history variables considered were length of military service, exposure to combat experience, history of alcoholism, number of previous hospitalizations, and severity of external precipitating stress. In "case studies," the format is either that of O↔O, seeking in an intensive study of a single individual to describe relationships among current organismic variables, or S←O, tracing through a careful retrospective exploration of earlier stimulus experiences those which may account for current organismic variables.

ACHIEVING CONTROL AND REPRESENTATIVENESS

To rephrase an earlier statement, an ideal research design is one that increases the internal and external validity of the study by minimizing or counteracting the effects of confounding and limiting factors. This is achieved, essentially, by two procedures: manipulation and randomization. In the previous chapter, the several sources of variability that determine the character and generalizability of research results were grouped into four categories. The first, the "research variables," comprise the elements and focus of the research hypotheses. The second category, termed "confounding the limiting factors," are sources of influence that obscure or distort the findings, or restrict their generalizability. It is the task of the research design to surmount the problems stemming from this second group by exploiting the procedures of manipulation and randomization; through these two methods, confounding and limiting factors are transformed into "manipulated" and "randomized" variables, the third and fourth of the sources of variability in a study.

Manipulation

By procedures of selection and arrangement, investigators may construct a research design that diminishes the contaminating effects of confounding factors, and extends the range of conditions and persons to which his findings may be generalized. The two principal methods by which this is accomplished are *planned uniformity* and *systematic variation*.

Planned Uniformity. The most common method of controlling potentially confounding factors is to hold them constant, that is, to assure that they have an equable impact upon other variables. In this way, whatever corrupting effect they produce will be uniform or consistent.

For example, ward behavior of patients may vary as a function of such variables as the hour of the day; to assure that clinical ratings of these behavior are not contaminated by variations in the time in which observers record their judgments, they are requested to make their appraisals at a set hour each day. Similarly, if it is anticipated that differences in therapist personalities may confound the results of an efficacy study comparing two treatment techniques, the investigator may enlist the same therapist for both procedures; in this way, variations in results that might stem from differences among therapists are nullified.

Confounding effects produced by measurement operations may also be controlled by procedures of planned uniformity. Thus, to obviate contaminating variations among raters in their judgments of patient behavior, the investigator may provide the raters with a manual containing explicit guidelines as to the exact behaviors that are to be observed, and precise instructions and numerical scales for indicating their magnitude. To further assure uniformity, raters may be indoctrinated through preresearch training sessions during which "errors" and idiosyncratic habits are carefully eliminated; for example, they may be asked to rate and rerate standardized samples for training and comparison (reliability) purposes.

Imposing uniformity upon extraneous variables does effectively decrease their potential confounding effects, *but at the price of lost generalizability*. Thus, in his attempt at control, the investigator may have arranged conditions that are so artificial or unusual as to diminish the significance and relevance of his findings. Similarly, by constructing a rating scale that eliminated errors in subjective judgments, he may narrow the range of behaviors his raters observe so sharply that they miss significant aspects of patient activity. Likewise, if the sample selected for study is homogeneous with regard to a particular diagnostic syndrome, age group, and sex, then his results will not be applicable to patients in other diagnostic groups or of a different age or sex.

Systematic Variation. To surmount the loss of generality entailed in uniformity planning, the investigator may choose to employ the more complicated procedure of systematic variation. In this technique, potentially confounding variables are not only identified, but introduced into the design of the study as research variables. In a drug study where various drugs are to be compared, for example, rather than controlling the possible influence of age factors by selecting only those within a restricted range, the investigator may select patients of all ages, grouping them into several age brackets, and then examining what bearing the age variable has on his findings. By building new variables such as these right into the study design, the researcher not only controls their "confounding" effects but also extends the generalizability of his findings to patients of all ages. Moreover, through various statistical analyses he can determine not only the general impact of the drug, but establish drug-age "interactions"; that is, determine whether the efficacy of the drug varies with the age of the patient and whether different drugs are effective at different ages.

Randomization

The number of factors that can confound the internal validity of a study is often far greater than can be controlled by the manipulative procedures of planned uniformity and systematic variation. The potential impact of these nonmanipulable influences may be nullified by randomization methods, that is, techniques that distribute their perturbing effects in an unsystematic and chancelike fashion.

Randomization is employed for four principal reasons: (1) when extraneous variables have not been identified and, therefore, cannot be manipulated; (2) when extraneous variables have been identified, but cannot be feasibly arranged in either of the two manipulative procedures described above; (3) when it is deemed a more efficient or appropriate procedure than systematic variation as a method for achieving generalizability; and (4) when it is required to meet assumptions of the statistical test to be used in analyzing the research data.

Randomization is useful not only to manage extraneous influences that cannot be controlled by other means, but also to optimize the generalizability of data obtained with research samples. In a typical investigation, a researcher will select a sample from the population to which he wishes ultimately to generalize his findings, a procedure executed in accord with any one of several standard sampling methods (see Kish, 1953, 1965; Chein, 1959). Although a few investigators will choose their subjects in a *completely* random fashion, this method is appropriate only when one wishes to generalize one's findings to people-at-large. Truly random samples often generate findings that mask more selective and important effects. To pinpoint his results where it is most important, the investigator may select his subjects randomly, but only from the population to which he desires to generalize his findings. For example, if a new drug is administered to a random sample consisting of *all types* of patients, the results obtained might obscure its particular efficacy with certain pathological syndromes. To obviate this difficulty, the investigator may subdivide his sample in line with several potentially discriminating organismic variables (e.g., specific syndrome groups, degrees of chronicity, etc.), and then randomly select patients within each of these categories. In effect, he will have random samples that represent significant organismic characteristics; this procedure has enabled him to neutralize potentially confounding subject factors, while at the same time providing him with both generalizable and discriminable data.

Procedures of randomization are expected to distribute uncontrolled confounding factors in an unsystematic manner, such that the net effect will be that they will balance or cancel each other out. For example, it is not unlikely that differences among patients in their prognoses or in their ongoing life experiences will affect the outcome of treatment in an efficacy study of drug therapy. Though desirable, it is often impossible to make uniform or systematically vary these factors. To surmount this problem, the investigator may set up two patient groups, one on active drugs, the other on placebo. By assigning patients to both groups, in a *completely random manner,* he can safely assume that the effects of these uncontrolled prognostic and intercurrent factors will distribute themselves, *by chance,* about equally in both groups. Whatever unevenness in distribution may occur is taken into account in statistical analysis. Thus, statistical inference tests are constructed to tell the researcher whether his groups differ more than can be expected on the basis of random fluctuations; with the analytic calculations of these statistics in hand, he can state, with a specified "level of confidence," whether the resulting data can be attributed to sources other than that of chance alone.

EXPERIMENTAL DESIGNS

There are two features that distinguish experimental from other research designs: (1) control over both research variables and extraneous factors, and (2) design arrangements that maximize the plausibility of causal interpretations of data. In general, experimental studies are of the S→R or S→O→R variety; that is, they attempt to deduce the "causal" impact of certain stimulus experiences or organismic characteristics upon response behaviors. This is done by manipulating S and O variables, referred to as the *independent* variables of the study, and observing whether and how they are related to R variables, or what are termed the study's *dependent* variables. By minimizing the role of potential confounding factors, either through planned uniformity, systematic variation, or randomization, the research seeks to strengthen the conclusion that variations recorded in the dependent variables can be safely attributed to variations in the independent variables. He can feel confident in drawing such causal interpretations if: (1) his independent and dependent variables *vary concomitantly;* (2) manipulations of the independent variable have *preceded in time* the changes observed in the dependent variable; and (3) he has effectively *eliminated rival hypotheses* by controlling all influences that could arise from extraneous factors (Selltiz et al., 1959).

The three experimental designs we shall next outline facilitate causal interpretations by arranging the independent and dependent variables in a proper time order sequence under conditions that minimize or eliminate extraneous sources of influence. Our presentation of these designs will proceed from those of lesser internal validity to those of greater internal validity. To illustrate distinctions among procedures more clearly, we shall draw our examples mainly from one field of research, that of therapeutic efficacy. Much of what follows draws heavily from the extensive and illuminating discussions of Campbell and Stanley (1966).

Own-control Studies

The simplest and most economical of experimental designs compares research subjects to themselves. In this procedure, subjects are evaluated on a dependent variable both prior to and after the introduction of the independent variable. The first dependent variable measure is termed *the pretreatment score;* the second measure is termed the *posttreatment* score. Differences or shifts between pretreatment and posttreatment scores serve as a gauge of the influence of the independent variable. For example, Silverman and Spiro (1967) used a variant of the own-control design to study the effects of subliminally presented aggressive stimuli on the functioning of hospitalized schizophrenics. They obtained pretreatment or "baseline" measures of functioning (using three different tests) prior to the presentation of a series of menacing pictures, and then obtained posttreatment or "critical" measures immediately afterward. The independent variable was the presentation of different groups of aggressive stimuli; the dependent variables were the scores on the three tests of functioning. They hypothesized that dysfunction as measured by these tests would be increased following the experimental manipulation, and the difference between the "baseline" and "critical" scores served as their gauge of the influence of the independent variable.

The primary value of the own-control procedure is economy; that is, the investigator does not have to find and put together a separate well-matched "control group" composed of subjects with organismic characteristics that are comparable to an "experimental group." However, this single-group design has serious weaknesses. To illustrate with reference to studies of therapeutic efficacy, this design fails to control for: (1) "spontaneous" variations in the patient's state; (2) confounding life experiences that may generate changes between the pretreatment and posttreatment scores; (3) the ephemeral "placebo effect" wherein any manipulation might have influenced the dependent variable by changing the subject's expectation; and (4) features of the pretreatment testing which itself may produce change. In other words, patients may do "better" after treatment, not because of its intrinsic merits, but because of chance fluctuations in their mental health, the influence of beneficial extratherapeutic events, a disposition to improve because they expect to do so, or the effects of the pretesting experience, such as when a self-attitude questionnaire stimulates them to reexamine and alter their self-attitudes.

To minimize certain of the weaknesses of the single pre- and posttreatment procedures, Campbell and Stanley (1966) describe two own-control design variants, termed the "time-series" and "equivalent time-sample" experiments.

In the *time-series design,* subjects are administered multiple-response measures at several periods both before and after the introduction of the independent variable; for example, Cartwright and Vogel (1960) evaluated therapeutic patients with a number of test instruments immediately upon application, again immediately before therapy began, at a point in time after beginning treatment that was equal to the waiting period between the time of application and the beginning of therapy, etc. Improvement that holds up under repeated measurement decreases the plausibility that it is a result of chance fluctuation; furthermore, since the positive effects of placebo suggestibility usually last only a brief period, if the time series is extended well beyond the termination of treatment, the impact of this confounding factor should be overcome. The design, however, fails to control for the contaminating effects of extratherapeutic experiences; also, the experience of repeated multitesting may itself influence the course of treatment.

The *equivalent time-samples design* is an extension of the time-series procedure. In its principal form, the researcher alternates treatment and no-treatment periods, making appraisals before, after, and between each treatment period. In addition to the advantages of the time-series design, this method counteracts the effects of extratherapeutic environmental events since these will influence the scores following no-treatment periods as well as those that follow treatment. Remaining, however, are problems created by the effects of multiple evaluations. Despite this minor complication, the equivalent time-samples design is an effective procedure for maximizing internal validity in an own-control study.

Pre-Post Control-Group Procedures

Time-series and equivalent time-sample designs effectively control several potentially confounding influences, but both are fairly complicated and often inexpedient procedures, thereby negating the primary advantages of the own-control design, that of simplicity and economy. Comparatively speaking, the procedure known as the pre-post control-group design is no more complicated and often more efficient in avoiding the contaminating effects of extraneous influences.

In this procedure, as applied to studies of therapeutic efficacy, one group of patients receives the designated program of treatment, while a second, or control, group, comparable on all relevant organismic characteristics, does not. Following a pretreatment evaluation, subjects are randomly divided into experimental and control groups; only the experimental group receives therapy. Since both groups have been exposed to the effects of the initial testing evaluation, are subject to the influences of nontherapeutic events, and experience natural fluctuations of mood and behavior, these potentially confounding influences should be distributed equally in the posttreatment scores of both groups. Differences that show up on these latter scores can then be ascribed with confidence to the one feature that distinguished the two groups, that of the treatment experience. In short, the scores of the control group serve as a standard or baseline for gauging influences above and beyond those produced by nontherapeutic influences; since the only variable that differentiated these groups was the therapeutic experience, its effects, if any, should be evident when comparing their posttreatment scores.

Despite the seeming simplicity and efficiency of the control-group design, it does present several methodological problems and limitations. For example, great care must be given to assure that subjects in both groups are equivalent on all relevant organismic variables, for example, prognostic factors, suggestibility, etc. Another difficulty may stem from patient and therapist expectancies. For example, in a drug study, therapists may rate the treated group as improved, and the untreated group as unimproved, simply because they know which patients received medication and which did not.

Problems of biased judgments stemming from observer expectancies may be solved by relying on "blind" procedures. For example, in studies of psychopharmaceutic agents, an observer's anticipations and desires may distort his appraisals of a drug's efficacy. To surmount this problem, patients in an untreated control group may be given a "placebo," that is, an inert tablet or capsule that is physically indistinguishable from the chemically active agent. In a "double-blind" procedure, neither patients, therapists, nor raters are informed of this duplicity. As a consequence, potentially confounding effects arising from patient or therapist or rater expectancies will operate uniformly in placebo and chemically active groups; if patients on the "real" drug improve more than those on placebo, the role of patient or therapist or rater bias can safely be discounted (Lasagna and Meier, 1959; Chassan, 1967).

"Blind" procedures eliminate the effects of foreknowledge and expectation, but they do not separate other spurious ingredients of therapeutic outcome. At best, control group designs merely tell us that therapy was associated with improvement; they do not provide us with information such as whether the essential ingredient was the therapist's attitudes, the treatment atmosphere, the specific technique employed, and so on. To obtain answers to these more specific questions, it is usually necessary to arrange a "factorial" design.

Factorial Designs

Control-group designs achieve internal validity via the methods of planned uniformity and randomization; that is, extraneous variables are either kept constant or distributed in chancelike fashion between treated and untreated groups. Factorial designs depend on randomization procedures also, but they employ systematic variation in lieu of uniformity planning. As described earlier, systematic variation not only achieves control over potential confounding influences but also allows the researcher to discern the independent and interactive effects of these influences, and thereby extends the discriminability and generalizability of the study's findings. In studies such as these, the investigator includes "two or more variables, each varied in two or more ways and studied in all combinations" (Edwards and Cronbach, 1952).

One of the shortcomings of the basic control-group design, as noted above, is its failure to differentiate the separable ingredients that may comprise a total matrix of influences such as those subsumed under the term "therapy." This limitation does not apply in factorial designs; here, a number of independent elements are identified and simultaneously varied. For example, in psychotherapeutic research, several, rather than two, groups may be formed, each subjected to one or another of the ostensive ingredients that may influence the course and efficacy of therapy; for example, in a client-centered approach to treatment, one group may be exposed only to therapeutic "warmth and empathy," another to "directive" procedures, and a third to a composite of both.

To further extend the range of information provided, subjects may be separated in accord with differences on potentially relevant target symptoms or prognostic factors. Thus, a factorial design may be arranged in which different types of patients are exposed systematically to different types of therapy; for example, patients exhibiting either phobic or hypochondriacal disorders may be subjected to either behavior modification or client-centered methods in what is labeled a 2×2 design (2 factors, each with 2 levels) with the following hypothetical percent improvement rates.

	Behavior Modification	Client-Centered
Phobia	.85	.55
Hypochondriasis	.40	.70
Total	.625	.625

Had patients not been differentiated according to target syndromes, the overall or average result would have suggested that both forms of therapy were of equal efficacy. By a factorial design, however, it was possible to gather more refined information, specifically the relative superiority of the different treatment approaches with different symptoms disorders.

With factorial designs, as evaluated by statistical "analyses of variance," one may extract the patterns of influence and interaction of several simultaneously manipulated variables such as alternative types of therapy, different clinical syndromes, therapists with dissimilar personality characteristics, etc. Not only do these designs produce significant increments in the precision and generalizability of research findings but they also accomplish in one experiment what might otherwise require several separate studies; in other words, factorial arrangements are highly economical in that they allow one set of subjects to do the work of two or more. The greater the range of variables and the number of distinctions among them that can feasibly be arranged in these designs, the more generalizable and discriminable will be the data they provide.

In discussing the values of this procedure in psychopharmacologic research, Sherman offers the following comment (1959):

> In contrast to the traditional approach of holding all but one variable constant, in a factorial design the experimenter deliberately varies as many factors as he is interested in studying. This procedure is more comprehensive than other methods because interactions between variables as well as the main effect of each variable may then be studied. It is also more economical because a wide range of conditions are sampled using fewer subjects and observations than would be required in conducting separate studies for each factor.
>
> In brief, a factorial design can answer more than one question in a single

experiment. It can tell us not only that one drug is superior to another, but also under which treatment conditions and for which types of patients this superiority obtains.

From the wealth of information that could possibly be obtained from such a study, the basic advantage of a factorial approach is clear: *the more variables systematically investigated, the more comprehensive the information obtained.*

In view of the considerable evidence that changes in behavior are not merely a function of the drug itself, it is surprising that so many studies still neglect or attempt to hold constant all other relevant variables. Instead of excluding these nondrug sources of influence, we should recognize their existence and, by using a factorial approach, actually build them into our research designs. Only in this way can the combined influence on behavior of drug, situation, and person variables ever be ascertained and more valid knowledge of drug effects obtained.

Comment. The examples employed to illustrate the experimental designs discussed above deal with the events of "real" therapy. The basic format of each of these designs may also be employed in laboratory studies that simulate real-life situations.

In the classical laboratory experiment, modeled from studies in the physical sciences, researchers separate from their natural setting just those variables they consider essential to their purposes, and manipulate them in an artificial or contrived setting that will optimize the conditions for testing hypotheses. Thus, laboratory settings differ from other experimental contexts in that they *isolate* their research variables from extraneous sources of influence. By simplifying the complex of natural events in this manner, the researcher is able to observe, with clarity and precision, the exact consequences of his manipulated independent variables upon his dependent variables. Not only do these methods increase the "purity" of an investigation but they may also be necessary where practical or ethical considerations preclude the use of other designs. For example, new therapeutic drugs that *may* be harmful to patients must be tried out in laboratory animal studies before testing their efficacy with human clinical populations; similarly, it may be impossible to separate the various ingredients that comprise the processes of "real" therapy, but it may be feasible to isolate these elements in a laboratory setting.

Laboratory procedures have proven fruitful in the design of what is termed "therapeutic analogue" research; here, the components of therapeutic action are isolated and examined independently of the larger complex of which they are a natural part (Goldstein and Dean, 1966). Through these procedures, it may be possible to elicit the basic principles and essential ingredients of various therapeutic techniques, a task difficult to achieve even with the most sophisticated of nonlaboratory factorial designs.

Since laboratory methods are arranged and executed in settings that only simulate "real" conditions, the results they produce should not be generalized until they are further analyzed and verified in natural clinical settings.

NATURALISTIC DESIGNS

As described previously, naturalistic methods attempt to extract the elements of a naturally occurring complex of variables *without* the intrusions of direct manipulation or constraining controls. In contrast with experimental procedures, where special stimulus conditions are deliberately introduced to alter the responses of subjects, naturalistic techniques record subjects' responses as they exist, that is, as they happen to be, or as they happen to unfold, without manipulative interventions or intentional modification. Control and representativeness, where desired, are achieved *indirectly,* either through statistical means or by selective sampling and measurement procedures. At the very most, instruments are applied to elicit or highlight the subject's behavior repertoire; responses are brought into sharp focus for purposes of measurement clarity and precision, and are *not* products of experimental induction, that is, formed anew as a function of independent variable manipulation.

Naturalistic studies often uncover patterns of concomitant variation among research variables, but either lack control over extraneous sources of influence, or are unable to establish the time-order sequences among variables. Since they fail to meet the requisite threefold criteria noted previously, the data of naturalistic designs cannot be employed with confidence to confirm causal relationships. For example, certain designs are able to demonstrate both concomitant variation and time-order sequences (ex post facto methods, case studies, and field observation), but do not control extraneous variables sufficiently well to disqualify rival causal interpretations. Other naturalistic methods (survey procedures and correlational techniques) exhibit both concomitant variation and a reasonable degree of control over confounding factors, but are not designed to demonstrate the time-order relationship among variables.

In general, naturalistic methods are most suitable in research studies that aim to explore hypotheses, classify data, or describe existent relationships. As noted above, they lack the efficacy and power of experimental designs to establish cause-effect sequences. However, naturalistic procedures may provide useful data where controlled experimentation is either impossible, impractical, or unethical; despite their drawbacks and limitations, these designs may prove the only or most expedient procedure for investigating causal hypotheses.

The five designs that follow will be presented in a sequence beginning first with those of maximum measurement precision, sampling representation, and extraneous variable control, and continue, in rough order, to those of lesser precision, representation, and control. Since naturalistic designs serve different purposes and are characteristically employed to investigate problems in different substantive fields, the illustrations to be used will, of necessity, be drawn from divergent subject areas.

Correlational Techniques

Perhaps the best controlled and most precise of the nonexperimental methods are a variety of procedures subsumed for our purposes under the label *correlational techniques.* Essentially, these procedures seek to determine the magnitude of covariation, or interrelatedness, among naturally occurring variables.

Correlational methods are perhaps best known for their use in psychological test construction and evaluation. In psychopathological research, however, their use centers chiefly on problems such as: (1) discovering intrinsic commonalities among seemingly divergent variables; for example, do patients diagnosed as schizophrenics evidence particular types of biochemical aberrations not found in other equally deteriorated syndromes? (2) assessing similarities among clinical groups; for example, are obsessive-compulsives and hypochondriacs alike in their "basic" personality attributes? and (3) predicting future behaviors from current diagnostic signs; for example, can the profile pattern of the MMPI accurately forecast future reactions to drugs?

Using our simplified notational system, correlational techniques appear most suitable in studies that wish to describe $O \leftrightarrow O$, $O \rightarrow R$ and $R \leftrightarrow R$ relationships, or to establish $O \leftrightarrow O \rightarrow R$ predictions. We cannot undertake a discussion here of the numerous statistical methods used in correlational designs for that would involve us in logical and computational complexities that lie beyond the province of a text such as this.

Many hypotheses posed for correlational analysis are indistinguishable from those subjected to experimental procedures. Correlational methods, however, deal with organismic and response variables that already exist within the repertoire of the subject, rather than with variables that are experimentally produced. Shontz (1965) illustrates the similarities and differences of these two approaches in this brief quote:

If a psychological investigator cannot actually manipulate the levels at which an independent variable operates, he may employ other strategies to accomplish a comparable purpose. . . . One possibility is to select subjects who themselves represent different levels of the variable. For example, if an investigator cannot make people bright or dull, he can, at least, measure intelligence and separate his subjects into bright and dull groups. If he cannot manipulate anxiety levels successfully, he can select anxious and non-anxious subjects, as defined by scores on a suitable measuring instrument, for comparison on some behavior that he thinks will be affected by anxiety level. When he uses this approach, he is employing what is here called the *correlational method.*

A major extension of basic correlational statistics is known as *factor analysis.* Essentially, factor analytic procedures are mathematical computations designed to reduce large bodies of data to their fundamental commonalities and relationships by minimizing redundancies or overlapping. By scrutinizing the matrix of intercorrelations exhibited among a wide array of measures, as small a number of "factors" as possible are extracted to account for the pattern or distribution of scores.

Numerous factorial systems have been devised (Fruchter, 1954; Harmon, 1960), the specifics of which need not be detailed here; a useful summary of several of the applications of factor analysis of psychopathology, such as the appraisal of diagnostic test patterns and psychiatric nosologies, has been provided by Dahlstrom (1957).

In general, factor techniques have been employed to extract commonalities among three classes of data; Cattell summarizes these factor sources, which have been differentiated and labeled *R-,* *Q-,* and *P-*techniques, as follows (Cattell et al., 1947).

. . . . in *R-*technique we correlated test variables with regard to a series of persons; in *Q-*technique we correlate persons with regard to a series of tests. In *P-*technique we again correlate test variables, but with regard to a series of occasions and within a single person.

The R-technique is the most common of the factor approaches; in essence, it is designed to uncover commonalities among a wide variety of test measures taken only once by a group of subjects. The results of these tests are intercorrelated, providing evidence as to which measures are merely overtly different expressions of fundamentally similar traits, that is, belong together as elements of single factors.

The Q-technique, strongly espoused for personality appraisal by Stephenson (1952), follows the same factorial procedure as the *R-technique,* but instead of correlating test scores, intercorrelations are made among subjects; that is, the overall shape or profile of their scores are correlated in an effort to establish similarities among general response patterns. The intent is to discover which persons belong together as members of the same type or to gauge the extent to which individuals approximate certain ideal personality types. Alternatives to the *Q-technique,* but concerned also with assessing similarities in clinical diagnostic profiles, have been formulated by several investigators (Zubin, 1937; DuMas, 1947; Cronbach and Gleser, 1953; Nunnally, 1962; Overall, 1963; Gleser, 1968).

The *P-technique* differs from other factor analytic methods in that it is based on the data of a single individual who has taken the same set of measures repeatedly. Intercorrelations are obtained on the basis of consistencies among these measures, and the resulting factors represent the most stable scores over time. According to Cattell (1947), a combined factor analysis using *P-* and *R*-techniques should furnish the clinician or researcher with an accurate portrayal of both the essential and most durable personality features of an individual.

Methods by which both experimental and factor analytic procedures may be fruitfully combines in the study of personality and psychopathology have been described in detail by Stephenson (1952), Cattell (1952), Cronbach (1957), Katz et al. (1968), Mahrer (1970).

Survey Procedures

Included in this group of naturalistic designs are systematic procedures of data collection, usually employing statistical records, personal interviews, and mailed questionnaires, that seek to discover the relative incidence, distribution, and general relationships among variables in large and widely dispersed populations, or in samples of these populations (Campbell and Katona, 1953; Kerlinger, 1964). Survey techniques, typically formed as $0 \leftrightarrow 0$ studies, are used chiefly in psychopathology to uncover a variety of social psychological correlates of clinical syndromes (Durham, 1959; Plunkett and Gordon, 1960; Milbank Memorial Fund, 1961; Hoch and Zubin, 1961; Zubin, 1961).

In his review of "epidemiologic" studies, Morris (1964) notes the following uses to which this body of work may be put: (1) by establishing historical trends, medical planners may be alerted to disorders that are on the increase; (2) obtaining information on the general distribution and incidence data should facilitate more efficient health programming; (3) by identifying cases that are neither in formal treatment or on other records, knowledge is gained about pathologic features and syndromes beyond that obtained in the restricted setting of clinical practice; (4) gathering data on the sociologic distribution of a disorder should elucidate potentially significant etiologic events. Detailed reviews by Scott (1958), Hunt (1959), and Freeman and Giovannoni (1969) have illustrated the range of socio-cultural correlates of psychopathology that may be researched through systematic survey procedures, for example, rural-urban and intracity patterns, socioeconomic differences in prevalence rates and treatment availability, cross-cultural distinctions in clinical syndromes, etc.

Survey methods can furnish extremely valuable descriptive data, provided the sampling procedures used have gathered representative subjects, a feat of no simple proportions. Problems of patient mobility, unstandardized criteria for identifying syndromes, biases among sources for obtaining cases, are just a few of the obstacles to be faced in detecting and gathering representative samples. And not to be overlooked are the tremendous investments of time, skill, and money that are often required to complete a thoroughly reliable and unbiased survey.

Field Observation

Procedures included in this category may be referred to as "natural process" research in that observers record a series of unmanipulated events as they transpire in their real-life settings; from these observations, inferences are drawn about the relations and interactions of relevant variables.

Field studies are similar in certain respects to both experimental designs and survey procedures. Katz (1953) distinguishes them from surveys as follows:

> Although it is not easy to draw a fine logical distinction between a survey and a study of a field situation, there are practical differences which call for somewhat different techniques and skills. The difference is roughly between the greater scope of the survey and the greater depth of the field study. More precisely, two essential distinctions can be made. In the first place, the survey always attempts to be representative of some known universe and thus attempts both in the number of cases included and in the manner of their selection, to be adequately and faithfully representative of a larger population. This emphasis on sampling may or may not be found in a field study, which is more concerned with a thorough account of the processes under investigation than with their typicality in a larger universe. In a survey we always ask about the relative incidence, or distribution, of social variables or personality characteristics in the larger group with which we are concerned.
>
> The ongoing social and psychological processes are inferred in the survey from their statistical end-effects. In the field study, however, attempts are made to observe and measure the ongoing processes more directly. Specifically, this means that the field study either attempts observations of social interaction or investigates thoroughly the reciprocal perceptions and attitudes of people playing interdependent roles. Thus, a field study will provide both a more detailed and a more natural picture of the social interrelations of the group than does the survey.

Field studies are similar in format to experimental designs in that they examine S→R and S→0→R sequences. However, they are nonmanipulative and lack the systematic control over extraneous variables we normally associate with strict experimental procedures. For the most part, field methods are exploratory in character, identifying significant variables and generating speculative hypotheses that may be subjected later to more rigorous methodological designs.

Field methods, as applied in psychopathologic research, may be divided into two broad categories: *cross-sectional* and *longitudinal* studies.

The former comprises observational appraisals of a research population either at one time or over a short span of time; its objective is to evaluate, with varying degrees of measurement precision, the natural interplay of variables, usually in a social setting. Thus, these techniques have been widely used in studying problems such as the styles of interaction among families of severely disturbed patients (Bishop, 1951; Behrens and Goldfarb, 1958; Farina and Dunham, 1963), and the patterns of patient behavior or personnel relationships in mental hospitals (Stanton and Schwartz, 1954; Greenblatt et al., 1957).

Longitudinal studies consist of repetitive appraisals over a relatively long span of time, usually of a small number of subjects. The intent here, for example, would be to extract elements of developmental continuity among a group of children, or to record influences associated with changes from one assessment period to the next. Thus, in the work of Murphy (1962) and Thomas et al. (1963, 1968) efforts were made to trace developmental styles from infancy to childhood in the hope of disentangling the complex of forces involved in shaping distinctive and potentially pathological patterns of behavior. Prospective studies such as these represent an important new direction in searching out the chain of influences that lead to disorder; they contrast sharply with the practices of earlier researchers who leaned heavily on dubious retrospective reconstructions as their basis for unraveling the pathogenic sequence.

Field studies represent faithfully the "reality" of events, but they are "too loose and fluid," and possess insufficient controls over extraneous variables to serve as an effective basis for causal analysis. Whatever degree of instrumental and observational precision utilized in the study, the possibility always remains that factors other than those observed by the investigator may account for the recorded events. Nevertheless, these methods are of great value as preliminary "scouting" expeditions, scanning the field for what may follow as rigorously controlled research.

Ex Post Facto Methods

A central theme in most theories of psychopathology is the belief that early life experiences, such as parent-child relationships, family composition, or traumatic events, comprise an antecedent chain of events that give rise to and shape the character of later emotional impairments. Indeed, this assumption of developmental continuity serves as the basis for the standard clinical practice of gathering life-history data on newly admitted patients; knowledge of past events, when pooled together, is expected to provide the clinician with a clear understanding of the patient's impairment, and a basis for predicting its future course. The assumption of developmental continuity is the bedrock of most psychopathological theories, but there is a paucity of solid empirical evidence showing that life-history experiences are, in fact, causal determinants.

The problem plaguing investigators in this field is that studies of the causal effects of parental upbringing, home atmosphere, peer relationships, etc., simply do not lend themselves readily either to prospective longitudinal studies or to experimental manipulative designs, the only means by which cause-effect sequences can be demonstrated with confidence.

Faced with the unfeasibility or impossibility of longitudinal research and experimentation, researchers often turn to *ex post facto designs*. In this procedure, a group of individuals are identified who possess the trait or characteristic to be studied (e.g., anxiety syndromes, paranoid personality patterns). Then, by a retrospective investigation of their past histories, an attempt is made to deduce the distinctive events of their past which may have produced the trait in question (Greenwood, 1945; Chaplin, 1955). For example, in seeking to reconstruct some of the distinctive influences conducive to the development of paranoid traits, an investigator may set out to compare the features of the life histories of paranoids which differentiate them from their normal siblings. By carefully interrogating the parents of his subjects, he hopes to identify those elements of upbringing that may have generated their divergent developmental paths.

In contrast to longitudinal field methods and experimental designs, the logic of ex post facto research proceeds from effect to cause and not from cause to effect; to use the shorthand we have previously applied, these studies are of an S←O, rather than an S→O or S→R, nature. Kerlinger's (1964) definition summarizes this characteristic of ex post facto research as follows:

> Ex post facto research may be deemed as that research in which the independent variable or variables have already occurred and in which the researcher starts with the observation of a dependent variable or variables. He then

studies the independent variables in retrospect for their possible relations to, and effects on, the dependent variable or variables.

We can note only a few of the numerous pitfalls and complications of ex post facto studies. Causal interpretations must be viewed with suspicion since there is insufficient control, even in the best of designs where "experimental" and "control" groups are matched on numerous confounding variables, to countermand the plausibility of rival hypotheses; disentangling the many and varied sources of potential influence is so difficult that the investigator can never be confident that determinants other than those he has "controlled" or hypothesized have not been overlooked. More specifically, especially in studies that depend on retrospective reports, he faces the possibility that informants will fail to recall important past events and feelings, and selectively distort, in particular, unpleasant memories; thus, several investigators (Haggard et al., 1960; Yarrow et al., 1964) have found considerable unreliability in parental retrospective reports, and have noted that the greater the emotional involvement in an event, the less accurate is recall.

Case Studies

Tradition has the case study method as the principal instrument of clinical research. In this procedure, there is an intensive analysis of single individuals, their life histories, current feelings, thoughts, and behaviors, and the complex network of relationships among these naturally evolved and interdependent variables. Until the last three to four decades, almost all knowledge concerning the etiology, symptomatology, and therapy of psychopathologic conditions rested on the insightful observations and deductions of clinicians engaged in the careful study of unique or illuminating cases. Even today, this method is the most popular, and perhaps the most fruitful, approach for generating and exploring new clinical hypotheses; unquestionably, it continues to serve as the primary source of data where systematic experimental and naturalistic procedures are neither feasible nor possible.

The aims of case studies are similar to both ex post facto and correlational methods. Intensive explorations of individual patients, as exemplified in the work of Freud, are usually designed to uncover the developmental origins of current symptomatological patterns through retrospective means; in this quest, case studies are akin to ex post facto procedures in that both are arranged in an $S \leftarrow O$ format. Other case studies, best illustrated by Kraepelin's systemization of clinical syndromes, seek to reduce the diverse symptomatologies of mental patients to their essential commonalities or clusters; here, the case method is similar to the $O \leftrightarrow O$ or $R \leftrightarrow R$ pattern of correlational factor research.

What distinguishes case studies from other naturalistic methods is their "fluidity," their dependence on the observational and inferential skills of the clinician, their focus on unusual or fortuitous, and therefore unrepresentative, cases, their almost total lack of extraneous variable control, the imprecision of measurement procedures, and the highly subjective and impressionistic character of data recording and interpretation. Most often, the raw material of these studies unfold in the context of a two-person interaction, without the presence of external and objective sources to control and verify what transpires. Inevitably, the content of these diagnostic assessments and therapeutic interviews are subject to distortions of patient recall and clinician influence, both of which may shape the resulting data in ways consistent with theoretical and research preconceptions: Despite new sophisticated designs (Shapiro, 1966; Chassan, 1967; Davidson and Costello, 1969), and the use of instrumental techniques to record and control observer distortions (Gottschalk and Auerbach, 1966), most problems of confounding and interpretive bias remain unsolved (Bolgar, 1965).

Despite the "unconvincing" nature of case study reports, they serve a central heuristic purpose in psychopathologic research. Free of the constraints of more systematic methods, the investigator can draw upon the full range of his observational and intellectual powers to speculate and probe new ideas, to move flexibly and unimpeded in his explorations of the highly interwoven and qualitative character of natural pathologic functioning. Unconstrained by the demands and rigors of more formal procedures of inquiry, he may uncover new directions and subtleties that can rarely be generated in more tightly controlled studies. These new speculative notions may then, in turn, be investigated through more refined, objective, and systematic procedures.

CONFOUNDING AND LIMITING FACTORS
IN PSYCHOPATHOLOGICAL RESEARCH

In order to prevent his research variables from being masked or distorted or his efforts from being relegated to the waste-heap of rigorously exact but trivial or irrelevant work, the investigator in psychopathology must arrange a research design that eliminates the biasing effects of confounding factors and removes the constraints on generalizability produced by limiting factors. Deterrents to internal and external validity may be grouped into three categories, each of which may be seen as parallel to the research stimulus, organismic, and response variables.

The first, termed *situational factors,* are stimulus variables other than those intended for research study which bias the results or limit their representativeness.

The second category includes *subject factors;* these reflect organismic variables of the persons sampled for the research study which slant the findings in an undesirable way, or restrict their generalizability to the population they are intended to represent.

Measurement factors comprise the third group of confounding and limiting elements; these refer to distortions and inadequacies in the research response variables themselves, or in the manner in which they are gathered and analyzed.

Let us examine and illustrate each.

Situational Factors

The stimulus variables chosen for research investigation may not be the only ones that influence the course of the study or its findings; other stimuli, which we have termed "situational factors," extraneous to the intent of the hypothesis, may intrude themselves and play a determinant role in influencing the research results. Unless their effects are controlled, they will decrease the study's internal validity by confounding the research stimulus variables. This will make it impossible to assign the effects observed to the hypothesized variables since the presence of confounding factors exposes the results to rival or alternative interpretations.

With regard to external validity, if the research stimulus variables produce their effects by virtue of the special procedures and conditions of the study, then the findings obtained may not be generalizable to other settings and arrangements. Thus the interaction of the particular properties of the selected stimulus variables and the particular properties of the research situation may have been required to produce the findings; had different stimulus variables been chosen to operationally define the hypothesized stimulus concept, or a different research setting employed, the results may have taken another turn. The problem, in short, is that certain situational complexes may have less external validity than others.

Among the many situational factors that can prove confounding or limiting, three will be illustrated here: (1) settings and procedural arrangements; (2) researcher effects; and (3) intervening and intercurrent experiences.

Settings and Procedural Arrangements. In psychopharmacologic research for example, it is often assumed that patient reactions are solely a product of the chemical properties of the drug. This mistaken assumption fails to recognize that the effects observed are attributable, at least in part, to the situational setting within which the drug was administered. It has been well established that patients do not respond only to the pharmacologic agent alone. To illustrate, Slater et al. (1957) have shown that subjects who receive LSD (the research stimulus) while alone react quite differently than when they receive the drug in the company of others. Similarly, Nowlis and Nowlis (1956), reporting a series of extensive and ingenious studies on drugs in four-man groups, demonstrate unequivocally that styles of group participation shape the character of drug effects. In short, unless the confounding effects of the wider situational context are controlled or systematically manipulated, the internal validity of a research hypotheses may legitimately be questioned (Klerman, 1963).

With regard to matters of external validity, we might note, to continue with examples from psychopharmacologic research, that most investigators employ one route of drug administration (e.g., oral or intramuscular), one "average" dosage level given at a standard frequency, and follow a fixed period of treatment length. No consideration is given to the possibility that different results might ensue with different routes, levels, and lengths of treatment as has been well established in many systematic studies (Nash, 1959; Lasagna and Laties, 1959). In short, although an investigator may simplify the job of appraising the effects of a pharmacologic stimulus variable by restricting the range of its attributes (single dose levels, single routes, etc.), the resulting data may prove to be of limited generalizability.

Research Effects. Whether it be in survey interviewing, therapeutic interaction, projective testing, or laboratory experiment, a whole host of researcher attributes may intrude to shape the responses of subjects. Innumerable experiments have shown that researchers who differ in sex, age, race, feelings of anxiety, hostility, and warmth, or, most significantly, who have different desires or expectancies with regard to the outcome of their work generate significantly divergent responses in comparable settings and with comparable subjects (Rosenthal, 1966).

To illustrate again from psychopharmacologic studies, Sabshin and Ramot (1956) reported distinct relationships between therapist attitudes toward the efficacy of drugs and the response these drugs produced in patients; in effect, nuances in expression and subtle forms of communication, which either dilute or potentiate the usual chemical impact of the drug, are apparently conveyed by participating physicians. Similarly, in psychotherapy, Frank (1959, 1961) notes convincingly, in his illuminating and detailed reviews, that efficacy is linked to the faith of the therapist in the treatment technique he employs. Goldstein (1962) has systematically examined the complex and reciprocal pattern of patient-therapist expectancies as a factor in determining the character and efficacy of psychotherapy.

In summary, then, investigators who disregard or fail to control for the impact of researcher attributes and attitudes may decrease the internal validity of their studies; these extraneous factors may play a more significant role in shaping the results than the variables posited in the research hypothesis.

Distinctive characteristics of the researcher and his associates may have an important bearing also on problems of external validity. Thus, questions may arise as to whether data gathered under the direction of a "biased" investigator can be safely generalized. Clearly, some evidence must be provided, or some controls instituted, to assure that researchers (therapists, experimenters) typify in their personal attributes and attitudes the population and events they ostensibly represent, for example, therapists are part and parcel of the stimulus variable complex termed "treatment"; if the findings they generate are to be generalized, they should be a representative cross section of therapists who employ that treatment approach. Although it may be useful at first to enlist therapists whose views and talents are congenial to a particular mode of therapy, the success with which their efforts are associated cannot be assumed to be valid for therapists of different persuasions or aptitudes.

Intervening and Intercurrent Experiences. Both types of factors described above refer to situational events or conditions that operate in the same setting as those of the research stimulus variables; that is, they occur conjointly with the hypothesized variable as part of the same complex of influencing processes. In this section, we shall discuss problems that arise in studies which extend over a period of time; difficulties here stem from experiences that take place outside of the research setting (intercurrent experiences), or occur after the hypothesized stimulus variable has had its ostensive effect (intervening experiences). Both classes of situational factors can generate effects independent of those produced by the research stimulus variable, thereby confounding the results.

Frank (1959) comments on the role of intercurrent experiences on psychotherapy as follows:

> Treatment with younger persons may extend over a sufficient span so that processes of growth and maturation may contribute significantly to the changes observed. Improvement due primarily to extra-therapeutic occurrences, such as a change in job or social relationships, may be erroneously attributed to concomitant psychotherapy.

The problem of intervening experiences is especially serious in retrospective or longitudinal studies that attempt to attribute a significant role to a stimulus variable from the past. For example, clinical investigators in the 1930's were struck by the high frequency with which delinquent children were found to have disturbed relationships with their mothers; most notable in this regard was the ostensive role of prolonged maternal separation. Recognizing that retrospective clinical studies are subject to selective samplings, faulty memories, and biased reporting, the thesis was investigated more systematically, with increasing care given to proper methods of representative sampling and statistical analysis. As the findings of these studies accumulated, it became clear that only a small proportion of children who had been subjected to early maternal deprivation developed psychological difficulties. Moreover, many factors, other than that of disturbed early maternal relationships, contributed to subsequent pathological behaviors in cases where it occurred; these maladaptive outcomes depended, in large part, on the child's experiences *after* maternal separation, for example, the frequency and character of the child's subsequent relationships with adults, whether or not opportunities were provided for developing capacities and interests, etc. In short, although intervening experiences are difficult to disentangle, their "contaminating" effects must be teased out; otherwise, the internal validity of the study may have been seriously damaged.

Subject Factors

The results of most studies are seen as applicable to a particular population of people; it is mandatory, therefore, that subjects included in the study be representative of that population. There are recognized standards and procedures for selecting a representative sample, but meeting these requirements is easier said than done. Compromises are common, especially when the investigator has a readily available clinical group or other "captive" population, such as a hospital ward or a class of college students. The upshot of such compromises is that the generalizability of the study may be severely restricted, and that comparisons may be difficult to make between one study and another. For example, some investigators studying the effects of new pharmacologic agents select as their sample the "sickest" patients available, contending that it is this population with whom findings will be most significant; other researchers choose the "healthiest" patients, believing that a drug's efficacy should be tested with those who evidence a good prognosis. Obviously, favorable results obtained with prognostically good cases cannot be assumed to be valid for those with poor prognoses, and vice versa.

There are numerous other criteria by which investigators narrow the representativeness of their research sample; utilizing patients from a single diagnostic category, selecting only those who evidence particular "target symptoms" such as hostility or thought disorders, or patients of only a given age group, sex, or chronicity. Other researchers make no attempt at representational sampling, studying "at random" whatever patient population chances their way.

In this section, we shall again review a number of factors that confound and limit the data of psychopathologic research. Our attention, this time, will be directed to the consequences of those organismic variables we have termed confounding and limiting "subject factors."

Biased Groups. As noted above, there are numerous ways in which the sample chosen for study may fail to represent the population for whom the results are to be generalized. Matters of expedience and convenience often determine the subject population; "captive" audiences such as college students illustrate this notorious practice. Among the more typical groups chosen for psychopathological research, and whose selection often leads to confounded and ungeneralizable findings, are *volunteers* and *chronic hospitalized patients.*

There are many sound as well as practical reasons for exploiting "normal volunteers" as subjects. However, several investigators have shown that so-called normal people who volunteer for research exhibit a higher incidence of psychopathology than would be expected in an unselected "normal" population; in effect, then, "normal volunteers" are not quite normal, and results obtained with these subjects may not be assumed to characterize the population at large (Lasagna and von Felsinger, 1954; Riggs and Kaess, 1955). Of particular importance in this regard is the frequent use of "control-groups" volunteers to provide baselines for comparison with psychiatric populations. Pollin and Perlin (1958) have observed, however, that as many as half of typical volunteer groups display significant signs of psychopathology; with so high a proportion of disturbance, volunteer groups cannot be safely employed as "normal" baselines for comparative purposes. Along similar lines, Carr and Whittenbaugh (1968) found that significant differences in types and degrees of psychopathology exist between volunteer and nonvolunteer psychiatric patients; their findings raise serious doubts as to whether data obtained with patients who volunteer for research can be extrapolated to the larger psychiatric population they ostensibly represent.

Regarding internal validity, it is not uncommon for investigators to overlook the potential effects of confounding subject variables in their studies of hospitalized patients. To illustrate, numerous researchers have hypothesized that "schizophrenics" possess an intrinsic biochemical defect, deriving support for their contentions from a variety of metabolic indices gathered on hospitalized groups. What they fail to recognize is that metabolic dysfunctions may arise as a consequence of the hospital experience itself, as Kety illustrates in the following quote (1959):

> Most biochemical research in schizophrenia has been carried out in patients with a long history of hospitalization in institutions where overcrowding is difficult to avoid and where hygienic standards cannot always be maintained. . . .

In variety and quality the diet of the institutionalized schizophrenic is rarely comparable to that of the non-hospitalized normal control. . . .

It is not surprising that a dietary vitamin deficiency has been found to explain at least two of the biochemical abnormalities recently attributed to schizophrenia. It is more surprising that the vitamins and other dietary constituents, whose role in metabolism has become so clearly established, should so often be relegated to a position of unimportance in consideration of the intermediary metabolism of schizophrenics.

Suggestibility. Among the various ways in which contaminating influences can be minimized is to arrange a study under standardized conditions, that is, conditions that are objectively uniform. Despite these arrangements, subjects often perceive "constant" conditions in different ways, and fail, therefore, to react in the same manner to them. Although the researcher's intention is to elicit and record differences in subject response, these differences may stem from subject characteristics other than those assumed by the investigator. Among these confounding characteristics are organismic factors that "set" the subject to approach the standard conditions of the study in ways that systematically distort the data, for example, differences among subjects in the "social desirability" factor (Edwards, 1957), or in their "response styles" (Cronbach, 1946; Jackson and Messick, 1958, 1962).

Of particular importance in this regard is *suggestibility,* a trait referred to in therapeutic studies as "placebo reactivity," that is, a tendency to respond favorably to treatment whether or not the technique employed is genuinely effective. For example, several studies (Lasagna, et al., 1954; Beecher, 1959) have demonstrated that about one-third of all research subjects report relief from pain following injections of chemically inert (placebo) substances. Equally significant, though operating in an opposite fashion, Kornetsky et al. (1957) have found that a reasonably high proportion of patients are "negative reactors," that is, possess personality traits that incline them to "counteract" the usual physiological effects of real drugs.

In summary, if disproportionate numbers of therapeutically suggestible or nonsuggestible subjects are sampled in an efficacy evaluation, the "true" nature of the results will be obscured, or prove spuriously impressive.

Prognostic Attributes. There are no extraneous subject variables more crucial to the internal and external validity of therapeutic studies than those associated with prognosis. As Keisler (1966) has pointed out so persuasively, the myth persists that "patients at the start of treatment are more alike than they are different." Of course, researchers need not examine and control for every trait that may differentiate patients, even if that were possible. However, it is necessary when research samples are selected that organismic features which dispose patients to favorable or unfavorable treatment outcomes be carefully scrutinized. Obviously, intelligent, likeable, and verbal patients, who are not too sick to start with, are more promising therapeutic prospects than those who lack these positive attributes. The work of Zubin and his former associates at the New York State Psychiatric Institute (Zubin, 1959; Kline, 1959; Peretz et al., 1964) has pointed up many of the relevant prognostic factors conducive to differential therapeutic outcomes, especially in schizophrenic patients. To illustrate the range and diversity of these potentially contaminating influences, let us quote the following (Peretz et al., 1959):

> Our findings suggest that those factors associated with favorable outcome reflect a history of moderately effective adaptation prior to the onset of illness. Thus, marriage, extroversion, a good social history and good premorbid adjustment were the background factors associated with favorable outcome. Associated with onset and course of illness, sudden onset, demonstrable precipitating factors, a duration of illness less than 2 years, and the first attack or a history of previous remission were related to favorable outcome. Among the many symptoms studied, only the presence of good effect was related to favorable outcome in our sample. It is of interest to note how much more frequently the background factors and factors associated with onset and course of illness appear significantly related to outcome than do symptoms and signs.
>
> The significant morbid indicators are those reflecting a long history of lack of genuine affective relationships, isolation, conflict and lack of productivity. As specifically described for background factors they refer to unmarried, introverted, poor premorbid adjustment and poor social history. Among the factors associated with onset and course of illness pointing toward unfavorable outcome were onset prior to age 20, gradual onset, lucidity and coherence at the onset, absence of precipitating factors, chronic course and duration greater than 2 years. Unfavorable symptoms include hostility, irritability, externally directed aggression and constricted or diminished affect.

Since the list of prognostic indicators is so long, each investigator, perforce, must choose only those that are likely to vitiate his findings, and employ sampling procedures that will diminish their obscuring or biasing effects.

Measurement Factors

The techniques employed to gather and score responses depend, of course, on the levels of data and the research aims of a study. Rather crude instruments may be used in exploratory research to scan the range and character of subject responses; for example, simple unstructured interviews may serve as a bias for formulating hypotheses that may be worthy of later intensive study. Once the investigator's ideas begin to crystallize more sharply, he may decide to employ a formal questionnaire schedule or an itemized behavior rating checklist. Whatever measuring device is used, however, the possibility exists that it may confound the internal validity of the study, or possess features that limit its external validity. The measures themselves can influence the subject's responses; also troublesome are contaminating effects that stem from observer errors and distortions.

Instrument Characteristics. Students have an implicit faith in the methods of "scientific" measurement, but they fail to recognize that even the most sophisticated of tools are useless when applied in situations for which they were not designed. Thus, a test constructed for clinical diagnostic purposes may be gross and unreliable in appraising specific and tangible behaviors. Problems in internal validity arise as a consequence of other "defective" attributes of measurement instruments. In the following quote, Frank illustrates contamination in self-report inventories when used to gauge therapeutic improvement (1959):

> If the patient can clearly perceive the significance of the information he gives, the question arises of controlling for factors influencing his statements other than his internal state.
>
> In using scales which are relatively transparent to the patient . . . one must always keep in mind that the patient is telling the rater what he wants him to hear, so that changes in scores may be due more to changes in his attitude to the observer or to treatment than to genuine improvement.

To obviate such difficulties, investigators often employ oblique instruments such as projective tests; however, as Frank points out further, these devices "do not bear an obvious relationship to clinical improvement."

Of pertinence to matters of external validity is whether the measuring instrument employed correlates with other indices of the theoretical concept to the exclusion of others. Since all devices can tap only a sample of the characteristics it presumably represents, the result it portrays will depend on the specific items included. For example, the items included in a questionnaire that deals with therapeutic improvement may happen to deal with attitudes and feelings that patients are likely to change simply as a consequence of "getting things off their chest"; data obtained on these questionnaires will contrast sharply with those on an inventory that inquires into characteristics that are not so readily altered. Frank (1959) reports, further, that improvement ratings depend in part on whether a self-report scale is itemized and written, rather than global and oral; itemized scales remind patients of complaints that may have slipped their mind, resulting in appraisals that are less sanguine than those expressed orally in a face-to-face interview.

Researcher Observation and Judgment. As noted earlier, researchers, by virtue of their distinctive physical attributes and psychological attitudes, can influence the character of their subjects' responses. Researcher effects can take place in more ways than this. Examiners are often employed to record and evaluate the behavior of subjects; thus, they function as measurement instruments themselves, with all of the distortions and biases of human judgment. Not only are human observers prone to the many random errors that can arise from hasty, sloppy, and superficial observations, but more importantly, since investigators rarely are disinterested research participants, what they "see" and record may be subject to their unconscious desires and expectancies (Rosenthal, 1966).

Difficulties such as these are especially troublesome in rating psychopathological behaviors since clinical symptoms are highly complex and ephemeral, requiring the most subtle and refined of judgments; only highly trained, scrupulous, and objective observers can be expected to interpret events accurately and reliably. Unless adequate controls are instituted to counteract the systematic effects of biased observations, the study's internal validity is seriously jeopardized, and its results cast in doubt.

Along similar lines, most raters have had prior experiences with patients that serve as a frame of reference for their present judgments. Should their background exert an influence that prejudges their observations, the resulting data may be severely biased. Klerman (1963) discusses this problem in the following quote:

> It is well known that the criteria by which improvement is judged varies with the value systems and backgrounds of psychiatrists. At most reception centers and admission services, improvement is judged in terms of reduction of socially deviant behavior or amelioration of symptoms; while in institutions oriented about psychotherapy or social therapy, emphasis is placed not only upon symptom reduction but also upon deep personality change and the patient's development of more stable social adaptations.
>
> Even when research teams rely upon standard rating scales . . . it is still possible that the modal standards for rating used by mental health professionals vary with the treatment setting. The behavior the rater judges as "extreme" or "mild" depends, in part, upon the range of patients he is used to seeing.

In short, measurement data gathered through ratings in one setting may not apply, or be generalizable to another.

CONCLUDING COMMENTS

We have summarized several of the many complex steps and procedures involved in selecting a research design strategy for investigating psychopathological problems. What we have sought to stress is the importance of balancing rigor and relevance, that is, controlling extraneous influences that might misguide the results or their interpretation, while at the same time ensuring that the data are not trivial, but of reasonably broad practical and theoretical significance. Of course, the ideals of control and representativeness may be neither feasible nor necessary; this depends on the state of scientific skill and knowledge in a field, and the specific research goals envisioned by the investigator. In areas of rudimentary knowledge, the researcher may best spend his time exploring his ideas freely, examining the events and processes of his interest in a somewhat crude, uncontrolled, and unrepresentative fashion. As relationships among relevant elements become clearer to him, he may gradually refine his procedures to assure the increasing rigor of his techniques and the scope and relevance of the data they produce. Throughout each of these stages, what is needed most is a thorough familiarity with prior work and the creative vision to pursue important problems in an imaginative yet scientifically sound manner.

It is possible to systematically vary either situational, measurement, or subject confounding factors, transforming what may have been potentially contaminating influences into manipulable research variables; in this way, the investigator increases the scope of his study's generalizability, and the precision with which he may draw conclusions. For example, by identifying and systematically varying settings, time of day, therapists, etc., he controls their confounding effects, extends the range and types of situations to which his conclusions apply, and may be able to specify where, when, and with whom the results he obtains are more pronounced. Similarly, to counteract restrictions to generalizability which may result by employing a single measurement instrument, or observers with narrow biases, the researcher may use several types of appraisal techniques (e.g., ward behavior ratings, neurophysiological measures, projective methods), each of which are judged or scored by examiners of different persuasions. In short, by building into his study design, whether naturalistic or experimental, a variety of situations, measures, and subjects, the investigator achieves control, gathers information of wide generalizability, and may draw precise conclusions from his data.

CHAPTER FOUR

DATA COLLECTION
AND MEASUREMENT

This chapter will focus on the techniques by which contemporary investigators collect the data of psychopathology. Much valuable work is done with lower species, but space considerations require that we limit our attention to methods used with human subjects. Since data comprise the substantive content of research, a discussion of those instruments that elicit and measure psychopathological processes will fill out the "bare bones" of the more abstract issues of planning and design presented in earlier chapters.

The wisdom of tackling a research problem depends, in large part, on the availability and character of the instruments by which its data will be gathered. Theoretically important and beautifully designed studies may prove impossible to execute because there may be no technique available to tap the variables comprising the research hypothesis; thus, many a well-reasoned and well-formulated notion has had to be set aside until adequate devices were invented to elicit, discern, and quantify the concepts under inquiry.

Our goal in this chapter is to acquaint the student with some of the more commonly used techniques in psychopathology. The procedures to be presented will be differentiated, first, between those that are directly obtained from patients and those that are obtained from records, artifacts, and/or people other than the patients themselves; we shall label these as direct and documentary methods, respectively. Direct procedures will be our primary focus and they will be divided in terms of the four previously discussed basic data levels: biophysical, intrapsychic, phenomonological, and behavioral.

Data collection techniques provide "operational measures," those concrete procedures that elicit, highlight, and quantify the actions of research subjects. They deal, in effect, only with the response and organismic variables of a study, not with the stimulus variables. Some of these procedures gather relatively gross data as they occur in the natural course of events, for example, clinical observation, historical and personal documents; others are selective and highly refined instruments that amplify the subject's responses under relatively standardized conditions, for example, electroencephalogram, psychological tests, laboratory performance tasks.

Earlier, we outlined several criteria to be considered in selecting the instruments and measures of response and organismic variables; among them were discriminability, norm and variability estimates, reliability, validity, utility, and representativeness. These criteria apply equally to *all* methods of data collection, be they self-report inventories, physiological measures, projective techniques, or laboratory measures of motor performance. All-too-many researchers become engrossed in the one or two excellent features a particular instrument may possess; they fail, however, to recognize its shortcomings and limitations and end up either with precise trivialities or grandiose obscurities. No matter how elegant or complex a technique for gathering information about a variable may be, its user must judge it in terms of the same criteria as those who employ the simplest of devices.

We shall comment only sparingly on the adequacy of the methods to be described; in general, few satisfy the stringent set of criteria we have set forth. Most have been employed with sufficient frequency and fruitfulness, however, to justify their continuance as research tools. Rather than attempting an exhaustive description of data collecting techniques, we have focused on methods in each data class that we believe possess features that justify their greater use. Through these examples, we hope to acquaint the student as much as possible with the diversity of methods available, to indicate the special strengths of certain measures, to note the weaknesses and limitations of several frequently used but inefficient instruments, and to provide a background for the proper selection of relevant data collection techniques.

BIOPHYSICAL METHODS

Men have explored relationships between physical anomalies and patho-logical behaviors since the days of Hippocrates; however, it is only in the last 50 years that sufficient knowledge and technical skill has been avail-able to achieve reasonably precise and valid research data. During recent years, psychopathologic studies have been undertaken on such diverse functions as cardiac pressure and blood volume, skin temperature, chemi-cal changes in saliva and urine, muscle tension, eye movements, electrical activity in the brain, metabolic rate, and so on. Thorough reviews of the techniques and results of this growing body of work have been provided by Altschule (1953), Lacey (1959), Martin (1961), Brady (1962), Eiduson et al. (1964) and Stern and MacDonald (1965).

This section will survey some of the more fruitful methods employed in the recent literature to collect data at the biophysical level of observa-tion and conceptualization. These data may be studied for their own sake, or for purposes of relating them in some systematic way to data gathered either at the same or on other levels. It is possible at the biophysical level to further separate methods in terms of the specific types of data they col-lect, and it may be useful to add to our data level classification these dis-tinctions as well. Hence, biophysical methods will be subdivided in terms of three rather loosely differentiated data classes: the *physiochemical,* the *neurophysiological,* and the *anatomical.* The *first* refers largely to proce-dures involving biochemical measures and modifications; the *second* relates to nonchemical measures of physiological functioning, such as registered by polygraph recordings, blood volume measures, skin temperature varia-tions, etc., and to changes in physiologic functioning induced by electrode implantations; the *third* deals essentially with measures of gross body structure, and with surgical alterations in neural tissue. All of these proce-dures lend themselves to both experimental and naturalistic research de-signs.

In addition to differentiating the kinds of biophysical data collected, it is possible to classify the procedures by which biophysical data is gathered into two classes: incursive and nonincursive. Some methods may be spoken of as *incursive,* signifying an intrusion into normal bodily structures and functions. Here, the investigator seeks to observe the consequences of ana-tomic or chemical modifications of the natural processes of the organism; among these incursive procedures are the infiltration of drugs, the implant-ing of electrodes, and the extirpation of specific brain areas. *Nonincursive* techniques attempt to gather "inner" biophysical data in an indirect fashion, that is, without disrupting or infiltrating the intact biophysical substrate; an illustration would be the electroencephalogram (EEG), which picks up rhythmic neural activities generated within the brain from electrodes attached to the scalp; similarly, information about internal physiochemical functioning may be gathered by a number of analytic tests based on blood and urine specimens.

Physiochemical Indices

It was Gerard (1956) who formulated the now well-known phrase "No twisted thought without a twisted molecule." If we accept the thesis implied by Gerard, we should expect, in time, that scientists will detect some physiochemical abnormality for all "mental" aberrations. Unfortunately, as matters now stand, we cannot pinpoint which techniques will uncover these chemical correlates since we know little about the biophysical substrate of even normal psychological processes. The task would be vastly simplified if we had this knowledge; without it, contemporary researchers grope blindly, collecting reams of data whose connection and relevance to psychopathology can only be crudely guessed. Although serendipity has given rise occasionally to promising leads, for the most part what Maudsley wrote in 1895 still applies.

> The many diligent and elaborate chemical analyses of the urine which have been made by different inquiries in different countries, notwithstanding that the tabular exposition of them might fill a large volume, have failed to yield definite and constant results or to warrant any positive inference.

With this discouraging note as a precis, let us briefly examine three sources of physiochemical data: blood extracts, urine measures, and other body fluids. Details concerning these techniques will be bypassed since they involve technical matters beyond our current scope.

Blood Extracts. A variety of substances extracted from blood specimens have been posited as indices of psychopathology. Among the most frequently reported indices is that pertaining to *serum copper;* elevated measures of this substance have been correlated with an abnormally high globulin fraction, *ceruloplasmin,* a nonspecific oxidase of neurochemical acids and amines (Ozek, 1957; Domino, 1959). Several investigators have suggested that high ceruloplasmin levels are pathognomonic signs of schizophrenia; this has proven incorrect since increased levels are found in a wide variety of chronic nonpsychological disorders. Heath and his associates at Tulane (1957) contended, however, that the abnormal ceruloplasmin of schizophrenics was qualitatively different from that observed in other patient groups, coining the term "taraxein" to represent the elusive attributes of this blood serum fraction. In recent research, Heath has clearly distinguished taraxein from ceruloplasmin, claiming that taraxein is an antibody, and that schizophrenia was therefore an immunologic disorder (1966). Unfortunately, methods for extracting taraxein have proved extremely difficult and unreliable.

Considerable research over the years has focused on relationships between endocrine functioning and mental aberrations. The thyroid, one of the endocrine glands, produces a hormone, *thyroxin,* that can be estimated in blood serum by measuring protein bound iodine (PBI). Employing this delicate, though often unreliable, procedure, as well as the uptake of radioactive iodine by the gland itself, several researchers have reported relationships between thyroid functioning and schizophrenic subtypes (Bowman et al., 1950; Reiss, 1953; Cranswick, 1955). Later studies by Kelsey et al. (1957) suggest, however, that these relationships may be a function of dietary rather than psychopathogenic factors.

Urine Measures. The adrenal cortex has been selected most frequently among the endocrines as a source of pathogenesis. Although blood extracts can provide data on its two major products, the *17-ketosteroids* and the *corticosteroids,* urine measures have proved to be more stable indices over time. An indirect method for estimating adrenal activity, referred to as the *eosinophil count,* is used less frequently because of its high unreliability. Hoagland and his associates (1952, 1955) have reported that schizophrenics, as compared to normals, excrete more 17-ketosteroids and less corticosteroids. However, Eiduson et al. (1961) and Geller (1962) conclude from their studies that no differences exist in adrenocortical activity between normals and schizophrenics; differences that do occur seem best attributed to variations in diet and exercise associated with length of hospitalization.

A series of studies of the excretion of aromatic metabolites undertaken by McGeer et al. (1956a, 1956b) suggest various deficits among schizophrenics as compared to normals. However, these compounds are highly susceptible to dietary influences; moreover, aromatic indices are analyzed by paper chromatographic techniques, a procedure notably subject to interpretive error and bias.

Other Body Fluids. Three additional bodily fluids have been employed in studies of biopathology: cerebrospinal fluid, sweat, and saliva.

The cerebrospinal fluid, though requiring the tapping of an internal liquid, may be grouped along with the withdrawal of blood as essentially nonincursive indices. Well recognized as a sensitive index of organic disease processes in the central nervous system, its many constituents have also been analyzed in the hope of identifying pathologic conditions not usually considered to be of recognized biogenic origin, for example, schizophrenia. In a series of early studies, Gamper and Kral (1937) found that cerebrospinal fluids from schizophrenics were toxic to rabbits and mice, and Sogliani (1938) reported observing "catatonic" behaviors among injected mice. In more recent work, however, Shapiro (1956) could not duplicate either of these findings, and Bogoch (1958) concludes a review of research in this field by stating that most findings are equivocal, at best.

Studies dealing with variations in *perspiration* and *salivation* among severely disturbed patients have been conducted by several investigators. Smith and Sines (1960) report that certain odors were found more frequently among schizophrenics than in a matched group of nonschizophrenics. Fairly consistent evidence has been marshalled by Peck (1959) and Busfield and Wechsler (1961) to support the rather frequent clinical observation of reduced salivary output among depressed patients. No conclusions can be drawn from these studies, however, as to whether the findings are of a biogenic or psychogenic nature.

Neurophysiological Indices

There are delays in the processing and analysis of physiochemical properties; brief though it may be, an inevitable time lapse exists between the drawing of a blood and urine specimen, for example, and the assessment of their chemical attributes. Moreover, these properties are complex end-products, representing a composite result of a variety of influences that are difficult to separate and identify. Also, it is impossible with most physiochemical measures to keep a continuous record of events as they transpire within the body, or an immediate account of variations produced by specific external stimuli.

Few of the above-mentioned difficulties are found in the assessment of nonchemical physiologic functions. Many neurophysiologic measures are registered on *polygraphic devices* that provide an immediate and continuous record of changing bodily activities, or their associated electrical discharges. Typically, these instruments amplify minute signals that would

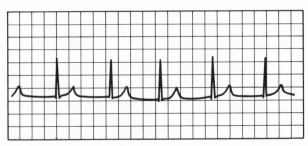

FIGURE 4.1   Polygraph recording.

otherwise be undetectable from recessed, though well-defined functional organs; variations over time in these amplifications are then transformed and recorded on a moving paper chart, furnishing a running account either of natural processes or responses elicited to external stimulations. These and other recording devices constitute the main source of neurophysiologic data in psychopathology research.

Five groups of data gathering devices will be presented in this section. The first, the electroencephalogram, focuses on the activities of the cortical centers of the nervous system; the remaining four tools—myographic, pupillographic, galvanic, and cardiovascular—record responses that reflect autonomic nervous system activities.

We can touch upon these instruments only briefly; an excellent presentation of the apparatus involved, and the procedures and complications of these devices, has been provided by Venables and Martin (1967).

Electroencephalographic Measures. The brain serves as the primary storehouse and coordinator of thought, feeling, and behavior. How to decode this information and analyze these functions without disrupting or damaging the brain's structure and protective coverings remains a matter for future research. In the interim, we must depend on rather gross instruments such as the electroencephalogram (EEG), a device first employed in 1924 by Hans Berger, a German psychiatrist. Although it was recognized early in the century that the metabolic processes of all living tissues generate electrical activity, the discharges of the intact nervous system were so minute and so vaguely understood that little interest was shown in them until Berger's seminal work. Attaching electrodes to the scalp, he amplified and recorded fluctuating voltages emanating from different regions of the intact brain. Adrian and Mathews (1934) replicated Berger's work and demonstrated convincingly that data so obtained could not be attributed to other organic processes such as muscle activity or circulatory pulsations; along with Gibbs, Davis, and Lennox (1935), they classified numerous EEG patterns associated with age, neurologic defects, activity level, etc.

Over the years, several frequency rhythms or wave patterns have been clearly distinguished. In general, these have proven of greatest value as a diagnostic aid in clinical neurology, especially in the identification of various structural lesions and epileptic subtypes. Among the normal cortical waves are those labeled the *alpha rhythm,* ranging from 8 to 12 cycles per second (cps), the *beta rhythm,* extending between 12 to 25 cycles, and the *delta rhythm,* falling between 0.5 to 4 cps. Typically, alpha rhythms are pronounced during relaxed wakefulness and when electrodes are placed above the occipital and parietal brain areas; the beta is notable during periods of alertness and in conjunction with the frontal and central regions; delta waves are prominent during sleep. Desynchronization, that is, a flattening of wave patterns, occurs in periods of marked excitement; dysrhythmia, a more or less irregular or chaotic wave sequence, often signifies a cerebral lesion. Because recordings in the standard EEG are taken from the intact skull, data is limited essentially to brain processes in cortical regions; electrical discharges from subcortical and other more deeply recessed areas are susceptible to measurement only through incursive techniques such as deep electrode implants.

Useful reviews of findings employing the EEG have been furnished by Ellingson (1956); Glaser (1963), Hill and Parr (1963), and Stern and MacDonald (1965). Attempts to correlate EEG patterns with various forms of nonorganic psychopathologies have not been notably successful, although abnormalities do occur with some frequency among patients categorized as schizophrenics and sociopaths; the significance of these latter findings, however, is unclear. Efforts to make prognostic judgments about schizophrenics on the basis of EEG measures have likewise been futile. Besides its recognized value as a neurological diagnostic tool, the EEG has been most useful in recent years as a research instrument in studies concerned with patterns of arousal and alertness (Lindsley, 1959; Malmo, 1961) and with identifying stages of sleep.

Biophysical theorists assume that patients differ in their physiochemical capacity to deal with the normal stresses of life. In line with this thesis, numerous investigators have attempted to unravel physiochemical defects by infiltrating into the body various stimulating or sedating drugs, and examining differences among patients and normals in their responsiveness to them. Such procedures might provide a biologic basis for differentiating patients syndromes and, more pragmatically, identify biochemical remedial agents that will be specific to the patient's particular deficits.

Among the various drugs employed in these studies are amo-barbital, methacholine, pentothal, atropine, chloralose, etc. (Fink, 1968). Following administration, their effects are assayed on any of a number of biophysical measures—pupillary and galvanic skin responses, conditionability, and, most commonly, EEG and blood pressure indices. Two procedures, the sedation threshold, using the EEG as the response measure, and the mecholyl test, using blood pressure as the response measure, have gained considerable favor among researchers, and have been used as "tests" for predicting treatment responsivity.

The *sedation threshold* technique, devised by Shagass (1954; 1956), consists of the intravenous administration of a barbiturate on a bodyweight basis, with its quantitative effects recorded on the EEG. It has been described as follows (Shagass and Kerenyi, 1969):

The sedation threshold . . . is a determination of the amount of sodium amytal required to bring about quantitative changes in the EEG. In developing this test, it was reasoned that the amount of a sedative drug required to reach a particular level of central nervous system depression should be proportional to the degree of tension or anxiety present in the individual receiving the drug.

To determine the sedation threshold, sodium amytal is injected at the rate of 0.5 mgm./Kg. of the body weight every 40 sec. until well after the time when the patient's speech is slurred. The sodium amytal solution is prepared so that 1 cc. contains 0.5 mgm./Kg. and 1 cc. is given at the beginning of every 40 sec. interval. The bifrontal EEG is recorded.

The clinical use of the sedation threshold determination arises from its ability to distinguish between various clinical psychiatric syndromes, and from the fact that such differentiation may be used to predict the outcome of electroconvulsive therapy.

Procedurally, an observer notes visually that the threshold has been exceeded by behavioral signs such as speech slurring or sleep. The beta EEG response has been continuously recorded from the frontal regions, usually by an electronic frequency analyzer. This generates an S-shaped curve of the rate of beta activity; the sharp inflexion of the curve denotes the sedation threshold, and the corresponding drug dosage required to produce it can be visually established. Shagass (1958) reports considerable success in differentiating various clinical conditions (Figure 4.2) with this technique,

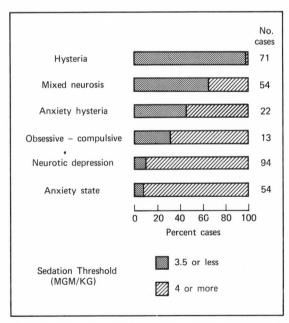

FIGURE 4.2. **Proportion of high and low thresholds in various neurotic groups (Shagass, 1958).**

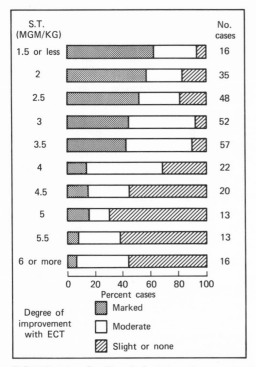

FIGURE 4.3. **Quality of short-term inprovement with ECT as a function of the pre-treatment sedation threshold (Shagass, 1958).**

as well as predicting response to electroconvulsive therapy (Figure 4.3). These findings have been questioned by Martin and Davis (1962, 1965); both they and Ackner and Pampiglione (1959) encountered numerous methodological difficulties with the sedation technique and failed to replicate Shagass' findings.

Electromyographic Measures. Activation of muscles produces electrical discharges that can be recorded in a manner similar to the EEG; measurement is made by means of the electromyograph (EMG). The typical EMG wave is much more erratic than that observed on the EEG, evidencing rapid bursts of high frequencies when the muscle is energized and low frequencies during periods of relaxation.

The EMG has been most frequently employed to record otherwise undetectable signs of emotional tension. For example, in a series of electromyographic studies, Malmo and his associates at McGill University (1951, 1961) have been able to demonstrate clear differences among psychotics, neurotics, and normals in response to a variety of startling and stressful conditions; Figure 4.4 illustrates recordings taken at neck and arm muscles in response to different magnitudes of thermal stimulation; similar distinctions have been noted in a series of studies by Whatmore and Ellis (1958, 1959, 1962). In an experimental study, Malmo et al. (1957) were able to demonstrate the effects of an interviewer's attitudes (criticism versus praise) upon EMG reactions in a clinical subject. Goldstein (1964), in her extensive review of the literature on measures of muscle tension, notes, however, that uniformity in research procedures will be necessary if comparable bodies of myographic data are to cumulate.

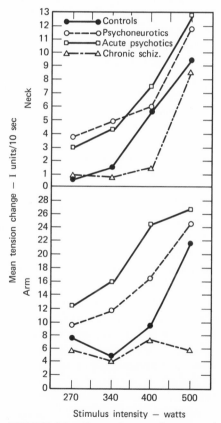

FIGURE 4.4. **Mean changes in arm and neck tension plotted against intensity of thermal stimulation (Malmo, Shagass, and Davis, 1951).**

Pupillographic Measures. At the turn of the century, Argyll Robertson detected pupillary changes associated with neurosyphilis; since then, numerous investigators have explored variations in the size and reflexive action of the pupil in the hope of identifying other psychopathologic conditions. Early explorations by Westphal and Lowenstein, employing rather crude measuring devices, led them to conclude that "catatonic schizophrenics" evidenced diminutions of the pupillary reflex, sufficient to distinguish them from both normals and other psychotics. Subsequent research has resulted in contradictory and confusing data, in part attributable to differences in the methods employed for assessing the pupillary response (Lowenstein and Lowenfeld, 1942; Hakerem, 1967).

Basically, the technique records responses to varying intensities of light stimuli upon the eye; decrements in the intensity lead to pupillary dilations, whereas increments results in contractions of the pupil. By systematically increasing and decreasing the light source, the rate of the response may be gauged. Recently, substantive stimuli (e.g., pictures of objects) have also been used in studies contrasting diagnostic groups. In the most commonly used procedure, serial photographs of the eyes are made under infrared illumination, and plotted against time. Because photographic methods are time-consuming, newer recording methods have recently been introduced, the most efficient of which are the photoelectric devices designed by Lowenstein and Lowenfeld (1958).

In reviews of pupillographic research with psychiatric patients, Martin (1961) and Hess (1968) summarize some of the more germane positive findings based on this technique and suggest that, though such findings are few and scattered, the instrument merits further use.

Psychogalvanic Measures. In contrast to the infrequent use of the pupillogram, psychopathologists have extensively employed psychogalvanic measures, that is, techniques that record changes in perspiration as gauged by skin resistance to small electric currents. The sweat glands close to surface of the skin are activated under conditions of tension or fear, reducing the skin's permeability to a current; if an electrode is placed in the palm of the hand, a notably sensitive region, changes in resistance consequent to provocative stimulation, termed the galvanic skin response (GSR), can be readily recorded on a polygraphic device known as the *psychogalvanometer.*

Despite their popularity, and the seeming simplicity of procedure, psychogalvanic methods are extremely susceptible to extraneous influences, and fraught with numerous technical complications that markedly diminish their effectiveness as a research tool. Thus, in discussing the GSR as an instrument for differentiating among clinical syndromes and normals, Martin (1961) comments as follows:

Landis summarized the available evidence in 1932, and drew attention then to the confused state of the findings concerning psychogalvanic activity in psychiatric patients, pointing out that there was no justification for using it as a measure of traditional psychological categories or personality traits. Since that time the topic has been vigorously pursued, and although additional results have hardly cleared the position, a general impression appears to have emerged that schizophrenics frequently demonstrate high resistance levels and diminished responsiveness, while neurotics show a lowered resistance level and increased responsiveness. But it is doubtful whether any such general impression can be substantiated; what is urgently required is a careful specification of the stimulus conditions under which any discrepancy in physiological activity might be observed.

Despite the above-noted limits, the psychogalvanometer has proved to be a highly useful device in a variety of experimental studies. For example, Dittes (1957) kept a continuous GSR record during 43 therapeutic sessions with a single patient; this enabled him to correlate variations in this "tension" index with the substantive content of the topics under discussion. In another neatly designed study, Lykken (1957) was able to distinguish among sociopathic subtypes by demonstrating differences among them in anxiety proneness; among the measures used was the speed with which a GSR response was conditioned to a painful stimulus.

Cardiovascular Measures. There are several instruments and procedures for assaying variations in the functioning of the cardiovascular system. The simplest of these cardiac measures are blood pressure, gauged by a *sphygmomanometer,* and heart or pulse rate. More complex indices are those of blood volume and blood flow at the surface of the body, obtained by calculating the skin temperature, and electrical discharges associated with contractions of heart muscles, which are registered on the *electrocardiogram* (EKG).

Increments in pulse rate and blood pressure consequent to emotional duress are well-known phenomena. Although the evidence is scanty, and at points contradictory, some consistent differences among pathologic conditions and normals have been recorded on these indices (Martin, 1961). Of particular interest is the recent development of tests based on blood pressure responses to autonomic drugs, as in the mecholyl test.

Several investigators have sought to test the thesis that the poor adaptive efficiency of psychiatric patients can be attributed to a slackness of central autonomic nervous system functioning. Among the techniques used to examine the validity of this notion are blood pressure responses to a variety of cholinergic and adrenergic drugs (Cyvin et al., 1956). The procedure most extensively employed is the *mecholyl test* (Funkenstein et al., 1949; Schneider et al., 1960). This consists of a record of the subject's systolic blood pressure measured once each minute for 25 minutes following the intramuscular injection of 10 mg. of the drug mecholyl, which serves as a neural stimulant. The response curves of subjects are classified in seven categories, varying from a markedly sagged curve with failure of the blood pressure to return to the premecholyl base level, to a curve at the opposite extreme where the drop is minimal and the homeostatic reaction exceeds the base line.

Despite questions concerning its reliability and validity as a measure of sympathetic nervous system reactivity (Cyvin et al., 1956; Thorpe, 1962; Rose, 1962), the mecholyl test has frequently been used to differentiate clinical groups, and to forecast patients' responses to biologic therapies; the results of these studies have been contradictory (Funkenstein et al., 1952; Alexander, 1955; Sloane and Lewis, 1956; Schneider et al., 1960).

Anatomical Indices

These techniques are used for the investigation of morphological structures correlated with and/or assumed to underlie psychopathological responses. Nonincursive studies of anatomy are limited essentially to measures of gross body morphology. Incursive studies include gross procedures such as postmortem and bioptic histopathological studies of diseased and damaged tissue; also employed are well-located surgical lesions of brain tissue and electrode implantation.

Morphological Techniques. Most morphological techniques are based on a threefold dimensional analysis of body fat, muscularity, and linearity. Although early anthropometric schemas classified people into three or four distinct body types, contemporary researchers recognize that morphological structure is best represented as mixtures of several body dimensions distributed in varying proportions.

The best known morphological index, that formulated by Sheldon (1940, 1942), derives from an analysis of photographs in which the relative dominance of three components of physique—body softness, muscularity, and linearity—are rated and quantified on a scale termed the somatotype; several limitations and complications of Sheldon's system have been noted in the literature (Millon, 1969).

Lindegard (1953, 1956) has developed an anthropometric index that includes measures of physical performance, such as gauged by hand grip strength and shoulder thrust, in addition to the usual structural components. Other researchers, basing their assessment variables on factor analyses of numerous body indices, have proposed more complex ways of calculating morphological patterns (Rees and Eysenck, 1945; Rees, 1959). More recently, in order to further refine the anthropometric analysis, investigators have proposed the use of a variety of intricate biomechanical procedures and measures of internal body composition. Rees (1961) has provided a detailed review of these techniques, as well as some of the research findings relating them to personality and psychopathology.

Histopathological Studies. Until this century, most knowledge of the biophysical substrate of pathologic conditions was gained by postmortem inspection of neural tissue in patients who had suffered some alleged brain disease or accidental brain damage. Autopsy procedures provide a visible source of data concerning nervous system defects, and are still usefully employed today by neuropathologists. More recently, brain tissue cultures obtained through biopsies with living patients have been extensively analyzed by the use of modern histochemical techniques, radioisotopes, and electron microscopy (Roizin, 1959; Solomon, 1967).

In general, both autopsy and biopsy procedures have proved useful only in well-known biophysical defect syndromes; anatomical correlates of "nonorganic" conditions have yet to be uncovered by these methods. Its most fruitful use in recent years has been in studies that investigate the consequences of early stimulus enrichment and impoverishment with rodents (Krech et al., 1963; Diamond et al., 1964; Bennett, et. al., 1964).

Surgical Lesions. The classical technique for establishing functional correlates of neural structures involves selective and measured removal of brain tissue. Rendering a segment of the nervous system inactive through extirpation, or through the severance of its connection to other regions, enables the investigator to record changes produced on a variety of biophysical or behavioral measures. Many refinements of surgical destruction and isolation have been developed in recent years, but the essential elements remain the same, that of identifying and mapping the structural correlates of psychological processes. Almost all of this work has been executed with lower species; the relevance of these findings for the behavior of intact human organisms remains to be demonstrated, especially as it may apply to higher cerebral functions that are more or less distinctive to man, for example, abstract thinking, verbal communication. Similarly, it must be recognized that a loss of function consequent to an incursive lesion does not "prove" that this function was uniquely subserved by the region in question (Meyer, 1961). Moreover, the behavioral consequences of surgical procedures are a product not only of the specified lesion but also of the organism's compensatory reactions and the secondary effects of body trauma, anesthesia, bleeding, etc. The fact that these techniques are of limited utility in human research can be readily judged by the sorrowful history of psychosurgical procedures.

Evaluative Comments

It is not uncommon for investigators who register great concern about the validity and reliability of "psychological tests" never to question the adequacy of biophysical measures; they appear to accept these measures as a matter of blind faith. The notable lack of success in gathering useful data with these measures is attributed, not to their intrinsic shortcomings, but to the complexities of the subject matter and to failures of human judgment; thus the assumption is made that once knowledge is greatly refined, and objective interpretive methods instituted, these instruments will give rise to data of great significance to psychopathology. Psychological test users need not be intimidated; their "subject" matter is no less complex, and biophysical measures exhibit more, rather than fewer, shortcomings and limitations. Most biophysical instruments generate less discriminating data, have fewer norms to guide interpretation, exhibit lower reliability coefficients, rarely are subjected to validity studies, and involve considerable expense and professional time. Yet, biophysical researchers go blithely on, acting as if their instruments were infallible. Let us note some of these deficiencies in brief detail.

1. Many biophysical methods produce data that are difficult to evaluate. Complex polygraphic records, such as obtained with the EGG or EMG, cannot be readily categorized into discriminable classes. Even with electronic frequency analyzers, most records, other than those with clearcut abnormalities, provide ambiguous results. Psychopathology that is easily detected clinically often is blurred or entirely missed with these "fancy" tools.

2. With few exceptions, the indices and techniques described lack normative data on relevant and distinguishable clinical populations, accounting, no doubt, for the high frequency with which the findings of one study fail to correspond to the results of others. Where clinical norms are available, they fail to provide data on relevant organismic characteristics such as age, chronicity, weight, etc. Moreover, most are based solely on clinically derived psychiatric diagnostic categories; these groups are notoriously heterogeneous. In short, where published, most norms are of questionable value as baselines for comparative studies.

3. Reliability studies are notably lacking among biophysical techniques; this deficiency is all the more lamentable since it is well known that mental patients tend to exhibit a high degree of variability over time. Thus, in referring to the mecholyl test, Grosz and Miller comment (1958):

> The day to day variability in the response patterns precludes the possibility of classifying patients on the basis of a single test. The marked instability of the test also contrasts with the presumably more stable characteristics with which they are being correlated. It is unlikely that correlates such as the diagnostic class, prognosis, and basic psychodynamic makeup, for example, could undergo similar fluctuations from day to day.

4. Low intercorrelations are found among biophysical measures that ostensibly represent the same psychological functions (Lacey, 1950; Martin, 1961); thus, data obtained with one measure of autonomic reactivity, for example, may not be duplicated if another index is employed. This raises serious questions about the validity of any single instrument as an index of a broader concept. Composite scores or profiles based on several instruments may be necessary if any confidence is to be given the results of a biophysical study.

5. The need for technical expertise and the complexity of several of the procedures described (e.g., sedation threshold, electrode implants, surgical lesions) are so great as to make them of limited utility. Of course, they are of value if they provide data that cannot otherwise be gathered; however, they should be replaced, where feasible, by equally valid, but more expeditious, instruments.

None of the problems enumerated above are unique to biophysical methods. We note them to point out the fact that research methodology in this field, contrary to the belief of most students, is as primitive as that employed in gathering data at other psychopathological data levels.

INTRAPSYCHIC METHODS

Intrapsychic concepts rarely are operationally defined. At best, they take the form of intervening variables, although they tend to be anchored rather loosely to the empirical events that signify their existence. Most are hypothetical constructs, metaphors, and analogies that are of undoubted heuristic value as clinical and theoretical tools, but are extremely elusive for purposes of systematic research.

Overt behaviors and phenomenological reports often serve as the basis for intrapsychic deductions; in fact, most of what clinicians infer about a patient's intrapsychic world is pieced together from data gathered through nonintrapsychic methods. In this section however, our focus will center on those techniques that uniquely gather intrapsychic phenomena, that is, those designed specifically to elicit and maximize their expression. Four such methods are currently employed: free association, dream analysis, hypnosis, and projective techniques.

Free Association

This classical psychoanalytic technique was developed by Freud to overcome obstacles to exposing the workings of the "unconscious mind." Since the unconscious is hidden, unusual prodecures had to be devised to evoke and lay bare its processes and contents. In addition to the then-established method of hypnosis, which Freud employed with inconstant success, he improvised two new techniques: free association and dream analysis. We shall present the first of these in this section; the second will be discussed later.

Let us quote from Erich Fromm, who succinctly described the logic of the free-association process and distinguished it from other features of the psychoanalytic interview (1955):

> What Freud discovered was that a person, even if he is not asleep and dreaming, even if he is not insane, even if he is not in a hypnotic trance, nevertheless, can hear the voice of his unconscious, provided that he does something which seems very simple: namely, that he leave the realm of conventional, rational thought, and permit himself to voice ideas which are not determined by the rules of normal, conventional thinking. If he does this, ideas emerge, not from his head but, as the Chinese would say, from his belly; ideas which are not part of his official personality, but which are the language of this dissociated, hidden personality. Furthermore, Freud discovered the fact that if I permit myself to associate freely, then these very thoughts which come from this dissociated realm attract other relevant and germane thoughts from the realm of the unconscious.
>
> Often several approaches are confused with the request for free association, particularly (a) the request for more information, and (b) the question as to what the patient thinks about a dream, or an occurrence. One should strictly differentiate between these three approaches: quest for information, for opinion, and for free association. In the quest for more information, the analyst asks the patient questions in order to clarify what he is saying, in order to bring out contradictions, in order to see, perhaps, where the patient is omitting something or distorting something. Such questions should be as precise, concrete, detailed, and clear as possible. Secondly, it is something else again if the analyst invites the patient to join him in rational thought about the meaning of certain things. To ask him, "What do you think this could mean?" "What is your idea about this or that behavior, or this or that incident?" This also is not free association. It does not make any difference whether it is phrased in the form of a question, or whether it is phrased in the form of a hypothesis. If I invite the patient to join me in reasonable thought about an object matter, then this is thinking, and not free association. And thirdly, there is free association in the sense of spontaneous association. We should indeed separate the latter from the former two, and be aware when we use free association as a tool, and when we do not use it.

In short, the free-association method seeks to unmask and unfold the linkages of the intrapsychic world by reducing to a minimum the processes of conscious selection and exclusion, or any other interference with the spontaneous expression of feelings and thought.

Useful though free association has been in furnishing clinical insights, it generates, like most interview procedures, extremely unwieldy data that is often entirely refractory to research management. Not only are these data bound by the usual limitations of human observation and judgment, but as Kubie (1960) has pointed out:

> . . . psychoanalysis has had to struggle with unique difficulties which are consequences of the fact that it has been dependent largely upon auditory data, with only minor visual additions. Because of the dominant importance and speed of the spoken work as an instrument of communication, because of the slower pace of writing, and because of the limited range of variations and the consequent relative stereotype of gesture and expression as methods of communication, the ear has been the major source of psychoanalytic data. To an even greater extent than visual data, auditory data are vulnerable to distortion both in the moment of perception and in recall.
>
> It is impossible to listen to ordinary speech without distorting our perceptual records of it. It is even less possible to take in and record and recall a string of free associations. They are distorted first at the time of perception, and again to an even greater degree in retrospect: this is true no matter how phonographic the mind of the listener. We can remember an entire sentence as a unit, but if we break up that sentence into syllables and scramble them, it becomes impossible to remember the same number of "nonsense" syllables. Yet free associations, when they are truly free in the technical analytic sense, approximate strings of ideas and words or even fragments of words and ideas without apparent relevance or pattern. Consequently, the task of perceiving and recalling truly free associations becomes so difficult that only a recording device can provide the raw data of analytic observations for critical qualitative and quantitative analysis as to content, meaning and form.

Fortunately, it is now possible to surmount man's fallible memory and distorted recollections by the use of video, motion picture, and sound recording techniques (Shakow, 1960; Gottschalk and Auerbach, 1966). Extremely promising and long overdue approaches to the systematic study of free association data have been initiated by Colby (1960) and Bordin (1966). For example, Bordin, using advanced students in clinical psychology, has obtained impressively high interjudge agreement on a series of rating scales that categorize both the flow and the content of tape-recorded free-association productions. Although not limited to free-association data, Dollard and Auld (1959) have devised a coding schema that focuses on the intrapsychic content of psychoanalytic interviews. With such procedures, a shift from exploratory single case studies as the major design to surveys and other designs will be possible.

Dream Analysis

Seventy years have passed since Freud published his classical interpretation of dreams. To him, this body of strange and seemingly nonsensical data represented, in part at least, memories and feelings that the dreamer dared not express in waking life; by decoding the disguises and distortions of this unconscious state, Freud's understanding of the intrapsychic mechanisms employed in the formation of neurotic and psychotic disorders was ostensibly enlightened. Little systematic research was done on the process of dreaming in the ensuing 50 years, and the interpretations that clinicians offered about the meaning of dream content remained entirely a matter of plausible speculation.

In recent years, there has been a burgeoning of interest and research concerning the neurophysiological correlates of dreaming. This began with the accidental discovery by Aserinsky and Kleitman (1953) of a direct relationship between nocturnal dreaming and bursts of rapid eye movement (REM). The outcome of this discovery has made the evanescent process of dreaming more accessible to study, and has led to an impressive series of investigations (Dement, 1964, 1965; Tart, 1965; Witkin and Lewis, 1967).

Although the ease of recognizing the REM state has greatly facilitated the monitoring of dreams, this clue has led, not to advances in the understanding of the content and psychological meaning of the dream, but to a marked increase in knowledge about the neurophysiology of the sleep state. Thus, this new and fresh avenue for unearthing intrapsychic data has resulted in substantive progress that goes little beyond that formulated by Freud 70 years ago.

There are two sources of "dream data" in addition to that produced during nocturnal sleep. The *hypnogogic reverie state* is a brief period of drowsiness shortly preceding the time of falling asleep; here, the subject is asked to keep on talking until he dozes off completely, recounting aloud his thoughts, feelings, and images, usually in a more disjointed and undirected manner than that generated in free association (Rapaport, 1951). The second data source is that of *daydreaming, the monologue interieur* in which persons fantasize and conjure up events that transcend the realities of past and present, or the probabilities of the future (Singer, 1966).

The intrapsychic analyses of dream content is fraught with even more complications than that encountered in the interpretation of free-association materials. Despite the impregnable faith that psychoanalytic writers have in dream analysis, there are no studies and few procedures by which the "meaning" they attribute to these data can be empirically confirmed or disconfirmed. As matters now stand, analysts provide only circumstantial evidence for the plausibility of their interpretations (Levy, 1963). The only conclusive evidence for the validity of these analyses would be through predictions and postdictions of behavior made independently of other sources of information.

Before such studies could be undertaken, however, considerable work must be done to operationally define, scrutinize, and categorize the data of dream reports, and to develop reliable criteria for rating and ascribing meaning to them; an important first step in this regard has recently been provided by Hauri et al. (1967). Two recent books (Witkin and Lewis, 1967; Singer, 1966) have summarized a number of experimental approaches employed to decipher the psychological process and content of nocturnal dreams and daydreams. Together with newer scales for rating dream reports, the techniques described in these works may serve to establish the necessary formal procedures for objectifying, quantifying, and ultimately validating the intrapsychic analysis of dreams.

Hypnosis

Brief note should be made of the principal forerunner of modern tools of intrapsychic exploration, that of hypnosis. Although it is of lesser significance today than before (e.g., the topic of hypnosis was not even listed in the subject index of the monumental 1965 *Handbook of Clinical Psychology*), this technique served a seminal role in pointing up the presence of unconscious ideas and emotions. It has had a spasmodic history since Freud's decision to forego its use at the turn of the century; although it continues to crop up in the research literature, questions still remain as to how it occurs and what elements constitute the hypnotic trance (Wolberg, 1959). Its status as an ancillary therapeutic technique seems well established, but it has borne little fruit as a device for explicating the content and processes of the intrapsychic world.

As with the techniques of free association and dream analysis, hypnosis provides the investigator with data that are shorn of the constraints of conscious selection and control. During the trance period, the patient withdraws his attention from the outside world, and is able to focus on aspects of his inner life that elude him in the wakeful state. With proper prodding, memory residuals of past experiences can be activated and brought to light; moreover, under proper conditions, the patient may display a vivid array of symbolic images and emotions that ostensibly reflect the primitive processes of the unconscious. Unfortunately, with the exception of a few exploratory forays (reviewed in Hilgard, 1961; Weitzenhoffer, 1953; Gordon, 1966), there are no truly systematic methods for organizing this wealthy fund of intrapsychic data.

In general, hypnosis has been employed in research merely to demonstrate the existence of unconscious phenomena; the well-known techniques of hypnotic memory recall and posthypnotic suggestion illustrate this approach. Experimental hypnotic studies of clinical processes have also been done. Some years ago, for example, Farber and Fisher (1943) showed that the form and content of dreams could be partially controlled by hypnotic suggestions; more recently, experiences implanted in the unconscious via hypnosis were systematically "treated" via two therapeutic approaches, as a means of comparing the efficacy of these techniques in relieving intrapsychic disturbances (Gordon, 1957).

Projective Techniques

Unquestionably, the most popular tools for eliciting, categorizing, and analyzing intrapsychic data are the methods labeled by Lawrence Frank in 1939 as projective techniques. In use for some time prior to World War II, they only began to flourish during the great surge of psychological testing in the late 1940's and 1950's. Although their underlying premises and rationales are not in question, subsequent validation research has shown that many of the diagnostic powers attributed to these techniques cannot be supported. Despite their sparse record in systematic evaluative research and their questionable superiority over other diagnostic instruments, there is still reason to believe that their promise as tools for exposing the realm of the unconscious will materialize. The inherent weaknesses of scoring, quantifying, and interpreting the more established of the older techniques are gradually being overcome (Holtzman et al., 1961; Zubin et al., 1965).

The value of the projective approach derives, at least in part, from the unusual character of the task presented to the subject. By providing an unstructured set of materials to which he is asked to respond, the subject is forced, so to speak, to draw upon his inner imaginative resources; moreover, he is likely to be unable to fathom the meaning or significance of his responses. Thus, unguided by the character of the task, and incapable of disguising what he may prefer to mask, he is apt to "project from within" perceptions and interpretations that disclose his emotional preoccupations, styles of thinking, ways of coping, etc.; in short, data that expose and illuminate his intrapsychic world.

Projective techniques have been classified in numerous ways as a means of highlighting their commonalities and differences (Frank, 1939; Sargent, 1945; Campbell, 1950, 1957; Cattell, 1951; Lindzey, 1960). Our discussion will be guided by the schema proposed by Lindzey, which stresses the type of response produced by the subject; by organizing our presentation in this way, the student may be led to consider projective techniques as instruments providing response variables, rather than as clinical tests. We have sought, in narrowing the list of techniques discussed, to mention the two or three methods in each category that are most commonly employed by researchers. Detailed presentations, critiques, and research reports using these techniques may be found in Buros (1965, 1969), Murstein (1965), and Zubin et al. (1965).

Associative Techniques. According to Lindzey's classification, associative techniques are those in which the subject is set to respond to a stimulus with the first word, thought, or image that occurs to him; the intent is to evoke an immediate reaction, that is, one without reflection and reasoning.

The oldest of these techniques, embodying in a standardized form certain features of Freud's then newly devised free-association method, was formulated by his erstwhile disciple Jung. This procedure, known as the word-association test, consists of a list of words, presented one at a time to a subject with the request that he respond to them with the first word that comes to mind. Although the word-association method still has its adherents, it has given way to other, more complicated methods. The idea of employing association as a projective procedure has been most extensively developed with the use of inkblots as the evocative stimulus.

Rorschach Inkblots. Not only is the Rorschach the most widely used clinical diagnostic instrument but it has also been the subject of over 3000 articles and books since its construction in 1921. Named after its originator, Swiss psychiatrist Hermann Rorschach, this instrument consists of ten symmetrical inkblots printed on separate cards; five are in shades of black and grey, and five are multicolored. In the standard administration, the subject is presented with one card at a time and asked to associate aloud the various impressions it suggests to him. The subject's responses are transcribed verbatim, and the timing and position in which the cards are held are likewise recorded. Following this initial associative phase of administration, the cards are again presented, one at a time, in a procedure termed the "inquiry"; here, the subject is asked to distinguish the various areas of each blot that contain the percepts he saw (the location score), and to describe the elements of the blot that suggested these perceptions (the determinant scores, such as form, movement, color, shading). In a frequently employed final step of administration, termed "testing the limits", the examiner probes more directly, seeking to elicit percepts and determinants that the subject failed to give in the associative and inquiry stages.

Several systems for scoring and interpreting the data of the Rorschach have attained a measure of popular recognition and use; among them are those of Rorschach himself (1942), Klopfer et al. (1954, 1956), Beck (1945, 1952, 1961), Piotrowski (1957), and Schafer (1954). In addition to scoring response locations and determinants, most of these systems evaluate the timing, content, popularity, and degree of correspondence between responses and the stimulus features of the cards. In addition to these data,

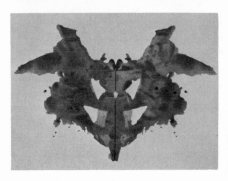

FIGURE 4.5. Card from the Rorschach Test. (Permission of Hans Huber Publisher, Berne, Switzerland.)

inferences on intrapsychic characteristics are frequently drawn from the ratios among various scoring categories and the sequential pattern of responses as they unfold between and within each card. The interpretive process is largely dependent on the experience and "intuitive" skills of the clinician.

As noted earlier, serious questions have arisen concerning the discriminability, reliability, and validity of the Rorschach. Nevertheless, the technique has gained immense popularity, and has been used extensively as an instrument in psychopathological research. For illuminating discussions of these issues, as well as a survey of studies relevant to psychopathology, see Zubin et al. (1965).

Holtzman Inkblots. Many derivatives of the Rorschach inkblot method have been devised. Among those of special, but limited, utility are the Levy Movement Blots and the Color-Cut-Out Test; the literature of both of these instruments, which attempt to highlight only one of the major "determinants" of inkblot perception, is discussed fully in Zubin et al. (1965).

The most promising of the newer Rorschach variants is the Holtzman Inkblot Technique (1961, 1966). This instrument consists of two sets of inkblots, comprising 45 cards each, and provides a system of administration, scoring, and interpretation that is better standardized and more "objective" than that of the traditional Rorschach technique. Holtzman has extracted 6 "factors" in an analysis of 22 scoring variables; these data were gathered with 15 different populations, ranging from normal children to adult psychotics. Recent studies of the discriminatory powers and validity of the instrument are impressive. Although its utility for clinical diagnostic purposes has not been adequately documented, its format is better suited for purposes of research than the Rorschach.

Construction Tests. Construction techniques, according to Lindzey's schema, call upon the subject to create a more or less elaborate imagina-

FIGURE 4.6. Card from the Thematic Apperception Test. (Permission of Harvard University Press, Cambridge, Mass.)

tive story, usually in response to a picture stimulus. No demand is made for immediacy in response; instead, the subject is asked to organize the suggestive features of the stimulus into a sequential plot or story theme.

Thematic Apperception Test (TAT). This instrument, devised by Morgan and Murray (1935), ranks second in popularity only to the Rorschach as a diagnostic test. Parts or variants of it have been extensively used in research.

The basic instrument consists of 31 cards (30 with pictures and 1 entirely blank), although only 10 or so are usually administered. In contrast to the totally amorphous character of inkblots, the figures and objects portrayed on these cards are entirely identifiable; the events, and the thoughts and feelings of the characters, are sufficiently ambiguous, however, to allow the subject to "read in" what may be taking place. One card at a time is presented in the standard administration; the subject is requested to formulate a theme or story that includes "what is happening, what the people involved are thinking and feeling, what led up to the events portrayed in the picture, and what the outcome will be."

In contrast to the Rorschach, with its three or four popular scoring and interpretive systems, the TAT has spawned numerous such procedures, none of which has caught on as "the standard" method. The rationale, and technique of several of these systems are well presented and discussed in Schneidman et al. (1951), Lindzey (1952), Murstein (1963), and Zubin et al. (1965); the latter two references also provide thorough and up-to-date reviews of evidence concerning the validity and reliability of the technique, as well as summaries of its use in psychopathologic research. Particularly notable for purposes of quantitative research are the standardized and objective administration and scoring procedures devised by McClelland (1953, 1958), and by Eron and his associates (Eron, 1950; Eron et al., 1950; Zubin et al., 1965).

TAT Derivatives. Several notable variants of the construction picture technique have been developed since the TAT was first introduced.

The Make-a-Picture-Story Test (MAPS), designed by Schneidman (1948, 1952), consists of 22 cardboard background scenes presented one at a time along with 67 cut out, movable human and animal figures. In contrast to the TAT, the respondent is free to compose his own scenes by selecting and placing the figures as he desires; he then constructs a story depicting his arrangement. Presumably, the subject will become more engrossed and display more of his intrapsychic world in stimulus situations that he himself has created than in those that are uniform and less· malleable; moreover, according to Schneidman, the examiner is able to discern qualities of performance (e.g., choice of figures, planning logic, etc.) that illuminate features of personality not observable in the standard TAT. Although it is of value as a diagnostic tool, the difficulties involved in standardizing and developing normative data make the MAPS of limited research utility.

Three TAT derivatives have been developed for adolescent and child populations. The *Children's Apperception Test* (CAT) is perhaps the best known and most frequently used of these clinical tools (Bellak, 1954); similar in construction and use is the *Blacky Pictures*, devised by Blum (1949, 1962). Both tests consist of cartoon drawings of animals about which the child creates a story; both were based on Freudian psychosexual theory and were designed specifically to elicit responses indicative of the child's experiences and manner of coping with the events ascribed to the Freudian stages of development. Research bearing on their reliability and validity is scanty or equivocal, and they have been infrequently used as instruments for investigational purposes.

The Michigan Picture Test (MPT), developed under the auspices of the Michigan Department of Mental Health (1953) for use with adolescents, illustrates many of the features of a well-constructed instrument, and is frequently commended for its careful design, adequacy of norms, and repeated attempts at cross-validation (Freeman, 1962; Zubin et al., 1965). Despite efforts to construct quantitative interpretive scales, the test is not measurably superior for research purposes to other projective techniques.

Completion Instruments. Completion techniques, to follow Lindzey's format again, usually consist of a series of suggestive but abbreviated stimuli which the subject is asked to fill out in any manner he wishes, consistent with the instructions provided him.

Among the methods grouped in this category are the *Picture-Frustration Test* (Rosenzweig, 1945) and the *Insight Test* (Sargent, 1955). The Picture-Frustration Test, providing a series of cartoon situations in which the subject is asked to supply a response to a frustrating experience, gained a measure of clinical and research use in the late 1940's and 1950's (Lindzey and Goldwyn, 1954), but has gradually lost its initial favor. The Insight Test, in which the subject is asked to furnish answers to problem situations, provides useful intrapsychic information, but has generated little research to date.

The most popular and simplest of the completion techniques are those in which the subject supplies a word or phrase to fill out an incomplete or truncated sentence. Several variants of the sentence completion method have been devised, the best known and most frequently researched of which is Rotter's *Incomplete Sentences Blank* (Rotter and Willerman, 1947; Rotter and Rafferty, 1952). Illustrative of the typical sentence "stems" completed by subjects are: "My mother always. . . ." "Suddenly, I. . . ." "A voice. . . ." "When I was a. . . ." "My greatest worry is. . . ."

In routine clinical work, the data provided through the sentence completion procedure are usually gleaned in a subjective fashion. Formal scoring methods have been devised by their test constructors, but apparently are rarely used. Goldberg (1965) has published a thorough and largely favorable review of the validity and research usefulness of these techniques.

Expressive Procedures. In these techniques there is as much emphasis placed on the manner or style with which the subject performs the task as on the end product of his efforts. Thus, in the two major expressive methods, drawing and play techniques, the subject allegedly reveals as much of himself in the process of carrying out what he does as in the character of his final creation.

Play techniques are employed almost exclusively with children. Formal scoring procedures are used rarely since the activity process is extremely fluid and difficult to capture with anything less than film or video recordings. The work of Levy (1933), Sears et al., (1953), Murphy (1956), and Bandura and Walters (1963) illustrate the range of variables (e.g., aggression, dependency) these techniques can evoke. More often than not, however, the data they furnish are used to represent behavioral rather than intrapsychic concepts.

Among the better known drawing techniques, with well-formulated scoring and interpretive guidelines, are those developed by Machover (1948) and Buck (1949). In Machover's *Draw-a-Person* procedure, the subject simply sketches a figure, and then, upon completion, is asked to produce a second "of the opposite sex." Buck's *House-Tree-Person* (HTP) technique requires the subject to produce free-hand drawings of a house, tree, and person, in that order, followed by an inquiry phase in which he is asked to describe or develop a story in conjunction with his productions. Despite the undoubted and steadfast clinical popularity of these two graphic techniques, their use as research instruments is infrequent, and evidence bearing on their reliability and validity has been largely negative (Swenson, 1957, 1968; Roback, 1968).

Evaluative Comments

The rich vein of information tapped by intrapsychic methods has been a boon to clinicians, but a source of perplexity and despair to researchers. More than any other group of techniques, intrapsychic methods generate data fraught with complexities that bewilder the most sophisticated of investigators. There are formidable, perhaps even insurmountable, problems inherent in the use of these techniques since intrapsychic processes are, by definition, unobservable; thus, their presence cannot be confirmed, logically speaking, and they cannot be exposed to objective and quantitative measurement.

Although hard-nosed scientists tend to be overly strict in their standards, they do have a point in claiming that one must "get hold of something tangible" with which to do the business of research. Moreover, intrapsychic concepts not only refer to intactile phenomena but they are also viewed to be intrinsically amorphous and pliant; thus, to complicate matters further, intrapsychic processes are considered unstable and fleeting, expressing themselves first this way and then that, meaning different things in one context than in another, or from one moment to the next.

The fact that the unconscious comprises a world of obscure and evanescent processes is not in question. What is troublesome are the serious problems these concepts create for research since they are difficult to tie down to empirical coordinates and cannot be investigated with precise and reliable measures.

In light of these difficulties, some researchers contend that it is futile, even meaningless, to study intrapsychic phenomena, and that to expend one's efforts on theories with so feeble a data base can only be futile. They assert, with reasonable justification, that more substantial progress can be made in explicating the genesis, structure, and therapy of psychopathology by excluding such data from the scientific enterprise (Skinner, 1954).

Although it may be that more fruitful research alternatives are available, the "reality" of intrapsychic events cannot be dismissed. The inevitable difficulties, and the marked paucity of reliable and valid instruments, should serve as a challenge, giving the scientist all the more reason to devote his energies to articulating the amorphous stream of intrapsychic events, and to developing methods by which this rich body of data can be transformed into researchable variables.

Even if one grants the difficulties posed by these concepts, intrapsychic measures must be gauged by the same criteria employed to judge other research instruments. Certainly, intrapsychic researchers cannot dismiss these criteria cavalierly and then expect sensible scientists to take their data seriously. Primitive instruments must be recognized as such, and the data they generate must be viewed with a healthy degree of skepticism, no matter how illuminating and promising they appear. Although this is not the place to labor the limitations and faults of these techniques, a few comments are in order.

1. Much of the difficulty of intrapsychic techniques stems from their dependence on clinical inference. Since the data in question cannot be directly observed and are often claimed to signify different intrapsychic processes in different contexts, it is impossible to assign them a standard or unequivocal meaning. To resolve these ambiguities, investigators typically interpret intrapsychic data in accord with the principles of certain "well-established" theoretical schemas. Facile and plausible though these interpretations may be, we know only too well the pitfalls of subjective appraisals; most intrapsychic theories are so malleable as to "explain" any set of findings, even those that patently contradict the theory. In short, intrapsychic methods lack a standardized and objective basis for data interpretation, leading all too frequently to controversial conclusions.

2. Intrapsychic methods are notoriously coarse; many provide only the crudest of guidelines concerning data interpretation. Inferences drawn from a global analysis of a dream or a free-association stream may prove "correct," but there is need to specify the particular elements of these complex responses that "cue" the inferences drawn. Where distinct scoring categories are established, it is possible to order the data into a series of quantitatively discriminable scales; at the very least, such intrapsychic methods meet the minimal criteria of researchable instruments.

3. The relative absence of normative information looms as a further limitation to the use of several of the intrapsychic techniques, for example, free association and dream analysis. Until data obtained with known and relevant population groups are available, the significance and comparability of findings gathered with these methods will be sharply curtailed.

4. The critical comments noted above would carry little import if intrapsychic methods were demonstrably valid in their present forms. Empirical validity, that is, evidence of an instrument's predictive accuracy and its capacity to differentiate among relevant criterion groups, is a pervasive issue with these methods since their interpretation is characterized, not by "proven" evidence of accuracy, but by speculative inferential "leaps." With the exception of projective techniques, practically no systematic evidence has been gathered to test the validity of intrapsychic methods. Numerous efforts have been made to evaluate the predictive and differential validity of several projective instruments; for the most part, these studies have yielded negative results, although some, rather meager, positive findings are scattered in the literature (Zubin et al., 1965). Although less discouraging, reliability data are far from satisfactory.

In conclusion, the general status of intrapsychic methods as research instruments leaves much to be desired. All of the techniques described are shot through with measurement and validation problems. Nevertheless, they do yield data that are obtainable in no other way. Until more objective and quantitative intrapsychic instruments are developed, their unique powers to tap this data level justify their continued use. Needless to say, they must be employed with circumspection and care, and efforts must be made to reduce the risks involved to a minimum.

PHENOMENOLOGICAL METHODS

The problems that beset research using intrapsychic data are not unique; similar complications arise in investigating all varieties of data, but most notably the phenomenological. Phenomenology represents the study of conscious experience, events as seen from the subjective frame of reference. As with intrapsychic data, the substantive content of phenomenological research deals with the unseen "private world"; such data are elusive, difficult to pin down or infer from observables, and therefore fraught with operational obscurities and methodological complexities.

Despite the inevitable hazards they involve, psychopathologists cannot afford the luxury of bypassing either intrapsychic or phenomenological data. The events they portray are "real"; they represent elements of experience that are no less significant than concrete observables and, therefore, must be tapped to fill out the entirety of our knowledge of the psychopathologic process.

Troublesome though these data may be to methodologically "pure" researchers, phenomenal events have been studied systematically since the "method of introspection" had its heyday in the first two decades of this century. Although this method fell into disrepute following the rise of behaviorism, the study of subjective conscious experience continued unabated, though "under various aliases," as Boring once put it (1953). In this section we shall review some of the many procedures employed to investigate this rich source of data. Although none fully resolve the problems inherent in researching subjective processes, most institute correctives to minimize their effects.

Three methods for gathering phenomenological data will be described. The first, *interview procedures,* consists of two major techniques: one seeks to deduce the patient's phenomenological state through a postinterview analysis of the content of his verbalizations; the other gathers specific types of information during the interview proper through a series of focused questions. In *self-report inventories,* the second of the methods discussed, the patient characterizes his attitudes toward self and others in response to a series of printed "test" questions. The third category of techniques, *performance measures,* tap ongoing phenomenological processes by subjecting the patient to a variety of perceptual and cognitive laboratory tasks.

Interview Procedures

The interview has been the backbone of clinical psychopathology, but it is only in the past 10 to 15 years that its components have been systematically analyzed, and its use as a source of "private" events has been exploited for purposes of research. Although many other techniques have been devised to uncover important phenomenological data, such as attitudes, memories, feelings, and self-evaluations, this chief tool of clinical information and detection has lagged far behind in scientific scrutiny and development. Fortunately, with the recent growth of interest in the therapeutic "process," increasing numbers of investigators have turned to an analysis of the elements and mechanisms of interview content and interaction.

We shall focus on the phenomenological significance of what is said in the interview. Two kinds of techniques have been employed to gather these data systematically: *postinterview content analysis* and *prearranged interview schedules.* The first categorizes the content of communication *after* it has been collected; the second organizes the interview in advance, thereby maximizing the probability that relevant data will initially be collected.

Postinterview Content Analysis. These techniques attempt to categorize and quantify the attitudes and feelings of a patient by reviewing and coding transcribed verbal communications. Although the "latent" qualities of these communications may be analyzed for their intrapsychic significance, content analysis generally focuses on the "manifest" or overt content of what is said; it takes communication data at its face value, accepting it as an indication of conscious experience and intent, rather than of unconscious distortion or symbolism. For this reason, we have included content analysis as a technique for deciphering phenomenological data; when content analysis contains interpretation of symbolism, it represents an intrapsychic method.

Many aspects of what is said in the interview can be categorized; the character of the categories selected will depend, of course, on the researcher's interest. These categories may code fairly simple and straightforward dimensions of content or rather subtle ones. Whatever the coding system developed, the researcher examines samples of interview transcripts and classifies specified units of the patient's verbalizations in accord with predetermined criteria. As he progresses in his transcript analysis, the relative frequencies of the various content categories begin to cumulate, providing him with a quantitative distribution of what was said. Through this procedure, he extracts a series of empirically anchored scores that transform the elusive free flow of communication into statistically manageable units; if the coding criteria are relevant and unambiguous, he should be assured of an accurate characterization of the attitudes and feelings conveyed by the interviewee. Excellent discussions of the steps and complications involved in devising a content analysis system may be found in Cartwright (1953), Berelson (1954), Selltiz et al. (1959), and Pool (1950).

Many features of the interview interaction, aside from content, can be subjected to systematic analysis. Each of the components of interview processes can be neatly separated now that we have at our disposal recording devices such as sound tapes, films, and videotape; for example, in an excellent early study, Geidt (1955) sought to compare the relative quality of information provided in interviews by presenting four types of data to clinical judges: (1) visual cues (silent film), (2) verbal content (verbatim written transcripts), (3) content plus auditory cues (sound alone), and (4) content plus auditory plus visual cues (complete sound film). In recent years, a number of investigators have begun to study not only nonverbal aspects of interview behavior, such as facial movements and gestures, etc. (Haggard and Isaacs, 1966; Ekman and Friesen, 1968; Mahl, 1968) but also a variety of noncontent facets of verbal behavior, such as total speaking time, ratio of adjectives to verbs, frequency of pauses, etc. (Matarazzo, 1961; Matarazzo et al., 1968). These latter techniques of analysis do not deal directly with the phenomenological content of the interview but with the subject's observable behavior; they will be discussed in a later section dealing with behavior research methods.

Attention in this section will be directed to procedures that focus primarily on verbal content. It should be noted before we proceed that the methodology of content analysis has been fruitfully employed to decode communications other than those contained in interviews, for example, suicide notes (Osgood and Walker, 1959); our discussion here, however, will be limited only to interview data.

The methods to be described have been divided into two groups: (1) those designed to elicit only one dimension of feeling or attitude, and (2) those that seek to analyze several phenomenological dimensions simultaneously. Thorough reviews of research employing these systems have been published by Auld and Murray (1955) and Marsden (1965).

Single Dimension Systems. Each of the two measures described in this section attempt to extract only one variable from the complex stream of ideas and feelings that unfold in the interview.

The *Discomfort Relief Quotient* (*DRQ*) was originally devised by Dollard and Mowrer (1947) as a method for measuring tension as expressed in written documents; its value in analyzing therapy transcripts was recognized shortly thereafter. The technique requires segmenting the protocol into "clause or thought units" according to definite rules, and then classifying each unit as an expression of discomfort (suffering, pain, unhappiness), or relief (comfort, pleasure, enjoyment), or neither. The DRQ is obtained by dividing the number of discomfort units by the total number of discomfort *and* relief units. In a typical research study, a sequence of quotients are calculated at various intervals both before, during, and after treatment, thereby providing a quantitative index of change in phenomenological discomfort.

The *Positive-Negative-Ambivalent Quotient* (*PNAvQ*), devised by Raimy (1948), categorized statements reflecting feelings toward self. The unit here is all words spoken by the interviewee between two responses of the interviewer. Six categories are coded: *P*—positive self-reference; *N*—negative self-reference; *Av*—ambivalent self-reference; *A*—ambiguous self-reference; *O*—no self-reference; and *Q*—nonrhetorical questions. The *PNAvQ* is obtained by dividing the number of *N* and *Av* units by the number *N, Av,* and *P* units. The final quotient may range between zero and one, with quotients closer to zero signifying greater self-approval.

Multidimensional Systems. In contrast to the content coding schemas presented above, the systems included here attempt to simultaneously categorize the same interview data on several dimensions. They are simply more encompassing and complex than the methods discussed earlier, and do not differ intrinsically in their technique or analysis.

The *Leary-Gill Omnibus System* (1959) illustrates how complex the analyses of content can be. The format employed is undoubtedly the most comprehensive and richly varied system yet formulated but, as with many such detailed and complicated devices, it has failed to enlist the interest of interview researchers. Although it consists of only five basic categories, there is a profusion of subcategories and modifiers that make the system extremely unwieldy. Essentially, Leary and Gill set out to devise not only a method of coding the final content of communication (the constituent category) but also interplay of both therapist and patient, and whether the subject matter under discussion was "discharged," "admitted to awareness," "admitted into speech," or elaborated "insightfully." These coding scales have not been used in published studies of interview material; the model upon which they were based, however, has been used for simpler content analysis schemas.

The *Holzman-Forman Five-Dimensional System* (1966) is a somewhat less cumbersome, but nonetheless comprehensive, set of content categories. The basic unit for coding (the meaning unit) is the sentence or logical segments thereof; statements of both therapist and patient are categorized. Five separate dimensions of each unit are coded where possible: (1) its grammatical structure, (2) its manifest content, (3) persons or objects relevant to the patient, (4) manifest expressions of approval or disapproval of the "other" in therapy, and (5) references to the "locus" of the patient's difficulty. Table 4.1 provides examples of the grammatical structure and manifest content categories. Although of recent vintage, the schema appears highly reliable and lends itself to research more readily than does the overly complex Leary-Gill system.

Gottschalk and his associates (Gottschalk and Gleser, 1964; Gottschalk et al., 1966) have devised a number of interview coding scales for cognitive disorganization and expressions of hostility and anxiety. Termed the *Affect and Cognitive Functioning Scales,* and operating from an intrapsychic frame of reference, the majority of categories included represent consciously voiced feelings and thoughts. Gottschalk's system depends on verbal content alone and classifies the patient's communications in terms of variables such as: (1) their frequency of occurrence per standard units of time, (2) the intensity of the affect expressed, and (3) the degree of personal involvement of the speaker with the event discussed. The relative ease of scoring, and the fact that the coding reliabilities and scale validities have been well documented, augurs well for the continued use of this system in psychopathology research.

Prearranged Interview Schedules. Whereas content analysis extracts relevant data *after* it has been gathered in a relatively unstandardized and free-flowing interview, the use of a fixed schedule of questions in a structured interview ensures that data relevant to research are obtained *during* the interview itself. Moreover, by organizing the interviewer's attention in advance to a uniform set of topical subjects, the prospects for gathering comparable data from all subjects is greatly enhanced. Although the casual air and flexibility of approach that characterizes unstructured interviews are lost when a standardized schedule is followed, more important to most research is the availability of specified classes of data collected under relatively uniform conditions.

Interview schedules and questionnaires are employed to gather a wide range of data relevant to psychopathology, for example, epidemiologic surveys, sociometric preferences, family case histories, etc. Space does not permit a discussion of these manifold uses, nor the problems and procedures involved in constructing and conducting either open-ended or prearranged interviews. The reader will find excellent presentations of these matters in Maccoby and Maccoby (1954), Kahn and Cannell (1957), Kornhauser and Sheatsley (1959), and Richardson et al. (1965).

We shall limit our attention in this section to interview schedules that focus on the patient's "mental status," that is, those that pose questions designed to detect such items as cognitive clarity and insight, emotional preoccupations, complaints, self-attitudes, mood, etc. By selecting a representative sample of patient verbalizations that can be reliably elicited and quantified, the resultant scores can be compared to appropriate norm groups or be used for purposes such as gauging changes consequent to therapy. The two interview schedules to be presented are notable for the care given their construction, the publication of normative data, and impressive evidence favoring their reliabilities and validities.

The *Psychiatric Status Schedule* (*PSS*) was devised by several research associates at the New York State Psychiatric Institute (Spitzer et al., 1964; Spitzer, 1966); it consists of a standardized interview schedule and a matching inventory of 492 precoded, dichotomous items of both pathological behavior and social adaption. The interviewer follows the prescribed order of the schedule to elicit a wide range of comments concerning the patient's symptoms and functioning during the past week. Most of the questions are open ended, enabling the patient to reveal not only the content but also the character of this thoughts and feelings. Juxtaposed opposite each question, or series of questions, are items comprising the inventory; these items characterize typical responses of subjects, and are rated

TABLE 4.1: Five-Dimensional System: Illustrations of Grammatical and Content Coding Units for Therapists and Patients

	Grammatical Structure	
Code and Primary Category	*Therapist*	*Patient*
A. Questions	How are you?	When was that?
B. Contentless interjections	Umhm.	Well.
C. Reflections (exact repetitions)	(After P: "It was there.") It was there.	(After D: "She's your mother.") She's my mother.
E1. Instructions.	Speak louder.	Give me a light.
E2. Demands	You will have to leave if you do that again.	Leave me alone.
E3. Agreements with the "other"	I see:	Yes.
E4. Disagreements with the "other"	I don't agree with you.	No.
E5. Statements having as subject neither the patient nor the therapist.	There's a nice pool here.	Mother doesn't like me.
E6. Statements having the patient as subject	You're angry.	I don't feel tired.
E7. Answers to the "other's" question	(After P: "Will he let me?") I should think so.	(After D: "Why are you doing that?") I'm just wiping off stain.
E17. Nonanswers to the "other's" questions	(After P: "Will he let me?") I'd be interested in what you think.	(After D: "Why are you doing that?") Do you want a cigarette?
E8. Statements having the therapist as subject	I'm going away next week.	You won't take me with you.
E9. Solicitous remarks	Here, here's your tea.	

TABLE 4.1: (continued)

	Grammatical Structure	
Code and Primary Category	*Therapist*	*Patient*
E10. Statements which are inexact repetitions of earlier verbalizations of the "other"	(After P: "In the long run, it won't be difficult.") It won't be hard.	(After D: "Why do you do that?") I do it.
E11. Nonmotivational, noninterpersonal questions about content which the "other" has introduced	(After P: "We played cards today.") On the ward?	(After D: "You're going out today.") When?

	Content	
Code and Primary Category	*Therapist*	*Patient*
G. Therapist's ideas and behavior	I am going to be away next week.	You came early.
C. Patient's behavior	Are you going home this weekend?	I didn't hit him.
A. Patient's feelings	Are you angry	I want to go back to the ward.
M. Patient's cognitive processes	What do you think?	I have an idea.
J. Patient's ideas of behavior of others and the external world	Does she like you?	They were talking about me.
B. Patient's symptoms	Do you have a headache?	The pills make me restless.
F. Therapist's feelings	I like your new haircut.	You are angry at me.
D. Patient's fantasies	Are you going to make yourself bigger than me now?	Kim Novak would like to marry me.

From: Holzman and Forman (1966).

as the interview proceeds by marking statements as true or false (Table 4.2). Although questions are posed in a casual manner, the fixed schedule and order of presentation ensures that data obtained with different interviewers will be comparable.

A few items call for relatively complex judgments, but most are brief, nontechnical descriptions of phenomenological attitudes or feelings, and recollections of recent behaviors or habits; in general, unconscious processes are not evaluated. Where necessary, optional follow-up questions are suggested to smooth the flow of the interview and for purposes of elaboration or clarification.

Numerous clinical and social subscales have been, and are being, developed via factor analysis; these will provide quantifiable indices not only of psychopathological symptom clusters (depressive mood, paranoid ideation) but also of role functioning, work adjustment, level of aspiration, etc.

Somewhat similar in format and procedure to the PSS is the *Structured Clinical Interview* (SCI), devised also by investigators associated with the New York State Psychiatric Institute (Burdock and Hardesty, 1964, 1966, 1968). It is briefer than the PSS and is designed to *evoke* immediate and salient pathology, rather than surveying a wide range of events and feelings associated with the patient's recent life. The interview consists of a schedule of open-ended questions, juxtaposed with an inventory of 179 items; as the interview progresses, these items are judged by the interviewer as *True* or *Not true* on the basis of the subject's responses and behaviors.

Since the focus of questioning is on current phenomenological attitudes and feelings, rather than on historical information or intrapsychic material, the instrument lends itself readily to repeated use, such as would be necessary in evaluating the extent of changes consequent to therapy. The data gathered are grouped into ten subscales: (a) anger-hostility, (b) conceptual dysfunctioning, (c) fear and worry, (d) incongruous behavior, (e) incongruous ideation, (f) lethargy-dejection, (g) perceptual dysfunctioning, (h) physical complaints, (i) self-depreciation, and (j) sexual deviance.

Self-Report Inventories

Robert Woodworth, a well-known American psychologist, was called upon in the First World War to devise a "psychological test" that would be more efficient and economical than the time-consuming psychiatric interview as an instrument for screening military inductees. The "test" he developed, known as the *Personal Data Sheet,* was essentially a self-administered interview in which the respondent replied to a standard series of printed questions dealing with his past and present habits, feelings, and attitudes. The inventory of items covered the same ground as that of the in-

TABLE 4.2: Psychiatric Status Schedule: Illustrative Items

Question Schedule	Inventory Items
Self-appraisal	*Self-appraisal*
How do you feel about yourself?	47 In appraising himself he indicates an inflated view of his value or worth [grandiosity].
Do you like yourself?	48 Accuses himself of being unworthy.
If unclear: (When you compare yourself with other people, how do you come out?)	49 Indicates he is bothered by feelings of inadequacy or that he doesn't like himself.
	50 Indicates he is bothered by feelings of having done something terrible [guilt].
Response to criticism	*Response to criticsm*
How do you feel when people criticize you?	51 Indicates he feels hurt or overwhelmed when criticized.
What do you do when people give you advice?	52 Indicates he gets angry when criticized OR that he customarily rejects or ignores advice.
Interpersonal relations	*Interpersonal relations*
How are you getting along with people? (What kinds of trouble do you have with people?)	53 Complains about the way peers or strangers treat him.
	54 Complains unduly about the way people in positions of authority or power treat him (e.g. staff members, police, employer).
	55 Complains unduly about member of family, friend or associate.
Whom do you feel you can trust the most? (Anybody else?) (Why?)	56 Indicates he cannot trust other people OR that he is unduly suspicious of their intent.
Who bothers or upsets you the most?	57 Mentions he feels people take advantage of him or push him around.

From: Spitzer, Endicott, and Cohen (1966).

terview, but saved considerable professional time. In this paper-and-pencil form, the interview was transformed into a well-standardized, highly efficient, and easily quantified measurement tool; these tools were labeled "self-report inventories." The fact that the "personal touch" and flexibility of the psychiatric interview was lost, and that answers had to be limited to fixed response categories such as "yes," "no," or "cannot say," was well compensated by the large number of subjects that could be assessed simultaneously and the simplicity and uniformity of both test administration and scoring. The inventory rapidly became a popular tool.

Authors of early self-report inventories selected their items on the basis of their *face validity,* that is, they "looked right" in that their content dealt with topics that had an *obvious* relationship to personality traits and psychopathology. Questions were raised, however, as to whether such items had relevance to any systematic theory of psychopathology, whether the sheer obviousness of the items invited deliberate misrepresentation on the part of the respondent, and whether such tests "really" discriminated among different pathological states. Several approaches to test validation were formulated to deal with these questions (Loevinger, 1957): *external* (empirical-criterion), *structural* (factorial-trait), and *substantive* (theoretical-rational).

The first approach, *external,* initiated with the development of the Humm-Wadsworth Temperament Scale (1935), and brought to its fullest refinement in the MMPI (Hathaway and McKinley, 1942), involves choosing items that have an empirically demonstrated correspondence with relevant external criteria, such as clinically diagnosed pathological types. Although the pool of self-descriptive items used in these empirically validated instruments were usually selected on face-valid grounds, the final items retained for the tests consisted only of those that held up when checked against real-life criteria (i.e., had predictive and/or concurrent validity).

The second procedure of validation, termed *structural,* is based on statistical and factor analytic procedures; its goal is to produce several homogeneous scales representing relevant traits of personality functioning with as small a number of items as necessary. In contrast to the external approach, which retains items on the basis of their empirically demonstrated correlations with significant clinical criteria, structurally validated tests select items that will ensure trait representativeness and internal consistency within scales.

The third method of validating self-report inventories, *substantive,* draws its items from a clearly formulated theoretical framework. The theory established a series of clinically relevant categories and provides a fund of diverse behaviors characteristic of patients in each category. Items that represent the typical behaviors of each clinical category are generated and then grouped, in accordance with the theory, to form the separate clinical scales of the inventory. In contrast to the two previous approaches to test validation, which may be viewed as empirical and statistical, the substantive method derives its items rationally in terms of a theoretical scheme. Since there are few theories of psychopathology from which self-report items can be rationally derived, the number of inventories constructed on this basis are few indeed. Ideally, inventories should be developed employing all three methods of item validation. No such clinical instrument is in current use, but several that follow this three-stage format are being constructed; one inventory of this type will be discussed briefly in later paragraphs.

For the present, we shall divide inventories into two groups, those which focus on a single clinical characteristic and those that encompass and distinguish among several such characteristics.

Single Dimension Instruments. These self-report inventories select and highlight one class of variables from the total personality matrix for analysis and measurement. Several personality dimensions have been isolated, but we shall limit our discussion to three of the more important and extensively research variables: *anxiety, affect-mood,* and *self-acceptance.*

Anxiety Scales. Because of its central role in psychopathology, anxiety has been a favorite concept for test constructors. Levitt (1967) provides an excellent review of the concept, describes more than ten recent "anxiety" inventories, and discusses, albeit briefly, the special attributes and limitations of each.

The most frequently used and researched of these inventories is *Taylor's Manifest Anxiety Scale* (1951, 1953), one of a number of instruments constructed from the 566 item pool of the Minnesota Multiphasic Personality Inventory (to be discussed later). The scale includes 225 of the MMPI items, of which only 50 contribute to the anxiety score; the remainder serve as "fillers" to disguise the intent of the measure. Although devised originally for use as a measure of an organismic variable in experimental studies of learning, the scale's success in distinguishing between normal and psychiatric populations has led to its wide use as an instrument in general psychopathological research.

There are other, less extensively researched, anxiety inventories that are worthy of note; among them are the *S-R Inventory of Anxiousness* (Endler et al., 1962), and the *State-Trait Anxiety Inventory* (Spielberger and Gorsuch, 1966).

Affect-Mood Scales. Despite the obvious importance of mood as an element of the personal experience of emotionally disturbed persons, it is only recently that systematic attempts have been made to devise quantifiable self-report instruments. Only a few of these inventories provide reasonably satisfactory evidence of reliability and validity; among them are the *Mood Adjective Checklist,* the *Multiple Affect Adjective Checklist,* and the *Personal Feeling Scales.* A brief description of each will suffice for our purposes.

The *Mood Adjective Checklist* (Nowlis 1956, 1965) attempts to capture moment-to-moment states of conscious mood. The list consists of 130 mood-related adjectives, for example, uncertain, apprehensive, carefree, down-hearted, which the subject is asked to read through rapidly and rate on a four-point intensity scale reflecting his feelings while taking the test. Factor analysis of intercorrelations among responses from several populations have resulted in eight mood factors, for example, aggression, anxiety, depression, social affection. The sensitivity of this instrument to experimentally induced drug states, sleep deprivation, boredom, emotionally charged films, etc., has been well documented by Nowlis and his associates.

Similar to the above, but even simpler to administer, is the *Multiple Affect Adjective Checklist* (Zuckerman and Lubin, 1966), which consists of some 60 items that are merely checked by the subject if he believes they characterize either his current or his general feelings, depending on the instructions provided. The instrument covers three areas with rationally derived scales: anxiety, depression, and hostility.

The *Personal Feeling Scales* (Wessman and Ricks, 1966) are completed daily for several days and summarize the intensity of several different feelings experienced during each day. There are 16 separate bipolar feeling categories, for example, elation-depression, harmony-anger, tranquility-anxiety, each graded on a 10-point scale; the subject is asked to record in the evening which of the 16 categories he rated as the "highest," "lowest," and "average," using the 10-point scale. Although this instrument has not been subjected to factorial analyses and has not yet been validated with psychopathologic populations, it is more richly differentiated and refined in structure than previous comparable tools, and promises to be a useful inventory for appraising complex mood variations over a number of days.

Self-Acceptance Scales. Central to most phenomenological theories is the notion that unfavorable self-evaluations comprise the essence of psychopathology, and that changes toward higher self-esteem are the sine qua non of successful therapy. To measure the self-concept variable, researchers have devised inventories in which the subject characterizes both his actual self, as phenomenologically perceived, and his ideal self, that is, what he would like to be. Discrepancies between actual and ideal ratings comprise a self-acceptance measure.

The most common format for these self-report evaluations are sorting procedures in which the subject distributes a series of descriptive statements, printed on individual cards, into a graded series of categories depicting the degree to which the items are "like" or "unlike" himself. In a typical study, Rogers and Dymond (1954) had patients perform a "self-sort" and an "ideal-sort" both prior to and after client-centered therapy; they gauged the effectiveness of treatment by the extent to which the discrepancy between the initial self-ideal sorts decreased on resorting after therapy.

Comparisons between actual and ideal ratings are employed in the *Self-Ideal-Other-Q-sort* (Rogers and Dymond, 1954), the *Inter-personal Checklist* (LaForge and Suczek, 1955), and the *Adjective Checklist* (Gough and Heilbrun, 1964). Other instruments probe self-evaluations directly; among these measures are the *Self-Acceptance Scale* (Berger, 1952), the *Self-Rating Inventory* (Brownfain, 1952), and the *Self-Evaluation Questionnaire* (Farnham-Diggory, 1964). Several of these instruments have been carefully developed, but there is little empirical data bearing on their validity with distinct psychopathologic syndromes.

Multidimensional Instruments. It is often useful for research purposes to employ an inventory that encompasses a more extensive range of personality characteristics than tapped by the single dimension instruments described above. Several such inventories have been devised; we shall concentrate on three instruments that typify the external, structural, and substantive approaches to test construction and validation.

Minnesota Multiphasic Personality Inventory (MMPI). There is little question but that the MMPI, developed by Hathaway and McKinley (1942), is currently the most popular self-report inventory, ranking along with the Rorschach and TAT, not only as "standard" instruments of psychopathologic analysis, but as the three most extensively researched clinical tools. More than 2000 articles and books have been written about it, and more than 200 tests have been devised using the question items of which it is composed.

The construction of the MMPI was thoroughly empirical. An original pool of over 1000 items, to which subjects responded "true," "false" or "cannot say," was reduced to 566 items on the basis of their demonstrated success in discriminating between psychiatric patients and "normal" adults. More specifically, patients were divided into subdiagnostic groups, and items that discriminated a particular psychiatric group from normals were categorized together to form a scale; each of these psychiatric scales was keyed so that the greater the number of items on a scale endorsed by a subject, the more similar he was assumed to be to the particular diagnostic group with which the scale was first constructed. Nine different clinical scales were developed in this fashion, as well as four validity scales to check against errors, evasiveness, and deception. Table 4.3 provides a brief description of the characteristics purportedly tapped by each of the 13 original scales.

In scoring the inventory, the number of responses keyed to each scale is totaled; this total is converted into standard scores, known as T-scores, and plotted on a profile sheet. A T-score of 50 corresponds to the average number of items on a scale responded to in the keyed direction by "normal" persons; T-scores of 70 or higher are considered to indicate the presence of pathological signs that characterize the clinical population with

TABLE 4.3: Interpretation of the Validity and Clinical Scales of the Minnesota Multiphasic Personality Inventory

Validity Scales	?—indication of cautiousness or defensiveness; too high a score invalidates the test.
	L—the extent to which the subject was motivated to put himself in a good light, to avoid admission of even the mildest of personal defects or conflicts.
	F—the degree to which the test has been invalidated by carelessness or by tendencies to exaggerate complaints and to give an unduly "bad" picture.
	K—more subtle measure than L or F of "test-taking" attitudes; the higher the K-score, the more "defensive" the subject.
Clinical Scales	1. Hs—hypochondriacal trends; all the major organ systems and physical complaint areas are sampled by the items scored on this scale.
	2. D—symptomatic depression.
	3. Hy—hysteroid trends; denial of conflicts, claims of superior personal adjustment, and presence of certain somatic complaints.
	4. Pd—a mixture of rebellious, resentful attitudes toward authorities, lack of positive emotional experiences, asocial trends, and interpersonal conflicts.
	5. Mf—psychological masculinity-femininity as revealed by interests and preferences.
	6. Pa—trends toward ideas of reference and influence, both subtle and more obvious paranoid mentation.
	7. Pt—presence of obsessive-compulsive trends, worries, phobias, and extreme anxiety symptoms.
	8. Sc—schizoid mentation and affect, including delusional trends.
	9. Ma—self-confidence, morale, and manic trends.

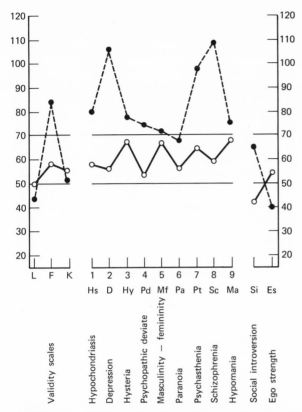

FIGURE 4.7. MMPI profiles for a 20-year-old male with a psychotic depression (dotted line), and after one month of daily therapy (solid line).

which the scale was developed. Figure 4.7 illustrates the profile of a depressed patient before and after treatment (note that the ?, or cannot say, scale has been deleted, and that two, more recently devised, clinical scales, Si and Es, have been added).

Although there is some question as to whether a valid picture of a patient's status can be gauged by examining his scores on a scale-by-scale analysis, the overall profile pattern has been shown in recent research to be a reasonably useful basis for diagnostic interpretation. Profile configurations, based on relative magnitudes of several T-scores, have themselves been empirically correlated with a variety of other diagnostic, as well as prognostic and therapeutic, variables. Thus, interpretation is guided by results obtained with known external correlates, and is not left to the speculative deductions of the clinician; in fact, these data have recently been

TABLE 4.4: Traits Measured by the Sixteen Personality Factor Questionnaire

Factor	Description
A.	Reserved, detached, critical, cool (Sizothymia, previously Schizothymia) versus Outgoing, warm-hearted, easygoing, participating (Affectothymia, previously Cyclothymia)
B.	Less intelligent, concrete-thinking (Low scholastic mental capacity) versus More intelligent, abstract-thinking, bright (High scholastic mental capacity)
C.	Affected by feelings, emotionally less stable, easily upset (Low ego strength) versus Emotionally stable, faces reality, calm, mature (High ego strength)
E.	Humble, mild, accommodating, conforming (Submissiveness) versus Assertive, independent, aggressive, stubborn (Dominance)
F.	Sober, prudent, serious, taciturn (Desurgency) versus Happy-go-lucky, impulsively lively, gay, enthusiastic (Surgency)
G.	Expedient, evades rules, feels few obligations (Low superego strength) versus Conscientious, persevering, staid, rule-bound (High superego strength)
H.	Shy, restrained, diffident, timid (Threctia) versus Venturesome, socially bold, uninhibited, spontaneous (Parmia)
I.	Tough-minded, self-reliant, realistic, no-nonsense (Harria) versus Tender-minded, dependent, overprotected, sensitive (Premsia)
L.	Trusting, adaptable, free of jealousy, easy to get on with (Alaxia) versus Suspicious, opinionated, hard to fool (Protension)
M.	Practical, careful, conventional, regulated by external realities, proper (Praxernia) versus Imaginative, wrapped up in inner urgencies, careless of practical matters, Bohemian (Autia)
N.	Forthright, natural, artless, sentimental (Artlessness) versus Shrewd, calculating, worldly, penetrating (Shrewdness)
O.	Placid, self-assured, confident, serene (Untroubled adequacy) versus Apprehensive, worrying, depressive, troubled (Guilt proneness)
Q1.	Conservative, respecting established ideas, tolerant of traditional difficulties (Conservatism) versus Experimenting, critical, liberal, analytical, freethinking (Radicalism)
Q2.	Group-dependent, a "joiner" and sound follower (Group adherence) versus Self-sufficient, prefers own decisions, resourceful (Self-sufficiency)
Q3.	Undisciplined, self-conflicting, careless of protocol, follows own urges (Low integration) versus Controlled, socially precise, following self image, compulsive (High self-concept control)
Q4.	Relaxed, tranquil, torpid, unfrustrated (Low ergic tension) versus Tense, frustrated, driven, overwrought (High ergic tension)

programmed into a computer, providing automated interpretive sugges-tions (Pearson and Swenson, 1967; Fowler, 1969). Useful empirically based guides to MMPI profile interpretation are furnished in Dahlstrom and Welsh (1960), Marks and Seeman (1963), and Gilberstadt and Duker (1965); the *MMPI Manual* (Hathaway and McKinley), revised last in 1951, has been outdated and will soon be replaced.

Sixteen Personality Factor Questionnaire (16 P-F). Whereas the MMPI exemplifies an inventory constructed by external or empirical-crite-rion methods, the *16 P-F Questionnaire* (Cattell, 1949, 1963) is a prime example of an instrument devised on the basis of structural- or factorial-trait procedures. In developing this instrument, Cattell amassed an impres-sive number of personality trait descriptions ultimately reducing them to 171 items, which he then intercorrelated to produce 12 factors. On the basis of these results, plus 4 additional factors identified in subsequent studies, Cattell prepared his 16 factor questionnaire, now available in three forms of 187, 187, and 106 items respectively. Table 4.4 summa-rizes the 16 personality dimensions purportedly measured by this instru-ment.

Considerable use has been made in personality research with the *16 P-F Questionnaire,* but there is a paucity of data on clinical populations. Moreover, although the construction of the instrument may have been im-peccable, it suffers many of the problems inherent in factor-based scales. Some have questioned whether the 16 separate dimensions are reasonably homogeneous and internally consistent, the sine qua non of the structural approach; and there is insufficient evidence that the scales are adequately reliable or relate empirically to significant external criteria. Cattell and his associates recognize these shortcomings, and are continuing, with skill and imagination, to further refine and validate their instrument.

Millon-Illinois Self Report Inventory (MI-SRI). The initial item pool for this instrument (Millon, 1972), consisting of over 3000 self-descriptive statements, was derived on a rational basis from a systematic theory of psychopathology (Millon, 1969); hence, it illustrates the substantive ap-proach to test validation in its initial stages of construction. Item lists for 19 theoretically based clinical scales (Table 4.5) were reduced so as to fur-nish two equivalent Provisional Forms of 566 statements each. Empirical studies with relevant and diverse clinical populations provided data for item analyses and refinements in scale homogeneity and reliability. Provi-sional Form items were eliminated on the basis of these studies, resulting in a single structurally validated Research Form of 566 statements. Cur-rent work investigating the correlation of scale scores and profiles with various criterion measures, such as clinical ratings, biographical data, and several perceptual and cognitive tasks, should furnish a basis for further

TABLE 4.5: Syndrome Scale Characteristics of the Million-Illinois Self Report Inventory

Scales	Syndrome Characteristics
Personality Patterns	
PD $_+$	Chronically asocial, flat, colorless, complacent, apathetic, unfeeling.
AD $_+$	Chronically apprehensive, shy, socially avoidant, mistrustful, ill-at-ease.
PD $_P$	Chronically docile, submissive, self-effacing, timid, dependent.
AD $_P$	Chronically gregarious, capricious, dramatic, flighty, exhibitionistic.
P1	Chronically narcissistic, pretentious, boastful, ungenerous, disdainful.
A1	Chronically aggressive, intimidating, competitive, controlling, domineering.
PA	Chronically conforming, methodical, rigid, conscientious, overcontrolled.
AA	Chronically negativistic, unpredictable, complaining, explosive, obstructive.
SS	Chronically schizoid, autistic, socially detached and self-alienated.
CC	Chronically cycloid; intense mood and behavior vacillation.
PP	Chronically paranoid, suspicious, delusional; intense hostility.
Symptom Disorders	
An	Symptomatically anxious, tense, overwrought.
PCD	Symptomatically phobic or dissociative.
H	Symptomatically hypochondriacal, fatigued, weary.
D	Symptomatically dejected, vaguely discontent and blue.
O-C	Symptomatically obsessive or compulsive.
Soc	Symptomatically sociopathic, antisocial, rebellious.
Psy	Symptomatically psychotic, delusional, depressive, confused.

item reductions and scale refinements. As these steps provide data for external validation, the final or Clinical Form of the instrument will be published for general diagnostic use. In the interim, the Research Form, derived from a systematic theory and displaying evidence of internal consistency and reliability, lends itself well as an instrument for a wide range of experimental studies.

Performance Measures

Phenomenological experience can be tapped by methods other than those which ask the subject directly to provide an introspective description of his inner feelings and attitudes. The techniques we have previously described are especially suited to the task of detecting the *content* of the subject's phenomenological world, but other procedures can and must be employed to uncover the *process* by which these phenomenal experiences are shaped and transformed. Data about process variables rarely are gathered by direct questioning; instead, they are inferred by observing the manner in which the subject identifies the events of his perceptual world and formulates them into ideas and concepts. It is through the subject's responses to specially devised "performance tasks" that the researcher is able to deduce cognitive styles and modes of perceiving. Although data obtained on these tasks are composed of overt verbal reports and behaviors, the focus of interest, however, is not the content of these responses, but the mediating processes they signify, that is, *how* the subject's phenomenological world operates, rather than *what* it contains.

The task employed to decipher phenomenological processes are far too numerous for us to attempt even a brief survey. For illustrative purposes, we shall present a sample of the more frequently used instruments. Additional examples, with associated research data, may be found in Zubin et al. (1957, 1960), Gardner et al. (1959), Uhr and Miller (1960), Eysenck (1960), Payne (1961), Inglis (1966), and Maher (1966, 1969).

For the sake of simplicity, we shall separate these methods into two categories: *perceptual tasks* and *cognitive tasks.* Few hard and fast lines can be drawn between complex theoretical concepts, such as perception and cognition; thus, it should not be surprising to find that the same performance task would be employed as a perceptual tool in one study and as a cognitive one in another.

Perceptual Tasks. It is quite natural that researchers would turn to the study of perception as one of the more promising avenues for uncovering psychopathologic processes; inflexibilities and distortions in the perceptual sphere characterize many clinical syndromes. Three tasks designed to uncover these processes will be described: the *rod and frame procedure,* the *embedded figures test,* and the *autokinetic phenomenon.*

Rod and Frame Procedure. This moderately complex instrument was designed by Witkin et al. (1954, 1962) as a means of differentiating two classes of patients: (1) those of a passive orientation and low self-esteem, termed field-dependent persons, and (2) those of a more active orientation who resist external sources of influence, labeled field-independent persons. Much research with this technique has involved determining which diagnostic subtypes fit into each class, for example, predicting that alcoholics are field-dependent persons.

The apparatus consists of a square frame coated with luminous paint, within which is mounted a similarly coated rod. The frame and rod are pi-

FIGURE 4.8.   Tilted seat and tilted-room apparatus (Witkin, 1962).

voted at their centers, but mounted on separate shafts, enabling them to be tilted from side to side independently of each other. The subject is seated firmly in a chair that can also be tilted to any one of several positions. The testing sessions take place either in a totally dark room or with the subject seated on an angle in a tilted room (Figure 4.8); in both arrangements, the coated frame and rod are the only objects that are visible. The subject is instructed to adjust the rod to the true vertical, that is, perpendicular to the earth's surface; the problem he faces is that he must gauge the true vertical when the chair in which he is sitting is tilted away from its usual vertical position, and the frame within which the rod is centered is likewise rotated in a misleading fashion. The true vertical can be reasonably guaged if the subject adjusts the rod in terms of body cues; if he succeeds in this adjustment, he is considered field-independent. Should the subject fail or use his body cues and be guided more by the misleading position of the frame, then he is considered to be field-dependent.

Embedded Figures Test. Originally devised as a clinical diagnostic tool by Gottschaldt (1926), this test has subsequently been used by numerous research investigators (e.g., Witkin, 1950; Gardner et al., 1959). The stimuli for this instrument consist of a small number of simple figures and a larger number of complex designs, each of which contains within it one of the simple figures (Figure 4.9).

In a typical procedure, the subject is shown one of the complex designs for a brief period; after it is removed, he is given one of the simpler figures for several seconds and told that it can be found embedded in the previously shown complex design; the simple figure is then removed and

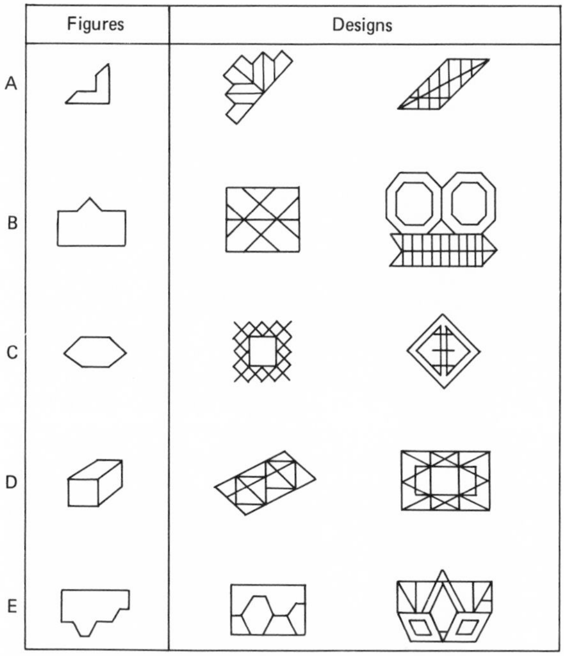

FIGURE 4.9.   Illustrative embedded figures items.

the complex design presented again. The time required to locate and trace the embedded figure with a stylus provides the score for each trial; several trials, matching different figures with different designs, comprise the test. Analysis is based on time factors, errors and distortions, and the qualitative comments made by the subject as he proceeds. Paper-and-pencil versions using multiple choice presentations of the embedded simple figure have also been developed.

Autokinetic Phenomenon. If a subject fixates a dimly perceived point of light in an otherwise totally darkened room, the light will usually appear to move to some extent; this apparent movement has been termed the autokinetic phenomenon. Several investigators (Sexton, 1945; Voth, 1947; Diamond, 1956) have recorded the responses of patients with differing syndromes to a series of repeated autokinetic exposures. The amount and pattern of movement perceived, the consistency or lack of consistency of these perceptions upon repetitive exposure, and the extent to which these subjectively perceived movements can be modified by social or other sources of external influence, are among the many measures that have been fruitfully employed.

Cognitive Tasks. It should not be surprising that the tools available to appraise cognitive processes are extremely diverse. Cognition, the process of knowing and thinking, is itself a multifaceted concept. It encompasses such varied activities as deductive and inductive reasoning, memory and retention, imagination and creativity, etc. The varied contents of cognition result in further subdivisions, thereby accounting for instruments that selectively focus on numerical, spatial, or verbal processes. Important personality dimensions, such as cognitive styles, provide another basis for differentiation. And a whole host of pathological symptoms, such as distractibility, rigidity, and overinclusion, may likewise be tapped and measured. Many performance tasks involve combinations of several cognitive operations, but it is beyond the scope of this chapter to cover even a small portion of these more encompassing tools. Two illustrations will have to suffice: *concept-formation sorting procedures* and *cognitive flexibility tests.*

Concept-formation Sorting Procedures. Perhaps the most popular and successful way of exposing and measuring styles and disturbances of cognition has been through concept-formation sorting tasks. First devised by Ach (1935), and developed for clinical use by Goldstein and Scheerer (1941), these procedures require the subject to discover, on his own, different but logical ways of categorizing a group of items. Most of the objects presented are selected with an eye to variations in color, shape, size, and content; Figure 4.10 illustrates the range of concepts that are possible using blocks only. The typical procedure consists of presenting the items simultaneously in a random assortment, and instructing the subject to put together those which he thinks belong together; following one successful conceptual grouping, he is asked to regroup the items differently. Scoring usually is based on the number of categories formed, the time to complete them, and a number of more qualitative indices that uncover cognitive styles and distortions.

Cognitive Flexibility Tests. Disturbances along the cognitive dimension of rigidity-flexibility are a major sign of psychopathology, according to many clinicians. Researchers have devised a number of tools to isolate and quantify these disturbances, usually with techniques that measure the

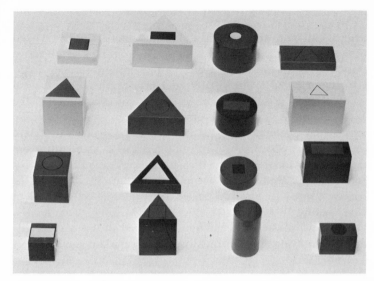

FIGURE 4.10. Typical items of a concept-formation sorting task; blocks can be sorted on the basis of characteristics such as color, shape, area, or volume (from Yacorzynski, 1965)

patient's ability to maintain a coherent train of thought, or his tendency to perseverate when a shift or change of set is appropriate.

One of the simplest of these procedures is the metalog test (Burdock et al., 1958) which requires the subject to produce, within one minute, as many different meanings to a simple stimulus word. Not only does this provide a gauge of the subject's flexibility in shifting conceptually, but it furnishes a qualitative index of cognitive preoccupations and distortions.

Another, and perhaps the most popular of these tasks, is *Luchin's water-jar test* (1942, 1951). In this procedure, subjects are presented with a series of arithmetic problems which require them to obtain a given quantity of water using any combination of three jars of known capacity. The first few of these problems can be solved only by a particular and complicated series of maneuvers that require the use of all three containers: these initial problems establish a "set" for solving the problems in a particular way. As the subject progresses, however, the problems can be solved quite simply by using only two of the jars. Measures along the dimension of cognitive rigidity-flexibility are obtained by noting how many of the problems that could have been solved by the two-jar method continue to be approached by the initial three-jar "set" procedure.

Evaluative Comments

Phenomenological data are more tangible and more readily evoked than those of the intrapsychic level, but both derive from highly subjective "inner" sources and are subject, therefore, to numerous distorting influences. What has contributed to the greater adequacy of phenomenological data is not so much their greater tangibility and ease of evocation, but the care with which potential sources of distortion have been avoided by those who have constructed phenomenological instruments. To illustrate, great pains were taken in the *Structured Clinical Interview* to standardize the data-gathering process and to ensure that idiosyncracies in interviewer questioning and interpretation were kept to a minimum. Similarly, in the MMPI, efforts were made to construct scales that would detect respondent evasiveness and "faking."

The three principal classes of techniques described in this section differ too greatly to be evaluated together; we shall separate them in this brief critical review.

1. The data of postinterview content analysis are often gathered in highly dissimilar settings; moreover, interviewers may have conducted their sessions in idiosyncratic fashions. Both of these factors decrease markedly the comparability of data, and it may not be possible to compensate for this lack of uniformity, even with clearly articulated systems of content analysis. Among other shortcomings of these systems is the lack of adequate normative data gathered on relevant psychopathologic groups; evidence for their validity in the psychiatric field is also almost nonexistent.

Data uniformity is not a problem with prearranged interview schedules; in fact, standardization at the input end is among their prime virtues. However, since most of these instruments are of recent vintage, there is little evidence that they provide a balanced cross section of factorially "pure" phenomenological data; moreover, minimal information is available of a normative nature, or of their validity as instruments of clinical discrimination or prediction. Such data are being accumulated.

2. Despite the highly structured character of self-report inventories, they are subject to distortions that may invalidate the data they furnish. For example, researchers cannot assume that all subjects interpret the items similarly, or that they have sufficient self-knowledge to reply informatively, or that they may not be dissembling or faking their replies. Few of the "single dimension" instruments described earlier were designed to obviate these problems, nor did their authors take adequate precautions to minimize their effects.

It is to the credit and distinction of the constructors of the MMPI that they established adequate "control" scales to avoid or detect these complications. Moreover, by validating their test items against relevant external criteria, they circumvented a variety of problems inherent in phenomenological data, such as respondent self-knowledge and test-taking attitudes; thus, it does not really matter "why" a subject responds as he does since the response, whatever its basis, correlates empirically with a known and significant external criterion. Unfortunately, evidence of the validity of the separate MMPI scales as instruments for discriminating among clinical syndromes has fallen far short of its developers' original expectations, although its validity in distinguishing broad categories such as psychoses, neurosis, and normality has stood up well.

Perhaps the factorial impurity of the MMPI scales accounts, in part, for their failure to correlate with clinically derived diagnostic dinstinctions. Cattell's 16 P-F questionnaire is composed of reasonably independent factors, but its scales have not been sufficiently validated empirically against external criteria of psychopathology. In fact, there is little normative data available on clinical populations, thereby decreasing its utility for comparative research studies.

3. Performance tasks are notably "objective" in procedure and lend themselves readily to quantification, their two chief claims to prominence among the phenomenological data collection methods. Their two principal shortcomings are the lack of normative data on pertinent pathologic groups, and their questionable generalizability. On this latter point, different instruments that deal ostensibly with the same perceptual or cognitive function intercorrelate rather poorly. This raises the serious question as to whether any one of them can be safely employed as operational measures of the more general perceptual or cognitive concept they have been selected to represent. For example, we cannot assume that findings on cognitive rigidity, gathered with the Luchin's water-jar test, will be replicated with any other operational measure of rigidity.

BEHAVIORAL METHODS

The behavioral approach is characterized in its strictest form by its exclusive focus on observable nonsubjective data. The subject matter is overt activity, the behavior of the person as he "moves about, stands still, seizes objects, pushes and pulls, makes sound gestures, and so on" (Skinner, 1956). Although researchers who work with phenomenological and intrapsychic concepts must, of necessity, draw upon observables, they depend primarily on subjective reports and use them to formulate and test notions about inner states or mediating processes. Behaviorists, in contrast, focus on "objective" observables, limiting their concepts to them, and eschewing, where possible, inferences and notions concerning "internal" and subjective events.

The behavioristic approach is difficult to pursue in its "pure" form when dealing with so complex a subject as psychopathology. Nevertheless, there are techniques that bypass such subjective data sources as phenomenological self-reports and intrapsychic projective techniques, and confine themselves, more or less, to overtly observable actions. Most pedagogic distinctions, however, have few counterparts in "reality"; thus, no hard and fast line will be found between the behavioral methods described here, and several of the methods of data collection discussed previously.

The techniques presented in this section will be separated into three subcategories: *systematic observation, verbal behavior analysis,* and *performance measures.* The *first* of these refers to methods that code and quantify either simple or complex behaviors and often require observer judgments for purposes of classification; moreover, inferences frequently are drawn about unobservable processes and internal dispositions. The *second* category of methods deal with the same speech materials as do a number of the previously described phenomenological tools, but contrast with those techniques in that they overlook the content and meaning of what is said and focus on the quantity, grammatical structure, or voice dimension of the verbal behavior. The *third* group of methods comprise objectively scored measures based on physical or tangible behavioral acts; in contrast to the other two categories, no judgments or inferences need be made in deriving these measures.

Systematic Observation

As just noted, observational methods typically call for classificatory and inferential judgments on the part of the researcher. In this section, we shall discuss several of the more systematic techniques of observation, that is, those which focus the observer's attention on specific and well-defined units of behavior and guide his judgments or ratings in such ways as to maximize their representativeness, reliability, and quantifiability.

Although unsystematic or impressionistic observations and judgments have a definite place in exploratory research, they tend to sample events in a scattered and capricious manner, are subject to recorder errors and biases and, typically, are cast in nonquantitative forms. Brief, but excellent, discussions of the problems of impressionistic observation have been furnished by Heyns and Lippitt (1954), Selltiz et al. (1959), Barker (1963), Kerlinger (1964), and Kleinmutz (1967).

The methods to be described in the following paragraphs can be considered to be "systematic" in that they employ procedures that minimize most of the pitfalls inherent in impressionistic observation. We shall divide these techniques in terms of their scope, that is, the range of events they encompass. The *first* group concentrates on specific expressive aspects of behavior, subtle components of the larger stream of activity that communicate thoughts and feelings nonverbally; they will be subsumed under the label, *micromomentary behavior analysis.* The *second* class of methods encompass a wide range of complex patient activities, both subtle and gross; they are commonly referred to as *behavior inventories and rating scales.*

Micromomentary Behavior Analysis. Every perceptive person recognizes that momentary body gestures and movements convey not only temporary feeling states but also more pervasive styles of behavior. Phrases common to our everyday language often capture the essence of these behaviors well, to wit, such descriptions as "shifty eyes," a "sly look," and an "arrogant walk."

Some 40 years ago, the study of expressive behavior was among the more richly investigated topics in psychology. However, since Allport and Vernon's systematic studies in 1933, interest in the subject markedly waned. Only in the past decade or so have the many possibilities of this fruitful source of psychopathologic data been rekindled. Guilford (1959), Brengelmann (1961), and Allport (1961) have brought the scattered literature of the prior 35 years up-to-date. But a more important impetus has been the recent growth of interest in therapeutic "process" research, with its concern for what transpires in the interview situation and what transient cues the therapist employs to guide his behavior. Equally important has been the availability of movie films and videotapes; with these recording instruments, the researcher can make permanent, for purposes of coding and analysis, the data of grimaces, gestures, and other fleeting movements.

Although categorizing techniques are still in a primitive stage of development, numerous investigators have initiated studies into nonverbal interview behavior in the hope of correlating these difficult-to-conceal forms of communication with such variables as speech content, unconscious emotional states, psychosomatic disorders, etc. (Ekman, 1964, 1968; Dittmann et al., 1965; Scheflen, 1965; Haggard and Isaacs, 1966; Deutsch, 1966; Mahl, 1968). Figure 4.11 illustrates the kinds of movements that can be recorded and quantified; more specifically, it represents one of a number of postural changes, communicative gestures, and idiosyncratic actions of a subject recorded at successive two-minute intervals during an initial interview. Although these findings are often used for purposes of inferring complex intrapsychic processes, the basic data consist strictly of objectively observable behaviors.

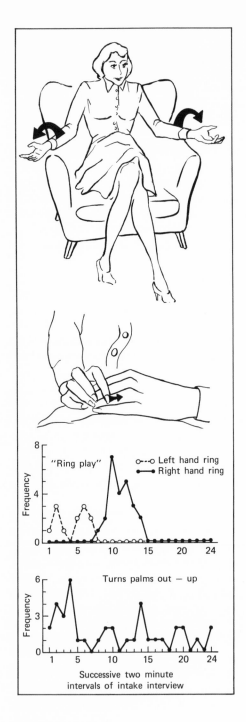

FIGURE 4.11. Micromomentary gesture analysis: a patient's communicative gesture of turning her palms out-up and ring play, first with her wedding ring on her left hand, then a ring on her right hand, and the frequency of these acts (Mahl, 1968).

"Ring play"
o--o Left hand ring
●—● Right hand ring

Frequency

8

4

0

1   5   10   15   20   24

Turns palms out — up

Frequency

6

3

0

1   5   10   15   20   24

Successive two minute
intervals of intake interview

Behavior Inventories and Rating Scales. Inventories and scales encompass a more varied and extensive range of clinically significant variables than do micromomentary measures. These instruments have grown in popularity in the past two decades, and literally dozens have been constructed since the development of the Phipps Psychiatric Clinic Behavior Chart (Kempf, 1915); Lorr (1960) has provided a thorough and reasonably up-to-date survey of over 25 inventories and scales.

The items comprising these tools generally are not single observations per se, but summary impressions derived from a series of observations. However, in contrast to most "free" descriptions of behavior, the rater is required to limit himself to checking or filling out a series of prespecified statements, judging all of the items pertaining to events he has observed. The standardized format of these instruments is one of their virtues since it permits the gathering of comparable data from various populations drawn from different settings. The uniformity in structure and the fixed number of precoded categories into which judgments must be placed transform into quantifiable units what would otherwise be discursive and qualitative clinical impressions.

The chief difference between inventories and rating scales relates to their discriminability. Inventories permit the choice of only "present" or "absent," that is, whether a behavioral item has or has not been observed. Rating scales refine this twofold discrimination by allowing the rater to record his judgment of the frequency or intensity of the behavior in question; thus, he may note whether the behavior is "intense," "strong," "moderate," "mild," "weak or absent." The format of some scales permits the rater an even greater measure of freedom by allowing him to check any point along a frequency or intensity continuum. In general, inventories are easier to complete since they demand less subtle judgments on the part of the observer; moreover, they usually consist of concrete and clearly delimited acts presented in fairly concise and straightforward descriptive language. By contrast, rating scales typically demand more discerning observations and sophisticated judgments; accordingly, the items tend to be cast in complex descriptive phrases that require rather keen and artful inferences on the part of the rater. Although rating scales would appear to provide a more sensitive index of individual differences and intraindividual changes, the evidence for the validity of their refined discriminations is lacking; moreover, rating scales rely to a greater extent on the inferential skills of the observer, a talent that is not notably common.

Three of the more carefully constructed rating instruments in current use will be described: the *Inpatient Multidimensional Psychiatric Scale,* the *Brief Psychiatric Rating Scale,* and the *Minnesota-Hartford Personality Assay.* It should be noted at the outset that none of these scales limit themselves exclusively to overt behavior; all include items or sections based on the phenomenological content of patient self-reports. However, in contrast to instruments such as the Structured Clinical Interview, to which they are akin, these scales do not depend on, nor are they administered with the explicit intention of questioning the patient and evoking subjective self-reports.

Inpatient Multidimensional Psychiatric Scales (IMPS): Lorr and his associates (1962) developed the IMPS after surveying numerous prior rating instruments and engaging in an extensive series of factor analytic studies; their goal was to obtain a quantified description of psychotic behaviors, and to extract their "underlying unitary variables."

The scale consists of 75 items that characterize behaviors observed and rated during an interview. The rater is advised to compare the patient to "normal" individuals of roughly the same age, sex, and social class. Each item is considered independently; that is, the interviewer is asked not to attempt to fashion a consistent diagnostic picture. Moreover, to minimize complex intrapsychic interpretations, he is advised to base his ratings on manifest behavior and "first order inferences"; about one-third of the items require that deductions be derived from the patient's verbalized feelings and thoughts, rather than his overt actions or behaviors. All judgments are made on an 8-point scale, ranging from "extremely" to "not at all." Table 4.6 illustrates a few of the items from the scale.

Lorr and his colleagues have extracted ten factorially based subscales from this instrument, cross-validating their findings with several different psychotic populations; the scales, they believe, represent relatively independent clinical syndromes that correspond, only in part, to the traditional nosological categories (Lorr et al., 1963); among them are "excitement," "hostile belligerence," "anxious intropunitiveness," "retardation and apathy," and "conceptual disorganization."

Brief Psychiatric Rating Scale (BPRS): The distinction of this instrument is its brevity (Overall and Gorham, 1962). It consists of 16 seven-point scales, each of which represents a discrete symptom feature. Sample items of the BPS are illustrated in Table 4.7. In contrast to the IMPS, ratings are made following an unstructured interview; judgments are of a summary or global nature, and are based on both overt behaviors and subjective self-reports.

The majority of items for the 16 scales of the BPRS were drawn from the longer IMPS; although some overlap is present, factor clusters derived by these two groups of investigators differ appreciably. Complex factor studies provide evidence of the instrument's internal consistency; higher-order clusters have been extracted, suggesting that the scale taps four major psychotic dimensions: depression, paranoid interpersonal disturb-

TABLE 4.6: Inpatient Multidimensional Psychiatric Scale: Illustrative Items

---

Compared to the normal person to what degree does he . . .

1. Manifest speech that is slowed, deliberate, or labored?

2. Give answers that are irrelevant or unrelated in any immediately conceivable way to the question asked or topic discussed?

    Cues: Do not rate here wandering or rambling conversation which veers away from the topic at issue (see item 4). Also, do not rate the coherence of the answer.

3. Give answers that are grammatically disconnected, incoherent, or scattered, i.e., not sensible or not understandable?

    Cues: Judge the grammatical structure of his speech, not the content which may or may not be bizarre.

4. Tend to ramble, wander, or drift off the subject or away from the point at issue in responding to questions or topics discussed?

    Cues: Do not rate here responses that are obviously unrelated to the question asked (see item 2).

5. Verbally express feelings of hostility, ill will, or dislike of others?

    Cues: Makes hostile comments regarding others such as attendants, other patients, his family, or persons in authority. Reports conflicts on the ward.

6. Exhibit postures that are peculiar, unnatural, rigid, or bizarre?

    Cues: Head twisted to one side; or arm and hand held oddly. Judge the degree of peculiarity of the posture.

From: Lorr et al. (1962).

ance, withdrawal-retardation, and thinking disturbance (Overall and Hollister, 1968).

Minnesota-Hartford Personality Assay (MHPA). This instrument is perhaps the most impressive tool devised in recent years for gathering behavioral data and recording clinical judgments (Meehl et al., 1965; Roche Report, 1966; Glueck and Stroebel, 1969). Eight thousand descriptive items were obtained from diverse sources; these were reduced to 1200 by eliminating duplications and unusual or rare behaviors. Fifty clinicians of divergent orientations were then asked to select items that were most descriptive of any two patients they know well. The 544 statements thus chosen were further reduced to 329 on the basis of factor analyses. Twenty factors were extracted from this final pool, covering such variables as "dis-

TABLE 4.7: Brief Psychiatric Rating Scale: Illustrative Items

---

3. *Emotional withdrawal*—deficiency in relating to the interviewer and the interview situation. Rate only degree to which the patient gives the impression of failing to be in emotional contact with other people in the interview situation.

   Not present   Very mild   Mild   Moderate   Mod. Severe   Severe
   Extremely Severe

4. *Conceptual disorganization*—degree to which the thought processes are confused, disconnected or disorganized. Rate on the basis of integration of the verbal products of the patient; do not rate on the basis of the patient's subjective impression of his own level of functioning.

   Not present   Very mild   Mild   Moderate   Mod. Severe   Severe
   Extremely Severe

5. *Guilt feelings*—over-concern or remorse for past behavior. Rate on the basis of the patient's subjective expereinces of guilt as evidenced by verbal report with appropriate affect; do not infer guilt feelings from depression, anxiety, or neurotic defenses.

   Not present   Very mild   Mild   Moderate   Mod. severe   Severe
   Extremely severe

6. *Tension*—physical and motor manifestations of tension, "nervousness," and heightened activation level. Tension should be rated solely on the basis of physical signs and motor behavior and not on the basis of subjective experiences of tension reported by the patient.

   Not present   Very mild   Mild   Moderate   Mod. severe   Severe
   Extremely severe

7. *Mannerisms and posturing*—unusual and unnatural motor behavior, the type of motor behavior which causes certain mental patients to stand out in a crowd of normal people. Rate only abnormality of movements; do not rate simple heightened motor activity here.

   Not present   Very mild   Mild   Moderate   Mod. severe   Severe
   Extremely severe

From: Overall and Gorham (1962).

turbances of affect," "hostile agressiveness," and "disorientation"; all 20 are noted along the horizontal axis in Figure 4.12.

Subsets of the basic 324 items were selected and grouped into two forms, one to be used by rating physicians (127 items), the other by nurses (118 items); Table 4.8 presents the instructions and illustrative items from the physicians scale. The rater assigns a value from 1 to 7 to each of the descriptive statements; this value represents his best judgment of the fre-

TABLE 4.8: Minnesota-Hartford Personality Assay: Instructions and Examples

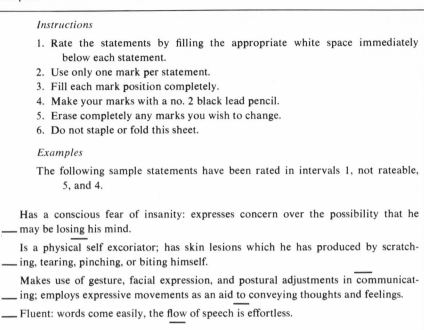

Instructions

1. Rate the statements by filling the appropriate white space immediately below each statement.
2. Use only one mark per statement.
3. Fill each mark position completely.
4. Make your marks with a no. 2 black lead pencil.
5. Erase completely any marks you wish to change.
6. Do not staple or fold this sheet.

Examples

The following sample statements have been rated in intervals 1, not rateable, 5, and 4.

Has a conscious fear of insanity: expresses concern over the possibility that he
___ may be losing his mind.

Is a physical self excoriator; has skin lesions which he has produced by scratching, tearing, pinching, or biting himself.

Makes use of gesture, facial expression, and postural adjustments in communicating; employs expressive movements as an aid to conveying thoughts and feelings.

___ Fluent: words come easily, the flow of speech is effortless.

Low |1| |2| |3| |4| |5| |6| |7| High |N R|

From: Meehl et al. (1965).

quency, intensity, and pervasiveness with which he has recently observed the characteristic in question. The scale is used as a quantitative index, with each category representing "how much" the patient demonstrates the behavioral item.

The completed assay form may be hand-tabulated or converted to punch cards and computer tapes. From these data a graphic representation of the patient's status on each of the 20 scales may be obtained. In general, scores falling between 45 and 60 are considered within the normal range, whereas those above 60 signify increasing psychopathology. Standard interpretations have been developed to correspond to varying scores on each of the scales. Arrangements can be made to have these interpretive comments printed out via an automated computer procedure, as illustrated in Figure 4.12. Although these statements provide only a crude

16-5 HAS A WELL FIXED PARANOID SYSTEM WITH DELUSIONS OF REFER-
ENCE AND PERSECUTION. HAS EXPERIENCED HALLUCINATORY EPI-
SODES.

15-5 HIS THOUGHT PROCESSES ARE SERIOUSLY DISTURBED WITH MARKED
EVIDENCE OF DEREISTIC THINKING, SEVERE COGNITIVE SLIPPAGE,
CONFUSION, AND ASSOCIATIVE DISRUPTION.

04-5 COMPLETELY WITHDRAWN AND ISOLATED FROM OTHERS.

05-5 HAS NO INSIGHT INTO, OR UNDERSTANDING OF THE MOTIVATIONS BE-
HIND HIS THOUGHTS AND BEHAVIOR.

02-4 HAS CONSIDERABLE DIFFICULTY IN CONFORMING TO SOCIAL EXPEC-
TATIONS, GROOMING, MANNER, AND DRESS FREQUENTLY INAPPRO-
PRIATE OR SOMEWHAT BIZARRE. TENDS TO STAND OUT AS
'DIFFERENT' FROM OTHERS.

19-4 GENERALLY SOMBER, MOROSE, RARELY CAN RESPOND WITH A SMILE,
NEVER JESTS OR JOKES, RARELY GETS ANY ENJOYMENT OUT OF LIFE.

09-3 OVERREACTS TO ANXIETY PRODUCING SITUATIONS AND CARRIES A
LOW CHRONIC LEVEL OF ANXIETY.

11-3 HAS A QUICK TEMPER. REACTS TO MINOR SLIGHTS WITH HOSTILE, AG-
GRESSIVE BEHAVIOR THAT AT TIMES IS DIFFICULT TO CONTROL.
SOMETIMES PETULANT OR QUERULOUS.

13-3 HAS SOME CONCERN ABOUT HIS MENTAL EQUILIBRIUM AND STABIL-
ITY, REQUIRING REASSURANCE FROM OTHERS REGARDING THIS.

01-2 SHOWS ADEQUATE AFFECTIVE CAPACITY, REACTS WELL TO SITUA-
TIONS WITH AFFECT APPROPRIATE IN BOTH QUALITY AND QUANTITY.

14-2 IS WELL INTEGRATED. DOES NOT EXPERIENCE DISTORTION OR DEPER-
SONALIZATION PHENOMENA EVEN IN PERIODS OF SEVERE STRESS.

12-2 WELL ORIENTED IN ALL SPHERES, WITH CLEAR, INTACT SENSORIUM.

20-2 SHOWS NO EVIDENCE OF SELF-DESTRUCTIVE TENDENCIES.

10-2 MAINTAINS A SATISFACTORY BALANCE BETWEEN INDEPENDENT,
SELF-ENERGIZING BEHAVIOR, AND ACCEPTANCE OF HELP WHEN NEC-
ESSARY.

08-2 IS ABLE TO RECOGNIZE AND ADMIT PHYSICAL SYMPTOMS WHEN PRES-
ENT.

17-2 SHOWS NO EVIDENCE OF WORRY OR CONCERN ABOUT HIS SEXUAL
ADJUSTMENT, ACCEPTS AN ADEQUATE HETEROSEXUAL ADJUSTMENT
AS PART OF HIS SELF-CONCEPT.

06-2 IS ABLE TO EXPRESS AND DEMONSTRATE APPROPRIATE FEELINGS OF
GUILT AND SHAME WHEN HE HAS BEHAVED IN AN UNACCEPTABLE
MANNER.

07-2 HAS REASONABLE CAPACITY TO ORGANIZE HIS DAILY ROUTINE WITH-
OUT EVIDENCE OF COMPULSIVE CONCERNS.

FIGURE 4.12. Computer print-out of Minnesota-Hartford Personality Assay may
be converted into a graph, as shown above, to demonstrate changes in the behavioral profile. In the case of this patient with paranoid-schizophrenia, the solid line
represents the behavioral profile 4 months ago and the dotted line indicates the
current profile. The profile is based on an evaluation of 20 factors and the degree
to which they are seen in the patient at the time of the rating. These factors are
identified at the right of the print-out and by number at the bottom of the graph.
Behavior rated above 60 and below 40 is generally abnormal. Narrative statements below the graph identify the factors and describe patient behavior; the first
figure (e.g., 16) to the left of the narrative statement identifies the factor while the
second figure (e.g., minus 5) indicates the number of standard deviations of the
patient from the group norm (Roche Report, 1966).

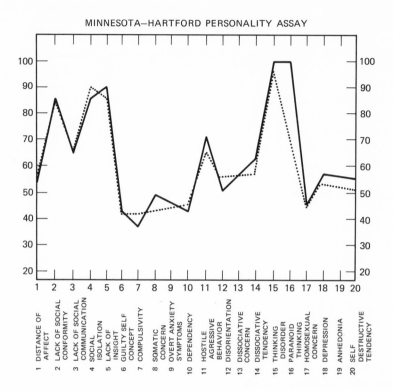

sketch of patient characteristics, they serve as a useful basis for more detailed personality appraisals.

Only a few empirical studies have been executed with this instrument. However, like its self-report prototype, the MMPI, considerable validity research has been undertaken and will be reported regularly in the literature.

Verbal Behavior Analysis

One distinction that may be made with regard to speech is the one between the manifest content of what is said, on the one hand, and the quantity, grammatical structure, and vocal properties of speech behavior, on the other. The manifest content of a communication conveys, essentially, phenomenological meaning, that is, ideas, memories, and feelings expressed consciously by the communicator. Of no lesser significance to psychopathology, according to several researchers, are a variety of behavioral

131

features intrinsic to the act of verbalizing that are incidental, however, to the content intended by the communicator. In this section, we shall briefly survey three ways of approaching these behavioral dimensions of speech: *noncontent analysis, word quotients,* and *dyadic interaction techniques.*

Noncontent Analysis. It is well recognized that emotions are conveyed not only in what a person says but also in how he says it, that is, in such noncontent properties of his speech as its timbre, frequency, quantity, tempo, and inflection.

Several investigators have sought to devise rating systems by which qualitative *paralinguistic* phenomena, such as voice tone and resonance, can be discerned and quantified (Starkweather 1956; Trager, 1958; Mahl, 1959; Dittman and Wynne, 1961); a careful review of these and related studies has been furnished by Kramer (1963). Unfortunately, progress along this line has moved slowly. As Dittmann and Wynne point out, indices that can be reliably coded (e.g., pitch and stress) appear to have little psychological relevance, whereas those which seem to be of psychological significance (e.g., rhythm, breathiness, resonance) are difficult to code reliably. Moreover, as Kramer has noted, no method devised to date has successfully obscured all traces of verbal content while, at the same time, maintaining the qualitative clarity of paralinguistic features. Despite the discouraging state of present affairs, further refinements are likely in the near future, enabling investigators to draw upon this important dimension of verbal behavior.

Less difficult to analyze is the quantity of verbal behavior, such as the ratio of *total speech to total silence behavior* during interviews. Matarazzo and his associates (1962, 1965, 1968) have explored the use of this simple index in numerous detailed studies, and have provided evidence for its intraindividual consistency and for its correlation with various clinical syndromes.

Words spoken per unit of time, or verbal rate, is another noncontent interview measure employed in psychopathology research. Goldman-Eisler (1954) has shown this index to be a fairly stable characteristic of verbal behavior, and Kanfer (1959) found that the rate of speaking increases when subjects discuss topics on which they were rated as poorly adjusted.

Word Quotients. Although the indices to be described in this section take cognizance of differences between words, words are coded strictly in terms of their formal attributes, rather than their personal or psychological "meaning." Thus, in contrast to procedures of content analysis, which classify words on the basis of their presumed phenomenological significance to the subject (e.g., discomfort or tension), behavioral analysis is based purely on the objective grammatical properties of words (e.g., nouns, adjectives, verbs).

The simplest of these coding methods is the *type-token ratio* (TTR), a measure of verbal diversification that merely notes the variety of words used in a verbal sample, regardless of their grammatical characteristics. The TTR is tabulated by dividing the number of *different* words (types) used by the *total* number of words spoken or written (token). For example, if 20 different words were employed by a subject when speaking a total of 50 words, the TTR would be .40; the higher the ratio, the greater the diversification. Early studies comparing schizophrenics and college freshmen by Fairbanks (1944) and Mann (1944) found the schizophrenic group to evidence generally lower TTR ratios (lower diversification), and greater inconsistency in ratios over a series of different word samples. Jaffe (1957, 1961), in more recent work with this index, has demonstrated that distinctive individual patterns occur among patients in their TTR values, and that dramatic shifts from these characteristic ratios occur at crucial periods in therapy.

More complex ratios may be tabulated when comparing words in accord with their grammatical properties. To illustrate, Fairbanks (1944) found that schizophrenics use significantly fewer nouns, prepositions, and adjectives than do freshman college students, and significantly more pronouns and verbs; these specific findings have not held up in subsequent studies, however. A commonly used word index is the *adjective-verb quotient* (Boder, 1940; Lorenz and Cobb, 1954). Computer techniques have been devised recently (Stone et al., 1962) which enable researchers to examine large quantities of data and to tabulate several word ratios simultaneously.

Dyadic Interaction Techniques. It is contended by some that significant events in psychotherapy cannot be understood without reference to the interaction between therapist and patient. Consequently, a number of investigators have devised techniques that seek to identify and measure the reciprocal interplay within two-man groups, termed *dyads*. These methods can be awesomely complex, given the number of categories required to represent the manifold dimensions and interdependencies involved, even in a two-way communication network. The schemas developed by Leary and Gill (1959), noted earlier, and those of Lennard and Bernstein (1960), Jaffe (1968), and Pande and Gart (1968) illustrate how complex a matrix is required to extract only a few components of the interactional process.

The most extensively used and thoroughly researched instrument for recording dyadic interview behaviors is *Chapple's Interaction Chronograph* (Chapple, 1939; Chapple and Arensberg, 1940). This rather complex electro-mechanical device is designed to code only the time aspects of interpersonal actions and communications, such as the frequency and duration of silences, speaking, interruptions, etc. Neither the content of what is said nor the character of the behavior is coded; similarly, no inferences are made about phenomenological states or unconscious motives. It was Chapple's assertion that data from these entirely objective records are more reliable and no less useful diagnostically or predictively than recording systems that require complex inferential judgments on the part of the observer.

In line with Chapple's thesis, Matarazzo and his associates (1962, 1965, 1968) have carried out detailed studies employing the Interaction Chronograph. For experimental purposes, they arranged a standardized interview divided into five distinct periods of communication interaction (Table 4.9); this enabled them to record interviewee responses as evoked by different types of interviewer behaviors. Employing the 14 coding categories of the chronograph, Matarazzo has demonstrated the stability of interviewee responses from session to session, correlations between the data of chronograph categories and those of content analysis systems, and a reasonable degree of accuracy in differentiating between normal and clinical groups.

Performance Measures

Behavioral performance data derive from tangible and discrete physical actions that the subject produces in a highly uniform and structured "test" situation (in contrast, for example, to micromomentary measures); moreover, they are recorded objectively, that is, without requiring observer judgments or inferences (in contrast, for example, to methods of behavior rating). These tasks illustrate "pure" behaviorism—overt actions that are recorded and measured objectively.

There are far too many behavioral measures to survey in a text such as this; detailed reviews may be found in King (1954, 1957), Hall (1957), Fleishman (1960), Spiker (1960), Yates (1961), Bachrach (1962), Krasner and Ullmann (1965), and Inglis (1966). Measures pertaining to two broad behavioral areas will be categorized and briefly described: *psychomotor tasks* and *learning tasks.*

Psychomotor Tasks. In the introduction to his excellent survey of psychomotor techniques, Fleishman states the following (1960):

> . . . psychomotor behavior somehow seems a more "uncontaminated," less ambiguous, and more direct measure of performance than is, let us say, verbal, conceptual, or even perceptual behavior. Most often, the experimenter can observe clocks or counters or he can obtain continuous records on some kind of moving tape. All this inspires confidence in the experimenter that he knows what he is measuring.

Not only do psychomotor tasks provide objectively observable and recordable data, but there is good reason to expect, given the dramatic ex-

TABLE 4.9: Standardized Interview and Coding Categories Used with Chapple's Interaction Chronograph

		Standardized Interview	
			Duration of Period
Period	*Type of Interviewing*	*Fixed Duration*	*Variable Duration*
1	Free	10 minutes	
2	Stress (silence)		12 failures to respond, or 15 minutes, whichever is shorter
3	Free	5 minutes	12 interruptions, or 15 minutes,
4	Stress (interruption)		whichever is shorter
5	Free	.5 minutes	
	Total	20 minutes	plus a maximum of 30 more minutes

Coding Categories

1. *Pt.'s Units:* The number of times the patient acted.
2. *Pt.'s Action:* The average duration of the patient's actions.
3. *Pt.'s Silence:* The average duration of the patient's silences.
4. *Pt.'s Tempo:* The average duration of each action plus its following inaction as a single measure.
5. *Pt.'s Activity:* The average duration of each action minus its following inaction, as a single measure.
6. *Pt.'s Adjustment:* The durations of the patient's interruptions minus the durations of his failures to respond, divided by Pt.'s Units.
7. *Interviewer's Adjustment:* The durations of the interviewer's interruptions minus the durations of his failures to respond, divided by Pt.'s Units.
8. *Pt.'s Initiative:* The percent of times, out of the available number of opportunities (usually 12) in Period 2, in which the patient acted again (within a 15-second limit) following his own last action.
9. *Pt.'s Dominance:* The number of times (out of 12) in Period 4 that the patient "talked down" the interviewer minus the number of times the interviewer "talked down" the patient, divided by the number of Pt.'s Units in the Period.
10. *Pt.'s Synchronization:* The number of times the patient either interrupted or failed to respond to the interviewer, divided by the number of Pt.'s Units.
11. *Interviewer's Units:* The number of times the interviewer acted.
12. *Pt.'s Quickness:* The average length of time in Period 2 that the patient waited before taking the initiative following his own last action.
13. *No. of Interruptions:* The number of times one interactee interrupted the other during the total interview (or a period thereof).
14. *Length of Interview:* The duration of the interview in minutes.

From: Saslow and Matarazzo (1959).

tremes of gross apathy and frenetic activity so characteristic of mental patients, that these instruments might be sensitive barometers of less intense forms of behavior pathology (King, 1954). These tasks will be divided into two subcategories: *simple motor measures* and *complex motor measures*.

Simple Motor Measures. These procedures usually require the subject to produce a relatively straightforward and uncomplicated movement. Most subjects have no difficulty in performing the task, and differences among them tend to reflect merely the speed and accuracy with which they achieve the assigned goal.

By far the most frequently researched of these tasks is *reaction time* in which the subject is asked to respond as rapidly as he can to a visual or auditory stimulus signal, usually by lifting a finger or pressing a switch; the elapsed time between the onset of the stimulus and the response serves as the score. Figure 4.13 illustrates a typical device employed in this task.

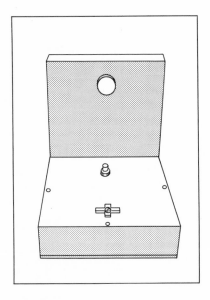

FIGURE 4.13. Reaction time apparatus.

Because of its frequent use, a vast array of data on both normal and clinical populations has accumulated for comparative purposes.

Much less researched than reaction time are *finger dexterity* tasks that require the subject to manipulate or place several tiny objects in a specified pattern; the number of items correctly arranged per unit time serves as the score. Among the better known of these performance tests are the *Purdue Peg Board* and the *O'Connor Finger Dexterity Test*.

An interesting, though not frequently used, device is the *Rotary Pursuit,* which measures large musculature precision and control (Figure 4.14). The instrument resembles a phonograph turntable that revolved at speeds between 20 to 80 rpm. The subject's goal is to keep a stylus in contact with a small target located near the edge of the disk; scores are based on the proportion of time the stylus is on target.

FIGURE 4.14. **Rotary pursuit apparatus.**

Complex Motor Measures. Two groups of tasks are included in this category. The first, as illustrated by the *Reaction Coordination Test* (King, 1954), requires the subject to execute a series of simple, but nonidentical, movements in an assigned sequence; for example, the subject must lift his finger from a key, cross a space, shift a peg from one hole to another, and then return his finger to the key. The second type of complex measure, exemplified by the *Mirror Tracing Test* (Peters, 1946), consists of sensorimotor coordinations that are either entirely novel or run contrary to the usual motor habits of the subject. Thus, in the tracing test, the subject is required to draw between two printed lines (¼-inch separation) forming the boundaries of a diamond or star. Following a series of practice runs in which the subject views the design directly, his direct vision is cut off by a shield and he must complete the task viewing the design and his hand in a reflected mirror image; scores are based either on the number of errors or the time required to complete the mirror trace without error.

Learning Tasks. Most forms of psychopathology are learned maladaptive coping styles resulting from the reciprocal interplay of constitutional and experiential factors. Unfortunately, little research has been done to demonstrate the sequence of interactions through which these learnings unfold. In fact, learning studies in psychopathology have only recently come to the fore; most of them focus chiefly on problems of therapeutic behavior modification and the discovery of differences in learning behaviors between various diagnostic groups. Until the past decade, there was no notable interest in the topic of learning at all; "styles" of learning were rarely considered important clinical symptoms, and the idea that learning principles might have some bearing on therapy was recognized by only a few scattered investigators. Fortunately, this serious lack in psychopathological research is rapidly being remedied. There has been an encouraging proliferation of new techniques in recent years, not only in developing methods of "behavior modification," but in discerning cognitive (phenomenological) and behavioral learning styles, as well.

In this section, we shall touch only briefly on two of the more traditional methods used to record and measure learning behaviors: *classical* (*respondent*) *conditioning methods* and *instrumental* (*operant*) *conditioning methods*. Although most of the work with these techniques has been done with animal subjects, human research with psychotic populations has increased sharply in recent years; useful reviews relevant to psychopathology may be found in Hall (1957), Spiker (1960), Jones (1961), Franks (1964), Huff (1964), and Maher (1966).

Classical Conditioning. The simplest procedure for promoting the acquisition of new response behaviors is known as classical conditioning. The manner in which this is accomplished proceeds as follows: an unconditioned stimulus (UCS) that previously elicited a response (UCR) is presented to the subject in close temporal proximity with a neutral stimulus (CS); by pairing the UCS and CS repeatedly, the CS alone ultimately evokes the response, now termed a conditioned response (CR).

Any number of rewarding or noxious stimuli have been paired with response behaviors to produce classically conditioned acquisitions. Among the measures used to gauge the progression of learning are: (1) the number of CS–UCS pairings required to evoke a preset level of consistency in CR behaviors, (2) the average time lag between the onset of the CS and the emission of the CR over a specified number of trials, and (3) the magnitude or strength of the CR. In most studies, the CR is usually a simple form of psychomotor behavior (e.g., eyeblink, finger lift), although a number of biophysical reactions also are commonly used (e.g., galvanic skin response).

Instrumental Conditioning. In instrumental conditioning, termed "operant conditioning" by followers of B. F. Skinner, a CS is presented to the subject, and, *if he performs the CR,* he is either given a reward or is permitted to avoid a noxious experience. In contrast to classical conditioning, the subject must himself learn to produce the required CR, rather than have it passively evoked by an unconditioned stimulus that naturally elicit it.

Instrumental conditioning studies are done with varying "schedules of reinforcement," that is, ratios between the number and rate of responses emitted, and the receipt of a reinforcement. For example, a reinforcement can be delivered for every correct CR (continuous reinforcement), after a fixed period of time (interval schedules), or after a fixed number of responses (ratio schedules). The most common measure of learning is rate-of-response per unit time.

Although the physical setting and recording procedures for studying instrumental conditioning were first devised in animal research, comparable arrangements have been constructed for work with humans. Lindsley (1956) has provided detailed specifications for the environmental enclosures, reinforcement delivery apparatus, and data collection equipment for use with clinical populations; Figure 4.15 depicts some of these materials. The automatic presentation of stimuli and the automatic recording of behavior responses that can be achieved with instruments such as these awards them a measure of "scientific purity" rare among psychological techniques used in psychopathology research.

Evaluative Comments

In contrast to phenomenological and intrapsychic data, the raw material of behavioral research is objectively observable; this simple fact in itself is sufficient to assure a reasonable degree of scientific respectability to behavioral techniques. However, the fact that these methods deal with overt data is no assurance that they satisfy other important criteria of "good" response measures. In the following paragraphs, we shall note a few of their shortcomings, dealing, in turn, with each of the three major categories discussed.

1. Not much can be said at this time concerning the usefulness of micromomentary research. Little data have been accumulated, and methodological techniques are still in their infancy; in short, despite the interesting character of these subtle forms of nonverbal behavior, there is no evidence to date to tell us whether these techniques will provide researchers with information that cannot otherwise be obtained more feasibly.

The use of trained observers employing well-constructed rating instruments has had a long and profitable history. Most inventories and scales are reasonably reliable, succeed in discriminating among patients, and possess adequate normative data for comparative purposes. Their dependence

(a)

FIGURE 4.15.   Operant conditioning setup. (a) Data recording room; hidden periscope enables observation of patient behavior for correlation with response records.

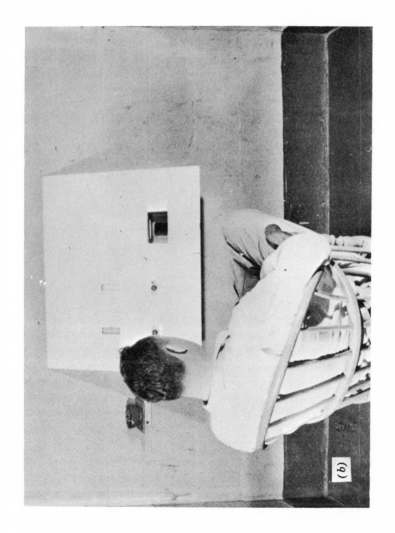

(b)

FIGURE 4.15. (b) Experimental room and apparatus; patient pulls knob on the left of the panel and periodically receives reward (candy, cigarettes) in magazine chute on the right. (Courtesy of O. Lindsley.)

on "clinical" judgments and inferences may create complications, however, since differences in the experience, skill, and orientation of raters may result in noncomparable data. The ultimate test, of course, is the empirical validity of these data as determined by their correlation with outside criteria, and their success in predicting future behaviors. Although progress has been made on this score, there is less information available than we would like for any of the instruments discussed.

2. Measures of verbal behavior are notably deficient in normative data. Although differing in their complexity of analysis, the question of utility can be raised with each. For example, there is no assurance that the expensive and time-consuming Interaction Chronograph procedure will generate data worth the energy and efforts expended. Only more laborious research will tell whether the "right" variables are being tapped by this, or any of the other methods of noncontent verbal analysis; and if they do uncover valid data, could they be gathered by more expeditious procedures?

3. The virtue of performance tasks is their objectivity, their quantifiability, and the ready availability of normative data. Questions arise, however, as to the relevance to psychopathology of these highly specific measures, that is, whether the refined and precise data they gather capture anything more than the most obvious and trivial aspects of the pathological process. That they enable the researcher to specify accurately what he is measuring is no guarantee that he is measuring anything worthwhile. The fact that low intercorrelations exist among different psychomotor measures makes one wonder whether any of them taps a behavioral dimension of sufficient generality to be of substantive significance. Moreover, these measures are extremely fragile, and sensitive to a host of subsidiary influences; thus, one may speculate as to whether differences on these performance tasks are chiefly a product of the patient's mood, interest, or attentiveness, rather than motor or learning processes.

None of these questions would be of significance if an adequate body of empirical evidence was available showing that these measures correlate significantly with relevant external criteria, or that they could be used fruitfully for therapeutic or prognostic purposes. Although research along these lines is in process, little of substance has been published to date.

DOCUMENTARY METHODS

A vast body of data may be gathered by researchers from sources other than those directly obtained from patients in the course of a study. These indirect procedures and sources will be referred to as documentary methods; they include statistical records to be found in publications or the files of various institutions, biographical data obtained through informants such as parents, siblings, and peers, and personal memorabilia such as in diaries and letters that had been produced by research subjects at some period prior to the study. A number of these sources are subject to research control and manipulation, for example, interviews with relatives; other, already available, sources of data furnish ready-made and relatively fixed information that must either be dealt with as they are, or recast to fit the goals and design of the study, for example, census data, diaries. Limiting though this latter group of materials may be, they often provide data that cannot be gathered through other means.

In general, documentary methods are employed in studies with exploratory and descriptive aims. Their greatest value lies in naturalistic research, particularly those formulated as survey, ex post facto, and case study designs. Since these data rarely lend themselves to experimental manipulation, their utility in confirmatory studies is limited.

To simplify matters, we shall categorize documentary methods according to their sources, differentiating three groups: *statistical records, biographic materials,* and *personal narratives.*

Statistical Records

In the following succinct statement, Selltiz et al. summarize the range and variety of statistical data available through institutional records (1959):

A considerable amount of statistical data on the behavior of its members is available in every literate community. Although these data have been accumulated primarily for purposes of administration and historical description, social science research can make good use of them. To neglect their existence often involves either a disregard of relevant information or, if the investigator laboriously collects data that already exist, a waste of effort.

The range of subject matter covered in available records, and the treatment of a subject received in such records, varies with the administrative needs for which they were originally collected. Many available statistical data refer to socioeconomic attributes of individuals. Thus, the census of a population contains information about age, sex, family size, occupation, residence, etc. Health statistics give birth and death rates and the like; federal, state, municipal, and private economic institutions collect and publish data on wages, hours of work, productivity, absenteeism, strikes, financial transactions, and so on. Many voluntary organizations have records not only of their own membership but of groups of people whom they serve. In addition, a small but steadily increasing body of data is being collected by various institutions on the psychological level proper. For example, schools, hospitals, social service agencies, personnel departments in industry, and similar institutions nowadays frequently administer psychological tests of various kinds to their entire populations.

The value of collating these data for epidemiologic survey research is inestimable; thus, important trends in the incidence of psychopathology may be traced by reviewing periodically published statistical reports on state and private hospital admissions; comparisons among geographic regions in the distribution pattern of syndromes can also be made; similarly, changes in type and duration of treatment may be gauged with reasonable accuracy; of particular value are studies concerned with relationships between socioeconomic, marital, and vocational variables, and the prevalence of psychopathology or the availability and character of therapy.

The documentary researcher should not only be acquainted with standard publications of statistical data but also evidence an altertness and ingenuity in uncovering equally fertile, if less known, sources of material. Published compliations provide only a small segment of what can be discovered by the enterprising investigator. Thus, hospitals, clinics, and schools generate reams of recorded, but uncompiled, material in the course of their day-to-day operations. Although lacking the precision and scientific rigor of more formal methods of data collection, this vast body of unassembled information will furnish an industrious researcher with an abundance of material that may be transformed into fruitful exploratory and descriptive studies.

Biographic Materials

Whereas statistical records provide quantitative measures about large and widely diversified populations, biographic methods generate qualitative data about the life history of single individuals. These procedures focus on the developmental background of the research subject, securing their data from sources in addition to that of the patient himself, such as family members, friends, physicians, school personnel, and employment authorities; in short, anyone who can furnish information relevant to the evolution of the patient's present state. Included in these biographical procedures are data pertinent to his family background, early upbringing, medical and educational history, home influences, peer relationships, work record, etc. Table 4.10 summarizes the kinds of information that were sought in a wide-ranging study of schizophrenia (Gerard, 1964).

Not only do biographic materials provide a useful supplement to other sources of research data, such as self-report inventories or projective tests but they also frequently comprise the substantive content of naturalistic case study and ex post facto designs.

A promising instrument for obtaining biographic information from rel-

TABLE 4.10: Social and Personal History Data (72-Item Check List)

1. Evaluation of informant
2. Factual background data regarding patient, patient's family, and the childhood community setting
3. Family mental illness history
4. Patient's development
    Birth
    Physical development
    Intellectual development
    Physical health during childhood
    Personality pattern
5. Parental personalities and interaction in family setting
    Mother personality pattern
    Father personality pattern
    Characterization of relationship
6. Parents' relationship to patient—patient to parents and sibling(s)
7. Patient's adjustment to school situation—socially and academically
8. Patient's adjustment to employment
    Job performance
9. Adolescent and adult social adjustment
    Pattern of sexual relationships
10. Onset of psychosis

From: Gerard (1964).

atives has been developed by Katz (1968). He outlines the rationale and characteristics of his "adjustment rating scale" as follows:

> The majority of the research which is aimed at describing and separating out patterns of symptomatology and behavior in the psychoses has dealt with their manifestations in the hospital setting. . . .
>
> The major gap in research in this area is the lack of objective information on the patient's behavior prior to entering the hospital. It is in the community that what is designated as psychopathology is initially manifested and identified. It is on the basis of such behavior that the patient is subsequently hospitalized, and despite the availability of detailed knowledge of his behavior following hospitalization, little knowledge exists of the relationship between behaviors in these two very different settings. . . .
>
> The authors felt that it would be salutary to depart from the expert's framework and to attempt, through the eyes of a lay observer, to reconstruct the nature of the behavioral pathology.

In this research we selected the close relative of the patient and tried to construct the reporting scheme, a rating inventory, so that the influence of emotional involvement would be minimized.

The rating inventory . . . is comprised of two kinds of items; psychiatric symptoms which have been translated into lay language; and items which describe the nature of the individual's social behavior.

These data were used to determine, through a factor analytic method, whether a set of measures could be developed to provide a profile of symptomatic and social behavior.

On the basis of these analyses, a preliminary list of 128 rated items was reduced to the 77 most salient ones. These were assigned to 12 factor clusters, representing the major areas of symptomatology and behavior that comprised the final inventory. Table 4.11 presents these items grouped to-

TABLE 4.11: Katz Adjustment Scales—Form R1: Relatives' Ratings of Patient Symptoms and Social Behavior—Subtest Clusters

(1) *Belligerence*

28. Got angry and broke things.
50. Cursed at people.
45. Got into fights with people.
113. Threatened to tell people off.

(2) *Verbal expansiveness*

100. Shouted or yelled for no reason.
106. Talked too much.
99. Spoke very loud.
105. Kept changing from one subject to another for no reason.
118. Bragged about how good he was.

(3) *Negativism*

46. Was not cooperative.
36. Acted as if he did not care about other people's feelings.
47. Did the opposite of what he was asked.
48. Stubborn.
56. Critical of other people.
51. Deliberately upset routine.
59. Lied.
37. Thought only of himself.
60. Got into trouble with law.

(4) *Helplessness*

93. Acted as if he could not make decisions.
74. Acted helpless.
92. Acted as if he could not concentrate on one thing.
3. Cried easily.

(5) *Suspiciousness*

40. Thought people were talking about him.
107. Said people were talking about him.
43. Acted as if he were suspicious of people.
108. Said that people were trying to make him do or think things he did not want to.

(6) *Anxiety*

19. Afraid something terrible was going to happen.
122. Said that something terrible was going to happen.
18. Had strange fears.
111. Talked about people or things he was afraid of.

23. Got suddenly frightened for no reason.
125. Talked about suicide.

(7) *Withdrawal and retardation*

76. Moved about very slowly.
8. Just sat.
80. Very slow to react.
70. Quiet.
17. Needed to do things very slowly to do them right.
84. Would stay in one position for long period of time.

(8) *General psychopathology*

5. Acted as if he had no interest in things.
12. Felt that people did not care about him.
30. Acted as if he had no control over his emotions.
31. Laughed or cried at strange times.
32. Has mood changes without reason.
33. Had temper tantrums.
34. Got very excited for no reason.
42. Bossy.
44. Argued.
52. Resentful.
55. Got annoyed easily.
67. Stayed away from people.
71. Preferred to be alone.
73. Behavior was childish.
79. Very quick to react to something said or done.
90. Acted as if he were confused about things; in a daze.
91. Acted as if he could not get certain thoughts out of his mind.
94. Talked without making sense.
97. Refused to speak at all for periods of time.

98. Spoke so low you could not hear him.
110. Talked about how angry he was at certain people.
119. Said the same things over and over again.
121. Talked about big plans he had for the future.
127. Gave advice without being asked.

(9) *Nervousness*

20. Got nervous easily.
21. Jittery.
38. Showed his feelings.
22. Worried or fretted.

(10) *Confusion*

85. Lost track of day, month, or the year.
86. Forgot his address or other places he knows well.
88. Acted as if he did not know where he was.

(11) *Bizarreness*

116. Talked about strange things that were going on inside his body.
26. Did strange things without reason.
25. Acted as if he saw people or things that weren't there.
124. Believed in strange things.
24. Had bad dreams.

(12) *Hyperactivity*

7. Had periods where he could not stop moving or doing something.
13. Did the same thing over and over again without reason.
6. Was restless.

Items within a cluster are listed in order of importance for interpretation of the cluster. Order is based on part-whole correlations of individual items with the cluster. *From* Katz (1968).

gether in their cluster categories. From data gathered with this instrument, Katz constructed several patient "types," and demonstrated that descriptions of pre-hospital patient behaviors provided by relatives correspond quite closely to ratings made by "clinically sophisticated" hospital personnel.

Personal Narratives

These sources of documentary data consist of phenomenological reports written by the subject in the form of autobiographies, diaries, and letters. They are distinguished from other phenomenological methods by the fact that they were produced as personal expressions entirely incidental to scientific study. It is the "free" character of these narratives, the natural flow of recollections, moods, and ideas, unmindful and undisturbed by the biases of theoretical preconceptions or research goals, that give them their special and often illuminating quality. Allport (1942) offers the following eloquent testimony favoring the use of personal documents:

> In psychology the font and origin of our curiosity in, and knowledge of, human nature lies in our acquaintance with concrete individuals. To know them in their natural complexity is an essential first step. Starting too soon with analysis and classification, we run the risk of tearing mental life into fragments and beginning with false cleavages that misrepresent the salient organizations and natural integrations in personal life. In order to avoid such hasty preoccupations with unnatural segments and false abstractions, psychology needs to concern itself with life as it is lived, with significant total processes of the sort revealed in consecutive and complete life documents.

Unfortunately, in the hectic pace of modern life, filled with facile diversions from self, fewer individuals than ever before invest the time and thought to reveal themselves in letter writing and diary composition. Valuable though these personal narratives may be in providing the subtleties of past moods and thoughts, they are a rare source of documentary data. With the exception of a few unusual circumstances, for example, suicide notes (Osgood and Walker, 1959) and diaries during social isolation (Burney, 1952), these materials are infrequent sources for systematic study. When they can be found in sufficient quantity and quality, they are most often evaluated through "content analyses," such as discussed earlier.

Evaluative Comments

There are two problems common to documentary methods: *the availability of uniform data,* and *the accuracy of the data.*

The problem of data uniformity is especially troublesome in survey research where the investigator may seek to collate and compare records obtained from several sources. For example, until completely uniform definitions and descriptions of clinical syndromes are established, epidemiologists may find that essentially similar pathologies are classified under different labels from one state to another. To illustrate further, it is almost impossible to obtain comparative national statistics on suicide rates since different countries "cover up" these events to differing degrees. Particular difficulties of this nature beset studies that seek to trace incidence or prevalence trends over time. In short, unless the definitions of terms, and the samples surveyed, are reasonably comparable, the resulting findings are simply not interpretable.

The accuracy of documentary materials is especially questionable in biographic and narrative data. Although researchers often assume that these sources represent with a fair measure of fidelity the life experiences they describe, notable discrepancies are quite common between the writer's recollections, and the realities of past events. We know well that mental patients are notoriously selective perceivers. Conscious falsification may be relatively uncommon, but only the most naive of investigators can argue that biographic sources and autobiographic materials are not biased by unconscious desires and needs.

CHAPTER FIVE

ANALYSIS AND INTERPRETATION

Having struggled through the complexities of setting up and executing a research study, an investigator still faces a variety of problems associated with analyzing and interpreting his findings.

Essentially, *analysis* refers to the process of categorizing and organizing data, that is, arranging the results of the study in a format that provides clear-cut answers to the questions that prompted the research. For the most part, the layout into which data are cast is determined by the form of the research hypothesis and the structure of the study design; for example, relationships among research variables are clearly set forth in a correlational hypothesis, and the analysis of these relationships follows in an almost mechanical fashion by a straightforward application of statistical correlational techniques.

The final phase of research, that pertaining to *interpretation* of the findings, is not an automatic process, since the investigator is usually inclined to draw conclusions that go beyond the specific results of his study. Interpretation, in its broader sense, consists, then, of generalizations from the research data, that is, seeing their broader theoretical implications, and connecting them in a logical fashion to some larger body of established research.

As Kerlinger (1964) has pointed out, interpreting a particular finding generally involves a three-step process. First, the investigator questions what is the finding's meaning within the study; that is, how consistent or inconsistent is the finding with the other data collected. Second, he asks what is the finding's meaning in terms of previously completed studies in the same area. And, third, he seeks the finding's meaning within the relevant theoretical framework—asking whether it is confirmatory or disconfirmatory.

There are certain "standard" analytic or interpretive steps followed in most descriptive and confirmatory studies; the data usually fit readily within conventional procedures of statistical methodology, and the results produced thereby tend to be linked to the theoretical schema from which the research hypothesis was derived. The particular statistical tests are often determined in advance by the research design, for example, the link between factorial designs and analysis of variance. Determination of statistical significance is the first step to be followed by a discussion of why it was—or why it was not—achieved.

This procedural clarity is not the case in exploratory investigations; having set out on an excursion into the "unknown," investigators may find themselves immersed in an unchartered sea of disconnected data whose order, analysis, and interpretation simply do not lend themselves to conventional rules and methods of appraisal. Exploratory ventures must first struggle then with basic matters of data management, that is, how to best simplify, categorize, and sharpen one's perception of the character of the variables that are likely to be most relevant and significant. Exploratory investigations need not be concerned with techniques of inferential statistics, the formal mathematical procedures that allow researchers to conclude, with varying degrees of confidence, whether the data they have sampled do or do not support an explicit and well-formulated hypothesis.

Data Management

Both practitioner and researcher are confronted in their everyday activities with vast bodies of data, more than they can reasonably absorb and analyze. Although the clinician manages somehow to extract meaning from the myriad events he encounters as he deals directly with patients, he does this in a rather fluid and nonquantitative fashion. In contrast, the researcher reduces the complexity of his data in two systematic ways: (1) grouping into separate categories events that exhibit commonalities; and (2) calculating one or another statistic that will describe essential properties of these categories.

Before proceeding, let us note that many psychopathologists shy away from matters of statistics. Whether this reluctance reflects a boredom or distaste for the "impersonality" of mathematical abstractions, an attitude not surprising among those whose life's work centers on human affairs, or whether clinicians feel intellectually intimidated or "frightened" by the esoteric symbols and logic of numerical processes, the sad fact is that few experience the genuine excitement of mathematics so common among physical scientists. Despite aversions and fears, most competent undergraduates can master the rationale and basic technical details of statistics; several excellent texts may be referred to for those who seek to learn more (Cochran and Cox, 1957; McNemar, 1962; Hays, 1963; Guilford, 1965; Edwards, 1968). No attempt will be made here to survey this extensive body of knowledge; we shall touch only lightly on some of the methods of data management and description and some of the techniques and problems of statistical inference and interpretation.

The simplest and most basic method of reducing the diversity of data is to group or order our measurements into general, but mutually exclusive, categories. Thus, rather than approaching each patient as a distinctive being, we may simplify matters by classifying him in accord with some feature or trait relevant to the purposes of research, for example, placing him in terms of a syndrome diagnosis, some age interval into which he may fall, his sex, marital status, etc.

The simplest way in which categorized data are quantified is through the well-known "frequency distribution." Data may be summarized in numerical form, or portrayed pictorially by means of a bar or line chart in which the total number of cases in each category is represented by some point or level on a chart. In psychopathology research, frequency distributions are especially appropriate for describing incidence and prevalence statistics found in epidemiologic studies.

A further way of simplifying, refining, and quantifying gross data is to calculate some summary statistic of these categories that will describe certain meaningful properties.

Among these statistics are measures of "central tendency," such as the *mean, median,* and *mode.* Scores such as these are particularly useful descriptive statistics; they provide the "average" of a set of numbers in order to "typify" the population included in a particular category, for example, calculating the average age of patients upon first admission to mental hospitals in a designated state. Such statistics simplify and make manageable what would otherwise be too scattered a body of data, and enable the investigator to deal with his findings in ways convenient to further analysis, for example, comparing admission ages in different states.

Another class of descriptive statistics, termed measures of "variability," summarize in a single number the important and complex characteristics of dispersion and diversity in the data. Thus, in addition to measures of central tendency, which describe only the midpoints of a distribution, variability statistics, such as the *range, variance,* and *standard deviation,* furnish information on its breadth and degree of scatter. With these calculations in hand, the researcher can, for example, determine how widely spread are the ages of patients upon first hospital admission, and the extent to which given patients deviate from the average age of admission.

In many studies, interest focuses on the degree of association between variables; thus, another important class of descriptive statistics are measures of "relation," most notably that of the *correlation coefficient*. Here, the researcher seeks to determine the direction and strength of association between different variables of research interest; for example, he may wish to establish whether age of admission is related to socioeconomic or marital status, type of disorder, residential locale, etc.

Statistical Inference

For practical reasons, and with few exceptions, most studies are based on a sample of subjects that ostensibly represents the larger population to which the results of the study are to be generalized; for example, data gathered in an experiment with a group of 40 randomly chosen hospital schizophrenics will be assumed to characterize schizophrenics-in-general. As noted, the practice of sampling is an inevitable part of research since it is rare that the entire population can be studied. Samples, however, present problems in that the particular group chosen may not generate data that accurately reflect the attributes of the larger population from which it was drawn. In other words, statistics from samples may fail to correspond to measures that would be obtained had the entire population been studied. These population measures are termed "parameters." The problem is that we wish to learn the population parameters, but for practical reasons must infer them from sample statistics. The task facing the investigator is that of determining the probability that the statistics he obtains with his research sample or samples represent the "true" parameter. By various calculational procedures, the reasonableness of the assertion of parameter-statistic equivalence can be gauged.

For psychopathology, there are two major relevant applications of inferential statistics, that is, those analytic procedures that are based on the fact that research samples provide only estimates of population parameters. First, much research in psychopathology is concerned with establishing relationships among specified variables; statistical inference methods can help establish whether the observed relationship, *as obtained with a sample,* can be attributed to a chance variation from a "true" zero relationship in the population. Second, a common question posed in psychopathology experimental designs concerns the significance of *differences* between research samples that have been subjected to dissimilar stimulus conditions (treatments); statistical inference methods can establish whether the observed difference is "real"; for example, whether the greater improvement rate reported in a group of pharmacologically treated patients, as compared to a nontreated or placebo control group, is "significantly" more than can reasonably be attributed to chance alone.

In appraising relationships or differences currently in psychopathological research, the common procedure is for the investigator to compare his results to the "null hypothesis," a proposition that states, in effect, that the resulting finding represents a chance occurrence and there is no real relationship or difference. In applying "tests of significance" to his findings, the investigator sets out to determine, via any one of a number of appropriate inferential statistical procedures determined by the study design, whether the resulting statistic exceeds the probability that the observed relationship or difference falls within the range of random sampling fluctuations or whether it lies beyond that reasonably attributable chance variations. If the calculated statistic is less than that associated with the "level of significance" chosen, for example, a probability of 5 out of 100, or the .05 confidence level, then the null hypothesis is accepted. If the calculated statistic is greater, meaning that the relationship or difference observed would occur by chance *less* than 5 percent of the time were the study repeated indefinitely, then the null hypothesis would be rejected; that is, the experimenter would feel confident that his result was a "real" rather than a chance occurrence.

Thus the confidence that the investigator places in his findings is based on probability estimates of statistical significance. Statistical inference based on probability estimates entails a certain amount of risk. For example, he may decide to reject the null hypothesis since his calculations show that the relationship or difference he obtained in his study would occur by chance less than 1 time in 20, that is, the .05 level of confidence. Although the odds are only 1 to 19 that his decision was wrong, improbable events do occur, and his study may be that 1 time in 20 when it did.

As probability decisions, statistical inferences are vulnerable to two kinds of risks. In what is known as a *Type I error,* the researcher mistakenly decides to reject the null hypotheses when it is true, resulting in a spuriously positive conclusion; for example, he may conclude that the differences recorded between two research samples signify that they represent different populations when, in fact, they represent the same population. On the other hand, in what is termed a *Type II error,* he may mistakenly decide to accept the null hypothesis when it is wrong; that is, he may dismiss the disparity in scores between his groups, attributing them to chance variations when, in fact, they do represent the presence of a real population difference; as a consequence, his analysis leads him to a spuriously negative conclusion.

To reduce a Type I error, that is, to decrease the risk of attributing significance to results that might result from chance, the investigator may choose a stringent level of significance; for example, he may decide to employ the .01 rather than the .05 level, thereby increasing the odds against chance as an explanation of his findings from 19 to 1 to 99 to 1. A decision of this sort, however, places the investigator in an awkward predicament; the more rigorously he protects himself against a Type I error, the more he increases the likelihood that he will fall prey to a Type II error, that is, overlook a real difference that fails to meet the stringent .01 level.

There is no easy solution to this problem, nor is there a clear-cut basis for deciding whether a Type I or Type II error would prove more disadvantageous. Researchers must gauge both the practical and scientific consequences of each type of error in the context of their specific studies, and then set their level of significance accordingly, within the bounds of scientific convention. The dilemma of Type I versus Type II errors have been partially resolved both logically and mathematically (Cohen, 1965, 1969); some have sought to minimize the incompatibility through methods that "optimize" the size of research samples (Mosteller and Bush, 1954; Kramer and Greenhouse, 1959), whereas others have suggested procedures of "sequential sampling" (Wald, 1947; Fiske and Jones, 1954). As with many of the topics that have been so briefly discussed in this chapter, the student must be referred to other sources to elaborate the rationale and technical details of these methods.

Interpretive Problems

The process of interpretation is essentially that of providing meaning to the analysis. More specifically, the investigator must decide: (a) what support there is for the originating hypothesis, and the theory from which it was derived; (b) what alternative explanations may reasonably account for the findings, since they rarely fit his expectations exactly; and (c) what new questions and implications arise from the data that may justify further research. Unless the study is unusually well designed, and its data woven tightly into a systematic theory, the interpretive process will include subjective appraisals and speculations, many of which may prove unwarranted and erroneous unless caution is taken.

We shall not discuss in this section interpretive problems that stem from theoretical disputation, faulty research designs, or issues arising from the validity or precision of measured variables; disagreements are inevitable among theorists of different persuasions, and matters of design and measurement, though crucial to the entire interpretive framework, have been discussed previously. Instead, attention will focus on five common errors in attributing meaning and significance to findings in studies that might otherwise be faultless. Those errors are found in studies using any of the four data levels.

Undue Importance Given "Statistical Significance". Let us begin our discussion of this interpretive problem with the following quote (Frank 1959):

Statistical measures of significance may be misleading in that a statistically significant finding need not be significant in the nontechnical sense of the term. The discovery of a very low correlation between variables which achieves high (statistical) significance . . . indicates, to be sure, that some relationship is present, but it may be so weak as to contribute practically nothing to an understanding of the phenomenon under study.

Statistical tests merely provide an answer to whether or not we can assert with confidence that the results of a study are more than can be attributed to chance variation alone. This determination is important, of course, but it is entirely secondary to the main purpose of research, which is whether the findings are of sufficient magnitude and importance to be relevant either to theoretical or practical ends. Unfortunately, it is in the nature of statistical tests that rather minute relationships or differences, when obtained on large samples, will be recorded as "statistically significant." The decision the investigator must make in examining these findings is not whether there is or is not statistical significance, but whether the magnitude of the observed finding is sufficiently large or meaningful to make it *worth* explaining in terms of its significance for psychopathology. The last thing researchers need spend their time on, given the number and variety of important problems facing the profession, are trivial, that is, substantively *in*significant significant findings.

Unwarranted Conclusions of Causality. Interpretations of causality are presumptive and often erroneous in studies that merely demonstrate a correlation between variables. Covariations tell us nothing about causation, despite the unhappy proclivity of many naive investigators to draw such conclusions. As discussed previously, attributions of cause-effect relationships must satisfy the threefold criteria of concomitant variation, time-order sequence, and the elimination of rival hypotheses; these criteria are fully met only in experimental designs. A significant correlation may be an important first step in demonstrating cause and effect, but it is no more than that.

Overlooking Alternative Hypotheses. The final results of a study are composed of many factors, not just one or two. Unless the investigator has taken pains to assure that *all* sources of potential influence have been controlled or systematically tested, he has no grounds for attributing his findings exclusively to the variable he has studied. Thus, in a design that compares a substantive hypothesis with the null hypothesis, the rejection of the null hypothesis (concluding that a positive result exists) does not "prove" the substantive hypothesis, but merely indicates that *some* effect or variable is operative. For example, finding a biochemical difference between schizophrenics and neurotics tells us only that such a difference exists, but tells us nothing regarding *why* it exists or what factors account for the difference; any one of several interpretive hypotheses, for example, constitutional differences, dietary experiences, chronicity, etc., may be equally valid as alternatives to the rejected null hypothesis. Here again is the danger posed by difficulties involved in attributing causality before all rival influences have been shown empirically to be insignificant.

Acceptance of Fortuitous Positive Results. Not uncommonly, especially in studies that simultaneously examine relationships among a vast number of variables, an investigator will come across statistically significant findings that were entirely unanticipated. Such unpredicted relationships may prove extremely illuminating, throwing light on potentially valuable aspects of a topic, and alerting the researcher to ideas that were never or only faintly grasped before.

Fortuitous findings such as these are not unmixed blessings. Given the flexibility of most theories and the speculative inclinations of most creative scientists, accidental "discoveries" are often cast by fanciful and convincing rationales into "proofs" of pet notions; quite frequently, the empirical validity of these "proofs" is inversely related to the fertility of the researcher's imagination.

Safeguards against spurious findings are particularly necessary in complex studies that set out to test the significance of numerous relationships and differences. Thus, if we were to employ the .05 level of confidence in a study comprising 100 or more statistical comparisons, it is *probable* that several significant results will turn up by chance alone. Unless these findings are immediately *cross-validated,* that is, treated as exploratory findings and replicated and substantiated in an entirely independent research study that is designed specifically to test their merit, they must be approached with suspicion.

Unjustified Generalizations. It is a prudent scientist who hesitates to draw conclusions that go beyond the specifics of his study; moreover, it is better to be the devil's advocate to one's own work and note its limitations and shortcomings before others point them out. The wisdom of this conservative philosophy regarding generalization is especially appropriate in psychopathology for several reasons: (1) criteria for defining concepts and variables differ markedly within the profession; (2) subject populations often comprise highly unstable persons who exhibit highly erratic behaviors, even in identical situational settings; and (3) most studies have not selected their samples in a random fashion, and depend for their results on small and biased populations. In short, it is best to be cautious in generalizing findings since the populations, behaviors, and events that give rise to these data may only partly apply elsewhere. Energies have been needlessly wasted by investigators seeking to follow-up results peculiar to the conditions of an earlier study.

It seems fitting to end the text with the reminder that a creative investigator goes beyond the logical and procedural tools we have provided as a guide. Well-designed and technically correct procedures reduce the possibility of methodological error, but it is the investigator's imagination and critical judgment that will determine the fruitfulness of his research efforts.

BIBLIOGRAPHY

Ach, N. Analyse des willens. Abt. 6 *Handb. d. biol. Arbeitsmeth. v. Abderhalden.* Berlin: Urban und Schwarzenberg, 1935.

Ackner, B., & Pampiglione, G. An evaluation of the sedation threshold test. *J. Psychosom. Res.,* 1959, **3,** 271–281.

Adrian, E. D., & Matthews, B. H. C. The interpretation of potential waves in the cortex. *J. Physiol.,* 1934, **81,** 440–471.

Alexander, L. Epinephrine-mecholyl test (Funkenstein test): Its value in determining the recovery potential of patients with mental disease. *AMA Arch. Neurol. Psychiat.,* 1955, **73,** 495–514.

Allport, G. *The use of personal documents in psychological science.* New York: Social Science Research Council, 1942.

Allport, G. W. *Pattern and growth in personality.* New York: Holt, Rinehart and Winston, 1961.

Altschule, M. D. *Bodily physiology in mental and emotional disorders.* New York: Grune and Stratton, 1953.

Aserinsky, E., & Kleitman, N. Regularly occurring periods of eye mobility, and concurrent phenomena, during sleep. *Science,* 1953, **118,** 273–274.

Auld, F., & Murray, E. J. Content-analysis studies of psychotherapy. *Psychol. Bull.,* 1955, **52,** 377–395.

Bachrach, A. J. (Ed.) *Experimental foundations of clinical psychology.* New York: Basic Books, 1962.

Bandura, A. & Walters, R. *Social learning and personality development.* New York: Holt, Rinehart and Winston, 1963.

Barker, R. G. (Ed.) *The stream of behavior.* New York: Appleton-Century-Crofts, 1963.

Beck, S. J. *Rorschach's test: II. A variety of personality pictures.* New York: Grune and Stratton, 1945.

Beck, S. J. *Rorschach's test: III. Advances in interpretation.* New York: Grune and Stratton, 1952.

Beck, S. J. et al. *Rorschach's test: I. Basic processes.* New York: Grune and Stratton, 1961.

Beecher, H. K. *Measurement of subjective responses.* New York: Oxford, 1959.

Behrens, M. J., & Goldfarb, W. A study of patterns of interaction of families of schizophrenic children in residential treatment. *Amer. J. Orthopsychiat.,* 1958, **28**, 300–312.

Bellak, L. *The Thematic Apperception Test and the Children's Apperception Test in clinical use.* New York: Grune and Stratton, 1954.

Bennett, E. L., Diamond, M. C., Krech, D., & Rosenzweig, M. R. Chemical and anatomical plasticity of brain. *Science,* 1964, **146**, 610–619.

Bercel, N. A. A study of the influence of schizophrenic serum on the behavior of the spider: Zilla-x-notata. In D. D. Jackson (Ed.), *The etiology of schizophrenia.* New York: Basic Books, 1959.

Berelson, B. Content analysis. In G. Lindzey (Ed.), *Handbook of social psychology.* Reading, Mass.: Addison-Wesley, 1954.

Berger, E. M. The relation between expressed acceptance of self and expressed acceptance of others. *J. Abnorm. Soc. Psychol.,* 1952, **47**, 778–782.

Berger, H. Uber das elektrenkephalogramm des menschen. *Arch. Psychiat. Nervenkr.,* 1929, **87**, 527–570.

Bishop, B. M. Mother-child interaction and the social behavior of children. *Psychol. Monographs,* 1951, **65**, (Whole No. 328).

Bishop, M. P. Effects of plasma from schizophrenic subjects upon learning and retention in the rat. In R. G. Heath (Ed.), *Serological fractions in schizophrenia.* New York: Harper and Row, 1963.

Blum, G. S. A study of the psychoanalytic theory of psychosexual development. *Genet. Psychol. Monogr.,* 1949, **39**, 3–99.

Blum, G. S. A guide for the research use of the Blacky Pictures. *J. Proj. Tech.,* 1962, **26**, 3–29.

Boder, D. P. The adjective-verb quotient. *Psychol. Rec.,* 1940, **3**, 309–343.

Bogoch, S. Fractionation and quantitative analysis of cerebrospinal fluid constituents with reference to neuropsychiatric disorders. *Amer. J. Psychiat.,* 1958, **114**, 1028–1035.

Bolgar, H. The case study method. In B. Wolman (Ed.), *Handbook of clinical psychology.* New York: McGraw-Hill, 1965.

Bordin, E. S. Free association: An experimental analogue of the psychoanalytic situation. In L. Gottschalk and A. Auerbach (Eds.), *Methods of research in psychotherapy.* New York: Appleton-Century-Crofts, 1966.

Boring, E. A history of introspection. *Psychol. Bull.,* 1953, **50**, 169–189.

Bowlby, J. *Maternal care and mental health.* Geneva, Switz.: World Health Organization, 1952.

Bowman, K. M. et al. Thyroid function in mental disease: A multiple test survey. *J. Nerv. Ment. Dis.,* 1950, **112**, 404–424.

Brady, J. V. Psychophysiology of emotional behavior. In A. Bachrach (Ed.), *Experimental foundations of clinical psychology.* New York: Basic Books, 1962.

Brengelmann, J. C. Expressive movements and abnormal behavior. In H. J. Eysenck (Ed.), *Handbook of abnormal psychology.* New York: Basic Books, 1961.

Brownfain, J. J. Stability of the self-concept as a dimension of personality. *J. Abnorm. Soc. Psychol.,* 1952, **47**, 597–606.

Buck, J. N. The HTP technique: A qualitative and quantitative scoring manual. *J. Clin. Psychol.,* 1949, **5**, 37–76.

Burdock, E. I., & Hardesty, A. S. Quantitative techniques for the evaluation of psychiatric treatment. In P. Hoch and J. Zubin (Eds.), *The evaluation of psychiatric treatment.* New York: Grune and Stratton, 1964.

Burdock, E. I. & Hardesty, A. S. Behavior patterns of chronic schizophrenics. In P. Hoch and J. Zubin (Eds.), *Psychopathology of schizophrenia.* New York: Grune and Stratton, 1966.

Burdock, E. I., & Hardesty, A. S. Psychological test for psychopathology. *J. Abnorm. Psychol.,* 1968, **73**, 62–69.

Burdock, E. I., Sutton, S., & Zubin, J. Personality and psychopathology. *J. Abnorm. Soc. Psychol.,* 1958, **56**, 18–30.

Burke, C. J. Additive scales and statistics. *Psychol. Rev.,* 1953, **50**, 384–387.

Burney, C. *Solitary confinement.* New York: Coward-McCann, 1952.

Buros, O. K. (Ed.) *The sixth mental measurements yearbook.* Highland Park, N. J.: Gryphon Press, 1965.

Buros, O. K. (Ed.) *Personality: Tests and measures.* Highland Park, N. J.: Gryphon Press, 1969.

Busfield, B. L., & Wechsler, H. Studies of salivation in depression. *AMA Arch. Gen. Psychiat.,* 1961, **4**, 10–15; **5**, 472–477.

Cameron, D. E. *Objective and experimental psychiatry.* New York: Macmillan, 1935.

Campbell, A. A., & Katona, G. The sample survey: A technique for social science research. In L. Festinger and D. Katz (Eds.), *Research methods in the behavioral sciences.* New York: Dryden, 1953.

Campbell, D. T. The indirect assessment of social attitudes. *Psychol. Bull.,* 1950, **47**, 15–38.

Campbell, D. T. A typology of tests, projective and otherwise. *J. Consult. Psychol.,* 1957, **21**, 207–210.

Campbell, D. T., & Stanley, J. C. *Experimental and quasiexperimental designs in research.* Chicago: Rand McNally, 1966.

Carr, J. E., & Whittenbaugh, J. A. Volunteer and nonvolunteer characteristics in an outpatient population. *J. Abnorm. Psychol.,* 1968, **73**, 16–17.

Cartwright, D. P. Analysis of qualitative material. In L. Festinger and D. Katz (Eds.), *Research methods in the behavioral sciences.* New York: Dryden, 1953.

Cartwright, R. D., & Vogel, J. L. A comparison of changes in psychoneurotic patients during matched periods of therapy and nontherapy. *J. Consult. Psychol.,* 1960, **24**, 121–127.

Cattell, R. B. *Manual for Forms A and B: Sixteen Personality Factor Questionnaire.* Champaign, Ill.: IPAT, 1949–1963.

Cattell, R. B. Principles of design in projective or misperception tests of personality. In H. Anderson and G. Anderson (Eds.), *An introduction to projective techniques*. Englewood Cliffs, N. J.: Prentice-Hall, 1951.

Cattell, R. B. The three basic factor-analytic research designs: their interrelations and derivatives. *Psychol. Bull.*, 1952, **49**, 499–520.

Cattell, R. B., Cattell, A. K. S., & Rhymer, R. M. P-technique demonstrated in determining psychophysiological source traits in a normal individual. *Psychometrika*, 1947, **12**, 267–288.

Chance, E. Content analysis of verbalizations about interpersonal experience. In . Gottschalk and A. Auerbach (Eds.), *Methods of research in psychotherapy*. New York: Appleton-Century-Crofts, 1966.

Chapin, S. *Experimental designs in sociological research*. (Rev. ed.) New York: Harper, 1955.

Chapple, E. D. Quantitative analysis of the interaction of individuals. *Proc. Nat. Acad. Sci.*, 1939, **25**, 58–67.

Chapple, E. D., & Arensberg, C. M. Measuring human relations: An introduction to the study of the interaction of individuals. *Genet. Psychol. Monogr.*, 1940, **22**, 3–147.

Chassan, J. B. *Research design in clinical psychology and psychiatry*. New York: Appleton-Century-Crofts, 1967.

Chein, I. An introduction to sampling. In C. Selltiz et al. (Eds.), *Research methods in social relations*. New York: Holt, 1959.

Clyde, D. J. Self-ratings. In L. Uhr and J. G. Miller (Eds.), *Drugs and behavior*. New York: Wiley, 1960.

Clyde, D. J. *Manual for the Clyde Mood Scale*. Coral Gables, Fla.: University of Miami Biometric Lab., 1963.

Cochran, W. G., & Cox, G. M. *Experimental designs*. New York: Wiley, 1957.

Cohen, J. Some statistical issues in psychological research. In B. Wolman (Ed.), *Handbook of clinical psychology*. New York: McGraw-Hill, 1965.

Cohen, J. *Statistical power analysis for the behavioral sciences*. New York: Academic Press, 1969.

Cohen, M. R., & Nagel, E. *An introduction to logic and scientific method*. New York: Harcourt, Brace, 1934.

Colby, K. M. Experiment on the effects of an observer's presence on the image system during psychoanalytic free-association. *Behavioral Sci.*, 1960, **5**, 197–210.

Cole, J. O. Classification in research on the prediction of response to specific treatments in psychiatry. In M. Katz et al. (Eds.), *The role and methodology of classification in psychiatry and psychopathology*. Washington, D. C.: Public Health Service, 1968.

Cranswick, E. H. Tracer iodine studies of thyroid activity and thyroid responsiveness in schizophrenia. *Amer. J. Psychiat.*, 1955, **112**, 170–178.

Cronbach, L. J. Response sets and test validity. *Educ. Psychol. Measmt.*, 1946, **6**, 475–494.

Cronbach, L. J. The two disciplines of scientific psychology. *Amer. Psychol.*, 1957, **12**, 671–684.

Cronbach, L. J., & Gleser, G. C. Assessing similarity between profiles. *Psychol. Bull.,* 1953, **50**, 456–473.

Cronbach, L. J., & Meehl, P. E. Construct validity of psychological tests. *Psychol. Bull.,* 1955, **52**, 281–302.

Cyvin, K. et al. Sympathicomimetics as diagnostic tests in psychiatry. *Acta. Psychiat. Neurol.* (Suppl.) 1956, **106**, 206–220.

Dahlstrom, W. G. Research in clinical psychology: Factor analytic contributions. *J. Clin. Psychol.,* 1957, **13**, 211–220.

Dahlstrom, W. G., & Welsh, G. S. *An MMPI handbook: A guide for use in clinical practice and research.* Minneapolis: University of Minnesota Press, 1960.

Davidson, P. O., & Costello, C. G. (Eds.) *N = 1: Experimental studies of single cases.* New York: Van Nostrand Reinhold, 1969.

Delgado, J. M. R. Electrodes for extracellular recording and stimulation. In N. Nastuk (Ed.), *Electrophysiological methods.* Vol. 5. New York: Academic Press, 1964. (a)

Delgado, J. M. R. Free behavior and brain stimulation. In C. Pfeiffer and J. Smythies (Eds.) *International review of neurobiology.* Vol. 6. New York: Academic Press, 1964. (b)

Delgado, J. M. R. Emotions. In J. Vernon (Ed.), *Introduction to psychology, a self-selection textbook.* Dubuque, Iowa: W. C. Brown, 1966.

Dement, W. C. Experimental dream studies. In J. Masserman (Ed.), *Science and psychoanalysis.* Vol. 7. *Development and research.* New York: Grune and Stratton, 1964.

Dement, W. C. An essay on dreams: The role of physiology in understanding their nature. In *New directions in psychology II.* New York: Holt, Rinehart and Winston, 1965.

Deutsch, F. Some principles of correlating verbal and non-verbal communication. In L. Gottschalk and A. Auerbach (Eds.), *Methods of research in psychotherapy.* New York: Appleton-Century-Crofts, 1966.

Diamond, M. C., Krech, D., & Rosenzweig, M. R. The effects of an enriched environment on the history of the rat cerebral cortex. *J. Comp. Neurol.,* 1964, **123**, 111–120.

Diamond, M. D. The ability of schizophrenics to modify responses in an interpersonal situation. *J. Consult. Psychol.,* 1956, **20**, 441–444.

Dittes, J. E. Galvanic skin response as a measure of patient's reaction to therapists' permissiveness. *J. Abnorm. Soc. Psychol.,* 1957, **55**, 295–303.

Dittmann, A. T., Parloff, M. B., & Boomer, D. S. Facial and bodily expression: A study of receptivity of emotional cues. *Psychiatry,* 1965, **28**, 239–244.

Dittmann, A. T., & Wynne, L. C. Linguistic techniques and the analysis of emotionality in interviews. *J. Abnorm. Soc. Psychol.,* 1961, **63**, 201–204.

Dollard, J., & Auld, F. *Scoring human motives: A manual.* New Haven: Yale University Press, 1959.

Dollard, J., & Mowrer, O. H. A method of measuring tension in written documents. *J. Abnorm. Soc. Psychol.,* 1947, **42**, 3–32.

Domino, E. F. Biochemical and physiological changes associated with schizophrenia.

In J. Cole and R. Gerard (Eds.), *Psychopharmacology: Problems in evaluation.* Washington, D. C.: National Academy of Sciences—National Research Council, 1959.

DuMas, F. M. On the interpretation of personality profiles. *J. Clin. Psychol.*, 1947, **3**, 57–65.

Dunham, H. W. *Sociological theory and mental disorder.* Detroit: Wayne University Press, 1959.

Edwards, A. L. Experiments: Their planning and execution. In G. Lindzey (Ed.) *Handbook of social psychology.* Reading, Mass.: Addison-Wesley, 1954.

Edwards, A. L. *The social desirability variable in personality assessment and research.* New York: Dryden, 1957.

Edwards, A. L. *Experimental design in psychological research.* (3rd ed.) New York: Holt, Rinehart and Winston, 1968.

Edwards, A. L. *The measurement of personality traits by scales and inventories.* New York: Holt, Rinehart and Winston, 1970.

Edwards, A. L., & Cronbach, L. J. Experimental design for research in psychotherapy. *J. Clin. Psychol.*, 1952, **8**, 51–59.

Eiduson, S., Brill, N. Q., & Crumpton, E. Adrenocortical activity in psychiatric disorders. *AMA Arch. Gen. Psychiat.*, 1961, **5**, 227–233.

Eiduson, I., Geller, E., Yuwiler, A., & Eiduson, B. T. *Biochemistry and behavior.* Princeton, N. J.: Van Nostrand, 1964.

Ekman, P. Body position, facial expression, and verbal behavior during interviews. *J. Abnorm. Soc. Psychol.*, 1964, **68**, 295–301.

Ekman, P., & Friesen, W. V. Nonverbal behavior in psychotherapy research. In J. Shlien et al. (Eds.), *Research in Psychotherapy.* Vol. III. Washington, D. C.: American Psychological Association, 1968.

Ellingson, R. J. Brain waves and problems of psychology. *Psychol. Bull.*, 1956, **53**, 1–34.

Endler, N. S., Hunt, J. M., & Rosenstein, A. J. An S-R inventory of anxiousness. *Psychol. Monogr.*, 1962, **76**, No. 537.

Eysenck, H. J. (Ed.) *Experiments in personality.* London: Routledge and Kegan Paul, 1960.

Eysenck, H. J. and Eysenck, B. G. *Eysenck Personality Inventory.* San Diego: Educational and Industrial Testing Service, 1963.

Fairbanks, H. The quantitative differentiation of samples of spoken language. *Psychol. Monogr.*, 1944, **56**, No. 255, 19–38.

Farber, L. H., & Fisher, C. An experimental approach to dream psychology through the use of hypnosis. *Psychoanal. Quart.*, 1943, **12**, 202–216.

Farina, A., & Dunham, R. M. Measurement of family relationships and their effects. *AMA Arch. Gen. Psychiat.*, 1963, **9**, 64–73.

Farnham-Diggory, S. Self-evaluation and subjective life expectancy among suicidal and non-suicidal psychotic males. *J. Abnorm. Soc. Psychol.*, 1964, **69**, 628–634.

Faris, R., & Dunham, H. W. *Mental disorders in urban areas.* Chicago: University of Chicago Press, 1939.

Ferguson, D. C., & Fisher, A. E. Behavior disruption in Cebus monkeys as a function of injected substances. *Science*, 1963, **139**, 1281–1282.

Ferrier, D. *The function of the brain.* London: Smith, Elder, 1876.

Fink, M. Neurophysiological response strategies in the classification of mental illness. In M. Katz et al. (Eds.), *The role and methodology of classification in psychiatry and psychopathology.* Washington, D. C.: Public Health Service, 1968.

Fiske, D. W. *Measuring the concepts of personality.* Chicago: Aldine, 1971.

Fiske, D. W., & Jones, L. V. Sequential analysis in psychological research. *Psychol. Bull.,* 1954, **51**, 264–275.

Fleishman, E. A. Evaluations of psychomotor tests for pilot selection. *Tech. Rep.* 1954, *AFPTRC-TR-54-131.*

Fleishman, E. A. Predicting advanced levels of proficiency in psychomotor skill. In G. Finch and F. Cameron (Eds.), *Symposium on Air Force human engineering, personnel, and training research.* Washington, D. C.: National Academy of Sciences—National Research Council, 1956.

Fleishman, E. A. Psychomotor tests in drug research. In L. Uhr and J. Miller (Eds.), *Drugs and behavior.* New York: Wiley, 1960.

Fowler, R. D. The current status of computer interpretation of psychological tests. *Amer. J. Psychiat.,* 1969, **125**, 21–27.

Frank, J. D. Problems of controls in psychotherapy as exemplified by the psychotherapy research projects of Phipps Psychiatric Clinic. In E. Rubinstein and M. Parloff (Eds.), *Research in psychotherapy.* Washington, D. C.: American Psychological Association, 1959.

Frank, J. D. *Persuasion and healing.* Baltimore: Johns Hopkins University Press, 1961.

Frank, L. K. Projective methods for the study of personality. *J. Psychol.,* 1939, **8**, 389–413.

Franks, C. M. (Ed.) *Conditioning techniques in clinical practice and research.* New York: Springer, 1964.

Freeman, F. S. *Theory and practice of psychological testing.* (3rd. ed.) New York: Holt, Rinehart and Winston, 1962.

Freeman, H. E., & Giovannoni, J. M. Social psychology of mental health. In G. Lindzey and E. Aronson (Eds.), *Handbook of Social Psychology,* (2nd ed.) Vol. 5, Reading, Mass.: Addison-Wesley, 1969.

Fritz, G. and Hitzig, E. Uber die elektrische Erregbarkeit des Grosshirns. *Arch. Anat. Physiol. Wiss. Med.,* 1870, **300.**

Fromm, E. Remarks on the problem of free association. *Psychiat. Res. Rpts.,* 1955, **2**, 1–6.

Fruchter, B. *Introduction to factor analysis.* Princeton, N. J.: Van Nostrand, 1954.

Funkenstein, D. H. et al. Psychophysiological study of mentally ill patients: Changes in reactions to epinephrine and mecholyl after electric shock treatment. *Amer. J. Psychiat.,* 1949, **106**, 116–121.

Funkenstein, D. H., Greenblatt, M., & Solomon, H. C. An autonomic nervous system test of prognostic significance in relation to electroshock treatment. *Psychosom. Med.,* 1952, **14**, 347–362.

Gamper, E., & Kral, A. Zur frage der biologischen wirksamkeit des schizophren-liquors. *Ztschr. Neurol Psyciat.,* 1937, **159,** 609–703.

Gardner, R. W. et al. Cognitive control: A study of individual consistencies in cognitive behavior. In G. S. Klein (Ed.), *Psychological issues*. New York: International University Press, 1959.

Geller, E. et al. Adrenocortical activity in relation to the severity of schizophrenia. *AMA Arch. Gen. Psychiat.*, 1962, **6**, 384–387.

Gerard, R. W. Comments. In J. Cole and R. Gerard (Eds.) *Psychopharmacology: Problems in evaluation*. Washington, D. C.: National Academy of Sciences—National Research Council, 1956.

Gerard, R. W. The nosology of schizophrenia: A co-operative study. *Behavioral Sci.*, 1964, **9**, 311–333.

Ghent, L., & Freedman, A. M. Comparison of effects of normal and schizophrenic serum on motor performance in rats. *Amer. J. Psychiat.*, 1958, **115**, 465–466.

Gibbs, F. A., Davis, H., & Lennox, W. G. The electroencephalograms in epilepsy and in impaired states of consciousness. *AMA Arch. Neurol. Psychiat.*, 1935, **34**, 1133–1148.

Giedt, F. H. Comparison of visual, content, and auditory cues in interviewing. *J. Consult. Psychol.*, 1955, **19**, 407–416.

Giberstadt, H., & Duker, J. *A handbook for clinical and actuarial MMPI interpretation*. Philadelphia: Saunders, 1965.

Glaser, G. H. (Ed.) *EEG and behavior*. New York: Basic Books, 1963.

Gleser, G. C. Quantifying similarity between people. In M. Katz et al. (Eds.), *The role and methodology of classification in psychiatry and psychopathology*. Washington, D. C.: Public Health Service, 1968.

Glueck, B. C., & Stroebel, C. F. The computer and the clinical decision process: II. *Amer. J. Psychiat.*, 1969, **125**, 2–7.

Goldberg, P. A. A review of sentence completion methods in personality assessment. In B. I. Murstein (Ed.), *Handbook of projective techniques*. New York: Basic Books, 1965.

Goldman-Eisler, F. On the variability of the speed of talking and its relation to the length of utterances in conversation. *Brit. J. Psychol.*, 1954, **45**, 94–107.

Goldstein, A. P. *Therapist-patient expectancies in psychotherapy*. New York: Pergamon, 1962.

Goldstein, A. P., & Dean, S. J. (Eds.) *The investigation of psychotherapy*. New York: Wiley, 1966.

Goldstein, A. P., Heller, K., & Sechrest, L. B. *Psychotherapy and the psychology of behavior change*. New York: Wiley, 1966.

Goldstein, I. B. Role of muscle tension in personality theory. *Psychol. Bull.*, 1964, **61**, 413–425.

Goldstein, K., & Scheerer, M. Abstract and concrete behavior: An experimental study with special tests. *Psychol. Monogr.*, 1941, **53**, No. 239.

Gordon, J. E. Leading and following psychotherapeutic techniques with hypnotically induced repression and hostility. *J. Abnorm. Soc. Psychol.*, 1957, **54**, 405–410.

Gordon, J. E. (Ed.) *Handbook of clinical and experimental hypnosis*. New York: Macmillan, 1966.

Gottschaldt, K. Verber den Einfluss der Erfahrung auf die Wahrnemung von Figuren. *Psychol. Forsch.*, 1926, **8**, 261–317.

Gottschalk, L. A., & Auerbach, A. H. (Eds.) *Methods of research in psychotherapy.* New York: Appleton-Century-Crofts, 1966.

Gottschalk, L. A. et al. The measurement of emotional changes during a psychiatric interview: A working model toward quantifying the psychoanalytic concept of affect. In L. Gottschalk and A. Auerbach (Eds.), *Methods of research in psychotherapy.* New York: Appleton-Century-Crofts, 1966.

Gottschalk, L. A., & Gleser, G. C. Distinguishing characteristics of the verbal behavior of schizophrenic patients. In *Disorders of communication.* Baltimore: Williams and Wilkins, 1964.

Gough, H. G., & Heilbrun, A. B. *Manual for the Adjective Check List.* Palo Alto, Calif.: Consulting Psychologists Press, 1964.

Greenblatt, M., Levinson, D. J., & Williams, R. H. (Eds.) *The patient and the mental hospital.* Glencoe, Ill.: Free Press, 1957.

Greenwood, E. *Experimental sociology.* New York: Kings Crown Press, 1945.

Gregor, A. A. *Leitfaden der experimentallen psychopathologie.* Berlin: Karger, 1910.

Grosz, H. J., & Miller, I. Two factors limiting the reliability of the mecholyl test: Variability in day-to-day responses and dissimilarity between simultaneous bilateral determinations. *J. Nerv. Ment. Dis.,* 1958, **127,** 417–429.

Gruenberg, E. M. Epidemiology and medical care statistics. In M. Katz et al. (Eds.), *The role and methodology of classification in psychiatry and psychopathology.* Washington, D. C.: Public Health Service, 1968.

Guilford, J. P. *Personality.* New York: McGraw-Hill, 1959.

Guilford, J. P. *Fundamental statistics in psychology and education.* (4th ed.) New York: McGraw-Hill, 1965.

Guilford, J. P., & Zimmerman, W. S. *The Guilford Temperament Survey: Manual of instructions and interpretations.* Beverly Hills, Calif.: Sheridan Supply, 1949.

Guilford, J. P., & Zimmerman, W. S. Fourteen dimensions of temperament. *Psychol. Monogr.,* 1956, No. 417.

Haggard, E. A., Brekstad, A., & Skard, A. On the reliability of the anamnestic interview. *J. Abnorm. Soc. Psychol.,* 1960, **61,** 311–318.

Haggard, E. A., & Isaacs, K. S. Micromomentary facial expressions as indicators of ego mechanisms in psychotherapy. In. L. Gottschalk and A. Auerbach (Eds.), *Methods of research in psychotherapy.* New York: Appleton-Century-Crofts, 1966.

Hakerem, G. Pupillography. In P. Venables and I. Martin (Eds.), *Manual of psycho-physiological methods.* New York: Wiley, 1967.

Hall, K. R. L. Conditioning and learning techniques. In J. Zubin (Ed.), *Experimental abnormal psychology.* New York: Columbia University Bookstore, 1957.

Hamilton, G. V. T. *An introduction to objective psychopathology.* St. Louis: Mosby, 1925.

Harmon, H. H. *Modern Factor Analysis.* Chicago: University of Chicago Press, 1960.

Hathaway, S. R., & McKinley, J. C. *Minnesota Multiphasic Personality Inventory.* Minneapolis: University of Minnesota Press, 1942.

Hathaway, S. R., & McKinley, J. C. *The Minnesota Multiphasic Personality Inventory Manual (Revised).* New York: Psychological Corporation, 1951.

Hauri, P., Sawyer, J., & Rechtschaffen, A. Dimensions of dreaming: A factored scale for rating dream reports. *J. Abnorm. Psychol.*, 1967, **72**, 16–22.

Hays, W. L. *Statistics for psychologists.* New York: Holt, Rinehart and Winston, 1963.

Heath, R. G. Schizophrenia: Biochemical and physiologic aberrations. *Intl. J. Neuropsychiat.*, 1966, **2**, 597–610.

Heath, R. G. et al. Effect on behavior in humans with the administration of taraxein. *Amer. J. Psychiat.*, 1957, **114**, 14–24.

Heath, R. G. et al. Behavioral changes in nonpsychotic volunteers following administration of taraxein; the substance obtained from the serum of schizophrenic patients. *Amer. J. Psychiat.*, 1958, **114**, 917–924.

Hebb, D. O. Alice in Wonderland, or, psychology among the biological sciences. In H. Harlow and C. Woolsey (Eds.), *Biological and biochemical bases of behavior.* Madison: University of Wisconsin Press, 1958.

Hess, E. H. Pupillometric assessment. In J. Shlien et al. (Eds.), *Research in psychotherapy.* Vol. III. Washington, D. C.: American Psychological Association, 1968.

Heyns, R. H., & Lippitt, R. Systematic observational techniques. In G. Lindzey (Ed.), *Handbook of Social Psychology.* Reading, Mass.: AddisonWesley, 1954.

Hilgard, E. R. Hypnosis and experimental psychodynamics. In H. W. Brosin (Ed.), *Lectures on experimental psychiatry.* Pittsburgh: University of Pittsburgh Press, 1961.

Hill, D., & Parr, G. (Eds.) *Electroencephalography.* New York: Macmillan, 1963.

Hoagland, H. Metabolic and physiologic disturbances in the psychoses. In Milbank Memorial Fund, *The biology of mental health and disease.* New York: Hoeber, 1952.

Hoagland, H. Steroid hormones and events in the nervous system. In K. Elliot et al. (Eds.), *Neurochemistry: The chemical dynamics of brain and nerve.* Springfield, Ill.: Thomas, 1955.

Hoch, P., & Zubin, J. *Comparative epidemiology of the mental disorders.* New York: Grune and Stratton, 1961.

Hollingshead, A. B., & Redlich, F. C. *Social class and mental illness.* New York: Wiley, 1958.

Holt, R. R. Experimental methods in clinical psychology. In B. Wolman (Ed.), *Handbook of clinical psychology.* New York: McGraw-Hill, 1965.

Holtzman, W. H. Inkblot perception and personality: The meaning of inkblot variables. In E. Megargee (Ed.), *Research in clinical assessment.* New York: Harper and Row, 1966.

Holtzman, W. H. et al. *Inkblot perception and personality: Holtzman Inkblot Technique.* Austin: University of Texas Press, 1961.

Holzman, M. S., & Forman, V. P. A multidimensional content analysis system: Applied to the analysis of therapeutic technique in psychotherapy with schizophrenic patients. *Psychol. Bull.*, 1966, **66**, 263–281.

Huff, F. W. Learning and psychopathology. *Psychol. Bull.*, 1964, **61**, 459–468.

Humm, D. G. & Wadsworth, G. W. The Humm-Wadsworth Temperament Scale. *Amer. J. Psychiat.*, 1935, **92**, 163–200.

Hunt, R. G. Socio-cultural factors in mental disorder. *Behavioral Sci.,* 1959, **4,** 96–106.

Inglis, J. *The scientific study of abnormal behavior.* Chicago: Aldine, 1966.

Jackson, D. N., & Messick, S. Content and style in personality assessment. *Psychol. Bull.,* 1958, **55,** 243–252.

Jackson, D. N. & Messick, S. Response styles and the assessment of psychopathology. In S. Messick and J. Ross (Eds.), *Measurement in personality and cognition.* New York: Wiley, 1962.

Jackson, D. N., & Messick, S. (Eds.) *Problems in human assessment.* New York: McGraw-Hill, 1967.

Jaffe, J. An objective study of communication in psychiatric interviews. *J. Hillside. Hosp.,* 1957, **6,** 207–215.

Jaffe, J. Dyadic analysis of two psychotherapeutic interviews. In L. A. Gottschalk (Ed.), *Comparative psycholinguistic analysis of two psychotherapy interviews.* New York: International University Press, 1961.

Jaffe, J. Computer assessment of dyadic interaction rules from chronographic data. In J. Shlien et al. (Eds.), *Research in psychotherapy.* Vol. III. Washington, D. C.: American Psychological Association, 1968.

Jones, H. G. Learning and abnormal behavior. In H. J. Eysenck (Ed.), *Handbook of abnormal psychology.* New York: Basic Books, 1961.

Kahn, R. L., & Cannell, C. F. *The dynamics of interviewing.* New York: Wiley, 1957.

Kanfer, F. H. Verbal rate, content and adjustment ratings in experimentally structured interviews. *J. Abnorm. Soc. Psychol.,* 1959, **58,** 305–311.

Katz, D. Field studies. In L. Festinger and D. Katz (Eds.), *Research methods in the behavioral sciences.* New York: Dryden, 1953.

Katz, M. M. A phenomenological typology of schizophrenia. In M. Katz et al. (Eds.), *The role and methodology of classification in psychiatry and psychopathology.* Washington, D.C.: Public Health Service, 1968.

Keisler, D. J. Some myths of psychotherapy research and the search for a paradigm. *Psychol. Bull.,* 1966, **65,** 110–136.

Kelsey, F. O., Gullock, A. H., & Kelsey, F. E. Thyroid activity in hospitalized psychiatric patients. *AMA Arch. Neurol. Psychiat.,* 1955, **112,** 170–178.

Kempf, E. J. The behavior chart in mental disease. *Amer. J. Insanity,* 1915, **71,** 761–772.

Kerlinger, F. N. *Foundations of behavioral research.* New York: Holt, Rinehart and Winston, 1964.

Kety, S. S. Biochemical theories of schizophrenia. *Science,* 1959, **129,** 1528–1532.

King, H. E. *Psychomotor aspects of mental disease.* Cambridge, Mass.: Harvard University Press, 1954.

King, H. E. Psychomotor techniques. In J. Zubin (Ed.), *Experimental abnormal psychology.* New York: Columbia University Bookstore, 1957.

Kish, L. Selection of the sample. In L. Festinger and D. Katz (Eds.), *Research methods in the behavioral sciences.* New York: Dryden, 1953.

Kish, L. *Survey sampling.* New York: Wiley, 1965.

Kleinmuntz, B. *Personality measurement.* Homewood, Ill.: Dorsey, 1967.

Klerman, G. L. Assessing the influence of the hospital milieu upon the effectiveness of psychiatric drug therapy: Problems of conceptualization and of research methodology. *J. Nerv. Ment. Dis.,* 1963, **137,** 143–154.

Kline, N. S. Neuropsychiatric disorders. In S. Waife and A. Shapiro (Eds.), *The clinical evaluation of new drugs.* New York: Hoeber, 1959.

Kline, N. S. et al. The selection of psychiatric patients for research. *Amer J. Psychiat.,* 1953, **110,** 179–185.

Klopfer, B. et al. *Developments in the Rorschach Technique.* Vol. I. *Technique and theory.* Yonkers-on-Hudson, N.Y.: World Book, 1954.

Klopfer, B. et al. *Developments in the Rorschach Technique.* Vol. II. *Fields of application.* Yonkers-on-Hudson, N.Y.: World Book, 1956.

Kogan, L. S. Principles of measurement. In N. Polansky (Ed.), *Social work research.* Chicago: University of Chicago Press, 1960.

Kornetsky, C., Humphries, O., & Evarts, E. V. Comparison of psychological effects of certain centrally acting drugs in man. *Arch. Neurol. Psychiat.,* 1957, **77,** 318–324.

Kornhauser, A., & Sheatsley, P. B. Questionnaire construction and interview procedure. In C. Selltiz et al. (Eds.), *Research methods in social relations.* New York: Holt, 1959.

Kraepelin, E. *Ueber die Beinflussung einfacher psychisher Vorgange durch einige Arzneimittel: Experimentelle Untersuchungen.* Jena, 1892.

Kramer, E. Judgment of personal characteristics and emotions from nonverbal properties of speech. *Psychol. Bull.,* 1963, **60,** 408–420.

Kramer, M., & Greenhouse, S. W. Determination of sample size and selection of cases. In J. Cole and R. Gerard (Eds.), *Psychopharmacology: Problems in evaluation.* Washington, D. C.: National Academy of Sciences—National Research Council, 1959.

Krech, D., Rosenzweig, M. R., & Bennett, E. L. Effects of complex environment and blindness on rat brain. *AMA Arch. Neurol.,* 1963, **8,** 403–412.

Kubie, L. S. Psychoanalysis and scientific method. *J. Nerv. Ment. Dis.,* 1960, **131,** 495–512.

Lacey, J. I. Individual differences in somatic response patterns. *J. Comp. Physiol. Psychol.,* 1950, **43,** 338–350.

Lacey, J. I. Psychophysiological approaches to the evaluation of psychotherapeutic process and outcome. In E. Rubinstein and M. Parloff (Eds.), *Research in psychotherapy.* Washington, D. C.: American Psychological Association, 1959.

LaForge, R., & Suczek, R. F. The interpersonal dimension of personality: III. An interpersonal check list. *J. Pers.,* 1955, **24,** 94–112.

Lasagna, L., & Laties, V. G. Problems involved in the study of drug-modified behavior in normal humans. In J. Cole and R. Gerard (Eds.), *Psychopharmacology: Problems in evaluation.* Washington, D. C.: National Academy of Sciences—National Research Council, 1959.

Lasagna, L., & Meier, P. Experimental design and statistical problems. In S. Waite and A. Shapiro (Eds.), *The clinical evaluation of new drugs.* New York: Hoeber, 1959.

Lasagna, L., Mosteller, F., von Felsinger, J. M., & Beecher, H. K. A study of the placebo response. *Amer. J. Med.*, 1954, **16**, 770–779.

Lasagna, L., & von Felsinger, J. M. The volunteer subject in research. *Science*, 1954, **120**, 359–361.

Leach, B. E., Byers, L. W., & Heath, R. G. Methods for isolating taraxein: A survey of results. In R. G. Heath (Ed.), *Serological fractions in schizophrenia*. New York: Harper and Row, 1963.

Leary, T., & Gill, M. The dimensions and a measure of the process of psychotherapy. In E. Rubinstein and M. Parloff (Eds.), *Research in psychotherapy*. Washington, D. C.: American Psychological Association, 1959.

Lennard, H. L., & Bernstein, A. *The anatomy of psychotherapy: Systems of communication and expectation*. New York: Columbia University Press, 1960.

Levitt, E. E. *The psychology of anxiety*. Indianapolis: Bobbs-Merrill, 1966.

Levy, D. M. Use of play technique as experimental procedure. *Amer. J. Orthopsychiat.*, 1933, **3**, 266–277.

Lindegard, B. Variations in human body-build. *Acta Psychiatrica & Neurologica*, 1953, **86**, 1–163.

Lindegard, B., & Nyman, G. E. Interrelations between psychologic, somatologic, and endocrine dimensions. *Lunds Universitets Arsskrift*, 1956, **52**, 1–54.

Lindeman, J. E., Fairweather, G. W., Stone, G. B., Smith, R. S., & London, I. T. The use of demographic characteristics in predicting length of neuropsychiatric hospital stay. *J. Consult. Psychol.*, 1959, **23**, 55–60.

Lindsley, D. B. Psychophysiology and motivation. In M. Jones (Ed.), *Nebraska symposium on motivation*. Lincoln, Neb.: University of Nebraska Press, 1958.

Lindsley, O. R. Operant conditioning methods applied to research in chronic schizophrenia. *Psychiat. Res. Rpts.*, 1956, **5**, 118–139.

Lindzey, G. Thematic apperception test: Interpretive assumptions and related empirical evidence. *Psychol. Bull.*, 1952, **49**, 1–25.

Lindzey, G. On the classification of projective techniques. *Psychol. Bull.*, 1959, 56, 158–168.

Lindzey, G., Lykken, D. T., & Winston, H. P. Infantile trauma, genetic factors, and adult temperament. *J. Abnorm. Soc. Psychol.*, 1960, **61**, 7–14.

Lindzey, G., & Aronson, E. (Eds.) *Handbook of social psychology*. (2nd. ed.) Vol. 2. Reading, Mass.: Addison-Wesley, 1968.

Lindzey, G., & Goldwyn, R. M. Validity of the Rosenzweig picture-frustration study. *J. Pers.*, 1954, **22**, 519–547.

Loevinger, J. Objective tests as instruments of psychological theory. *Psychol. Rpts.*, 1957, **3**, 635–694.

Loevinger, J. Conflict of committment in clinical research. *Amer. Psychol.*, 1963, **18**, 241–251.

Lorenz, M., & Cobb, S. Language patterns in psychotic and psychoneurotic patients. *AMA Arch. Neurol. Psychiat.*, 1954, **72**, 665–673.

Lorr, M. Rating scales, behavior inventories, and drugs. In. L. Uhr and J. Miller (Eds.), *Drugs and behavior*. New York: Wiley, 1960.

Lorr, M. et al. *Inpatient Multidimensional Psychiatric Scale Manual*. Palo Alto: Calif. Consulting Psychologists Press, 1962.

Lorr, M., Klett, C. J., & McNair, D. M. *Syndromes of Psychosis.* New York: Macmillan, 1963.

Lowenstein, O., & Friedman, E. D. Present state of pupillography: Its method and diagnostic significance. *Arch. Opthalmol.,* 1942, **27,** 969–993.

Lowenstein, O., & Lowenfeld, I. E. Electronic pupillography. *Arch. Opthalmol.,* 1958, **59,** 352–363.

Luchins, A. S. Mechanization in problem solving: The effect of *Einstellung. Psychol. Monogr.,* 1942, **54,** No. 6.

Luchins, A. S. On recent usage of the *Einstellung*-effect as a test of rigidity. *J. Consult. Psychol.,* 1951, **15,** 89–94.

Lykken, D. A study of anxiety in the sociopathic personality. *J. Abnorm. Soc. Psychol.,* 1957, **55,** 6–10.

Maccoby, E. E., & Maccoby, N. The interview: A tool of social science. In G. Lindzey (Ed.), *Handbook of social psychology.* Reading, Mass.: Addison-Wesley, 1954.

Machover, K. *Personality projection in the drawing of the human figure.* Springfield, Ill.: Thomas, 1948.

Macht, D. I. Pharmacologic reactions of normal and psychotic blood serums. *South. Med. J.,* 1950, **43,** 1049–1056.

Maher, B. A. *Principles of psychopathology.* New York: McGraw-Hill, 1966.

Maher, B. *An introduction to research in psychopathology.* New York: McGraw-Hill, 1969.

Mahl, G. F. Measuring the patient's anxiety during interview from "expressive" aspects of his speech. *Trans. N. Y. Acad. Sci.,* 1959, **21,** 249–257.

Mahl, G. F. Gestures and body movements in interviews. In J. Shlien et al. (Eds.), *Research in psychotherapy.* Vol. III. Washington, D. C.: American Psychological Association, 1968.

Mahrer, A. (Ed.) *New approaches to personality classification.* New York: Columbia University Press, 1970.

Malmo, R. B. Activation. In A. Bachrach (Ed.), *Experimental foundations of clinical psychology.* New York: Basic Books, 1961.

Malmo, R. B., Shagass, C., & David, F. H. Electromyographic studies of muscular tension in psychiatric patients under stress. *J. Clin. Exp. Psychopathol.,* 1951, **12,** 45–66.

Mann, M. B. The quantitative differentiation of samples of spoken language. *Psychol. Monogr.,* 1944, **56,** No. 255, 41–74.

Marks, P. A., & Seeman, W. *The actuarial description of abnormal personality: An atlas for use with the MMPI.* Baltimore: Williams and Wilkins, 1963.

Marsden, G. Content-analysis studies of therapeutic interviews: 1954 to 1964. *Psychol. Bull.,* 1965, **63,** 298–321.

Martin, B. The assessment of anxiety by physiological behavioral measures. *Psychol. Bull.,* 1961, **58,** 234–255.

Martin, I. Somatic reactivity. In H. J. Eysenck (Ed.), *Handbook of abnormal psychology.* New York: Basic Books, 1961.

Martin, I., & Davis, B. M. Sleep thresholds in depression. *J. Ment. Sci.,* 1962, **108,** 466–473.

Martin, I., & Davis, B. M. The effect of sodium amytal on autonomic and muscle activity in patients with depressive illness. *Brit. J. Psychiat.*, 1965, **11,** 168–175.

Matarazzo, J. D. Prescribed behavior therapy: Suggestions from interview research. In A. Bachrach (Ed.), *Experimental foundations of clinical psychology.* New York: Basic Books, 1961.

Matarazzo, J. D. The interview. In B. Wolman (Ed.), *Handbook of clinical psychology.* New York: McGraw-Hill, 1965.

Matarazzo, J. D. et al. Speech and silence behavior in clinical psychotherapy and its laboratory correlates. In J. Shlien et al. (Eds.), *Research in psychotherapy.* Vol. III. Washington, D.C.: American Psychological Association, 1968.

Maudsley, H. *The pathology of mind: A study of its distempers, deformities, and disorders.* London: Macmillan, 1895.

McGeer, P. L. et al. Aromatic excretory pattern in schizophrenics. *Science,* 1956, **123,** 1029–1030. (a)

McGeer, P. L. et al. Relation of aromatic amino acids to excretory pattern of schizophrenics. *Science,* 1956, **123,** 1078–1080. (b)

McGuighan, F. J. *Experimental psychology: A methodological approach.* Englewood Cliffs, N.J.: Prentice-Hall, 1968.

McNemar, Q. *Psychological statistics.* (3rd ed.) New York: Wiley, 1962.

Mednick, S. A., & Schulsinger, F. Factors related to breakdown in children at high risk for schizophrenia. In M. Roff and D. F. Ricks (Eds.), *Life history research in psychopathology.* Minneapolis: University of Minnesota Press, 1970.

Meehl, P. E. & Rosen, A. Antecedent probability and the efficiency of psychometric signs, patterns, or cutting scores. *Psychol. Bull.,* 1955, **52,** 194–216.

Meehl, P. E., Schofield, W., Glueck, B. C.., & Clyde, D. J. *Minnesota-Hartford Personality Assay.* Hartford: Institute of Living, 1965.

Megargee, E. I. (Ed.) *Research methods in clinical assessment.* New York: Harper and Row, 1966.

Meyer, V. Psychological effects of brain damage. In H. J. Sysenck (Ed.), *Handbook of abnormal psychology.* New York: Basic Books, 1961.

Michigan Department of Mental Health. *Michigan Picture Test Manual.* Chicago: Science Research Associates, 1953.

Milbank Memorial Fund. *Causes of mental disorders: A review of epidemiological knowledge,* 1961.

Miller, N. E. Experiments relating Freudian displacement to generalization of conditioning. *Psychol. Bull.,* 1939, **36,** 516–517.

Millon, T. *Theories of psychopathology.* Philadelphia: Saunders, 1967.

Millon, T. *Modern psychopathology.* Philadelphia: Saunders, 1969.

Millon, T. *Millon-Illinois Self-Report Inventory Manual: Provisional and Research Forms.* (Limited to research investigators), 1972.

Mischel, W. *Personality and assessment.* New York: Wiley, 1968.

Morgan, C. D., & Murray, H. A. A method for investigating fantasies: The Thematic Apperception Test. *AMA Arch. Neurol. Psychiat.,* 1935, **34,** 289–306.

Mosteller, F., & Bush, R. R. Selected quantitative techniques. In G. Lindzey (Ed.), *Handbook of social pshchology.* Reading, Mass.: Addison-Wesley, 1954.

Murphy, L. B. *Personality in young children.* New York: Basic Books, 1956.

Murphy, L. B. et al. *The widening world of childhood.* New York: Basic Books, 1962.

Murstein, B. I. *Theory and research in projective techniques (emphasizing the TAT).* New York: Wiley, 1963.

Murstein, B. I. *Handbook of projective techniques.* New York: Basic Books, 1965.

Nowlis, V. Research with the Mood Adjective Checklist. In S. S. Tomkins and C. E. Izard (Eds.), *Affect, Cognition and personality.* New York: Springer, 1965.

Nowlis, V., & Nowlis, H. H. The description and analysis of mood. *Ann. N. Y. Acad. Sci.,* 1956, **65,** 345–355.

Nunnally, J. Analysis of profile data. *Psychol. Bull.,* 1962, **58,** 311–319.

Olds, J. Pleasure centers in the brain. *Scient. Amer.,* 1956, **195,** 105–116.

Olds, J. Self-stimulation of the brain. *Science,* 1958, **127,** 315–323.

Olds, J. Hypothalamic substrates of reward. *Physiol. Rev.,* 1962, **42,** 554–604.

Osgood, C. E., & Walker, E. G. Motivation and language behavior: A content analysis of suicide notes. *J. Abnorm. Soc. Psychol.,* 1959, **59,** 58–67.

Overall, J. E. A configural analysis of psychiatric diagnostic stereotypes. *Behavioral Sci.,* 1963, **8,** 211–219.

Overall, J. E., & Gorham, D. R. The Brief Psychiatric Rating Scale. *Psychol. Rep.,* 1962, **10,** 799–812.

Overall, J. E., & Hollister, L. E. Studies of quantitative approaches to psychiatric classification. In M. Katz et al. (Eds.), *The role and methodology of classification in psychology and psychopathology.* Washington, D. C.: Public Health Service, 1968.

Ozek, M. Untersuchungen uber den Kupferstoffwechsel im schizophrenen Formankreis. *Arch. Psychiat.,* 1957, **195,** 408–423.

Pande, S. K., & Gart, J. J. A method to quantify reciprocal influence between therapist and patient in psychotherapy. In J. Shlien et al. (Eds.), *Research in psychotherapy.* Vol. III. Washington, D. C.: American Psychological Association, 1968.

Paul, G. L. Behavior modification research: Design and tactics. In C. M. Franks (Ed.), *Assessment and status of the behavior therapies and associated developments.* New York: McGraw-Hill, 1969.

Payne, R. W. Cognitive abnormalities. In H. J. Eysenck (Ed.), *Handbook of abnormal psychology.* New York: Basic Books, 1961.

Pearson, J. S., & Swenson, W. M. *A user's guide to the Mayo Clinic automated MMPI program.* New York: Psychological Corporation, 1967.

Peck, R. E. The SHP Test: An aid in the detection and measurement of depression. *AMA Arch. Gen. Psychiat.,* 1959, **1,** 35–40.

Peretz, O., Alpert, M., & Friedhoff, A. Prognostic factors in the evaluation of therapies. In P. Hoch and J. Zubin (Eds.), *The evaluation of psychiatric treatment.* New York: Grune and Stratton, 1964.

Peters, H. N. The mirror tracing test as a measure of social maladaptation. *J. Abnorm. Soc. Psychol.,* 1946, **41,** 437–448.

Piotrowski, Z. A. *Perceptanalysis.* New York: Macmillan, 1957.

Plunkett, R. J., & Gordon, J. E. *Epidemiology and mental illness.* New York: Basic Books, 1960.

Pollin, W., & Perlin, S. Psychiatric evaluation of "normal control" volunteers. *Amer. J. Psychiat.,* 1958, **115,** 129–133.

Pool, I. (Ed.) *Trends in content analysis.* Urbana, Ill.: University of Illinois Press, 1959.

Raimy, V. C. Self reference in counseling interviews. *J. Consult. Psychol.,* 1948, **12,** 153–163.

Rapaport, D. *Organization and pathology of thought.* New York: Columbia University Press, 1951.

Rees, L. Constitutional factors and abnormal behavior. In H. J. Eysenck (Ed.), *Handbook of abnormal psychology.* New York: Basic Books, 1961.

Rees, L. & Eysenck, H. J. A factorial study of some morphological and psychological aspects of human constitution. *J. Ment. Sci.,* 1945, **91,** 8.

Reiss, M. Investigations into psychoendocrinology. *Internat. Rec. Med.,* 1953, **166,** 196–203.

Richardson, S. A., Dohrenwald, B. S., & Klein, D. *Interviewing: Its forms and functions.* New York: Basic Books, 1965.

Rickels, K. Psychopharmacologic agents: Patient and doctor variables. *J. Nerv. Ment. Dis.,* 1963, **136,** 540–549.

Riggs, M. M., & Kaess, W. Personality differences between volunteers and nonvolunteers. *J. Psychol.,* 1955, **40,** 229–245.

Roback, H. B. Human figure drawings: Their utility in the clinical psychologist's armamentarium for personality assessment. *Psychol. Bull.,* 1968, **70,** 20–44.

Roche Report. Applying computer procedures to hospital psychiatry. *Frontier Hospit. Psychiat.,* 1966, **3,** No. 19, 1–10.

Roff, M., & Ricks, D. F. (Eds.) *Life history research in psychopathology.* Minneapolis: University of Minnesota Press, 1970.

Rogers, C. R., & Dymond, R. F. (Eds.) *Psychotherapy and personality change.* Chicago: University of Chicago Press, 1954.

Roizin, L. Neuropathology. In S. Arieti (Ed.), *American handbook of psychiatry.* New York: Basic Books, 1959.

Rorschach, H. *Psychodiagnostics.* Berne: Hans Huber, 1942.

Rose, J. T. The Funkenstein Test: A review of the literature. *Acta. Psychiat. Scand.,* 1962, **38,** 124–153.

Rosenthal, R. *Experimenter effects in behavioral research.* New York: Appleton-Century-Crofts, 1966.

Rosenzewig, S. The picture-association method and its application in a study of reactions to frustration. *J. Pers.,* 1945, **14,** 3–23.

Rotter, J. B., & Rafferty, J. E. *The Rotter Incomplete Sentences Blank Manual.* New York: Psychological Corporation, 1952.

Rotter, J. B., & Willerman, B. The incomplete sentence test. *J. Consult. Psychol.* 1947, **11,** 43–48.

Sabshin, M., & Ramot, J. Pharmacotherapeutic evaluation and the psychiatric setting. *AMA Arch. Neurol. Psychiat.,* 1956, **75,** 362–370.

Sargent, H. D. Projective methods; Their origin, theory and application in personality research. *Psychol. Bull,* 1945, **42,** 257–293.

Sargent, H. D. *The Insight Test.* New York: Grune and Stratton, 1955.

Schafer, R. *Psychoanalytic interpretation in Rorschach testing.* New York: Grune and Stratton, 1954.

Schapiro, A. K. An attempt to demonstrate a catatonigenic agent in cerebrospinal fluid of catatonic schizophrenic patients. *J. Nerv. Ment. Dis.,* 1956, **123,** 65–71.

Scheflen, A. E. Communication systems such as psychotherapy. In J. H. Masserman (Ed.), *Current psychiatric therapies.* Vol. 5. New York: Grune and Stratton, 1965.

Schneider, R. A., Costiloe, M. S., Yamamoto, J., & Lester, B. K. Estimation of central sympathetic reactivity using the blood pressure response to methacholine (mecholyl). *Psychiat. Res. Rpts.,* 1960, **12,** 149–160.

Schneidman, E. S. Schizophrenia and the MAPS test. *Genet. Psychol. Monogr.,* 1948, **38,** 145–224.

Schneidman, E. S. (Ed.) *Thematic test analysis.* New York: Grune and Stratton, 1951.

Schneidman, E. S. Manual for the MAPS test. *Proj. Tech. Monogr.,* 1952, **1,** No. 2, 1–92.

Scott, W. A. Research definitions of mental health and mental illness. *Psychol. Bull.,* 1958, **55,** 29–45.

Scott, W. A., & Wertheimer, M. *Introduction to psychological research.* New York: Wiley, 1962.

Sears, R. R. et al. Some child-rearing antecedents of aggression and dependence in young children. *Genet. Psychol. Monogr.,* 1953, **47,** 135–236.

Sechrest, L. Incremental validity: A recommendation. *Educ. Psychol. Measmt.,* 1963, **23,** 153–158.

Selltiz, C., Jahoda, M., Deutch, M., & Cook, S. (Eds.) *Research methods in social relations.* (Rev. ed.) New York: Holt, 1959.

Senders, V. L. A comment on Burke's additive scales and statistics. *Psychol. Rev.,* 1953, **60,** 423–424.

Sexton, M. C. The autokinetic test: Its value in psychiatric diagnosis and prognosis. *Amer. J. Psychiat.,* 1945, **102,** 399–404.

Shagass, C. The Sedation Threshold: A method for estimating tension in psychiatric patients. *Electroenceph. Clin. Neurophysiol.,* 1954, **6,** 221–233.

Shagass, C. Sedation Threshold: A neurophysiological tool for psychosomatic research. *Psychosom. Med.,* 1956, **18,** 410–419.

Shagass, C. Neurophysiological studies of anxiety and depression. *Psychiat. Res. Rpts.,* 1958, **8,** 100–117.

Shagass, C., & Kerenyi, A. B. "Sleep" Threshold techniques. *Psychiat. Res. Rpts.,* 1959, **11,** 59–65.

Shakow, D. The recorded psychoanalytic interview as an objective approach to research in psychoanalysis. *Psychoanal. Quart.,* 1960, **29,** 82–97.

Shapiro, M. B. The single case in clinical-psychological research. *J. Gen. Psychol.,* 1966, **74,** 3–23.

Sheer, D. (Ed.) *Electrical stimulation of the brain*. Austin: University of Texas Press, 1961.

Sheldon, W. H., & Stevens, S. S. *The varieties of temperament*. New York: Harper, 1942.

Sheldon, W. H., Stevens, S. S., & Tucker, W. B. *The varieties of human physique*. New York: Harper, 1940.

Sherman, L. J. The significant variables in psychopharmaceutic research. *Amer. J. Psychiat.*, 1959, **116**, 208–214.

Shlien, J. M. et al. (Eds.) *Research in psychotherapy*. Vol. III. Washington, D. C.: American Psychological Association, 1968.

Shontz, F. C. *Research methods in personality*. New York: Appleton-Century-Crofts, 1965.

Silverman, L. H., & Spiro, R. H. Further investigation of the effects of subliminal aggressive stimulation on the ego functioning of schizophrenics. *J. Cons. Psychol.*, 1967, **31**, 225–232.

Simon, J. L. *Basic research methods in social science*. New York: Random House, 1969.

Singer, J. L. *Daydreaming: An introduction to the experimental study of inner experience*. New York: Random House, 1966.

Sjoberg, G., & Nett, R. *A methodology for social research*. New York: Harper and Row, 1968.

Skinner, B. F. Critique of psychoanalytic concepts and theories. *Scientific Monthly*, 1954, **79**, 300–305.

Skinner, B. F. What is psychotic behavior? In *Theory and treatment of mental disorders*. St. Louis: Washington University Press, 1956.

Slater, P. E., Morimoto, K., & Hyde, R. W. The effect of group administration upon symptom formation under LSD, *J. Nerv. Ment. Dis.*, 1957, **125**, 312–317.

Sloane, R. B., & Lewis, D. J. Prognostic value of adrenaline and mecholyl responses in electroconvulsive therapy. *J. Psychosom. Res.*, 1956, **1**, 273–286.

Smith, K., & Sines, J. O. Demonstration of a peculiar odor in the sweat of schizophrenic patients. *AMA Arch. Gen. Psychiat.*, 1960, **2**, 184–188.

Sogliani, G. Ricerca di proprieta catatonigene nel siero di sangue e nel liquor cefalorachidiano umano. *Cervello*, 1938, **17**, 253–279.

Solomon, S. Clinical neurology and neuropathology. In A. Freedman and H. Kaplan (Eds.), *Comprehensive textbook of psychiatry*. Baltimore: Williams and Wilkins, 1967.

Spielberger, C. D. Theory and research on anxiety. In C. D. Spielberger (Ed.), *Anxiety and behavior*. New York: Academic Press, 1966.

Spiker, C. C. Research methods in children's learning. In P. Mussen (Ed.), *Handbook of research methods in child development*. New York: Wiley, 1960.

Spitzer, R. L. The Mental Status Schedule: Potential use as a criterion measure of change in psychotherapy research. *Amer. J. Psychother.*, 1966, **20**, 156–167.

Spitzer, R. L. et al. The Mental Status Schedule: Rationale, reliability, validity. *Comprehen. Psychiat.*, 1964, **5**, 384–395.

Stanton, A. H., & Schwartz, M. S. *The mental hospital*. New York: Basic Books, 1954.

Starkweather, J. A. Content-free speech as a source of information about the speaker. *J. Abnorm. Soc. Psychol.*, 1956, **52**, 394–402.

Stephenson, W. Some observations on Q-technique. *Psychol. Bull.*, 1952, **49**, 483–498.

Stern, J. A., & McDonald, D. G. Physiological correlates of mental disease. In P. Farnsworth et al. (Eds.), *Annual review of psychology.* Vol. 16. Palo Alto, Calif.: Annual Reviews, 1965.

Stern, J. A., Ulett, G. A., & Smith, K. Effect of blood plasma from psychotic patients upon activity levels of white rats. *Amer. J. Psychiat.*, 1958, **115**, 465–466.

Stevens, S. S. (Ed.) *Handbook of experimental psychology.* New York: Wiley, 1951.

Stevens, S. S. Measurement, psychophysics, and utility. In C. Churchman and P. Ratoosh (Eds.), *Measurement: Definitions and theories.* New York: Wiley, 1959.

Stone, P. J. et al. The general inquirer: A computer system for content analysis and retrieval based upon the sentence as a unit of information. *Behavioral Sci.*, 1962, **7**, 1–15.

Swenson, C. H. Empirical evaluation of human figure drawings. *Psychol. Bull.*, 1957, **54**, 431–466.

Swenson, C. H. Empirical evluations of human figure drawings.: 1957–1966. *Psychol. Bull.*, 1968, **70**, 20–44.

Tart, C. T. Toward the experimental control of dreaming: A review of the literature. *Psychol. Bull.*, 1965, **64**, 81–90.

Taylor, D. W. et al. Education for research in psychology. *Amer. Psychol.*, 1959, **14**, 167–179.

Taylor, J. A. The relationship of anxiety to the conditioned eyelid response. *J. Exp. Psychol.*, 1951, **41**, 81–92.

Taylor, J. A. A personality scale of manifest anxiety. *J. Abnorm. Soc. Psychol.*, 1953, **48**, 285–290.

Thomas, A. et al. *Behavioral individuality in early childhood.* New York: New York University Press, 1963.

Thomas, A., Chess, S., & Birch, H. B. *Temperament and behavior disorders in children.* New York: New York University Press, 1968.

Thorpe, J. G. The current status of prognostic test indicators for electroconvulsive therapy. *Psychosom. Med.*, 1962, **24**, 554–567.

Torgerson, W. *Theory and methods of scaling.* New York: Wiley, 1958.

Trager, G. L. Paralanguage: A first approximation. *Stud. Linguist.*, 1958, **13**, 1–12.

Uhr, L., & Miller, J. G. (Eds.) *Drugs and behavior.* New York: Wiley, 1960.

Underwood, B. J. *Psychological research.* New York: Appleton-Century-Crofts, 1957.

Underwood, B. J. *Problems in experimental design and inference.* New York: Appleton-Century-Crofts, 1966.

Venables, P. H., & Martin, I. *Manual of psycho-physiological methods.* New York: Wiley, 1967.

Voth, A. C. An experimental study of mental patients through the autokinetic phenomenon. *Amer. J. Psychiat.*, 1947, **103**, 793–805.

Wald, A. *Sequential analysis.* New York: Wiley, 1947.

Weitzenhoffer, A. *General techniques of hypnotism.* New York: Grune and Stratton, 1953.

Wessman, A. E., & Ricks, D. F. *Mood and personality.* New York: Holt, Rinehart and Winston, 1966.

Whatmore, G. B., & Ellis, R. M. Some motor aspects of schizophrenia. *Amer. J. Psychiat.,* 1958, **114,** 882–889.

Whatmore, G. B., & Ellis, R. M. Some neurophysiologic aspects of depressed states: An electromyographic study. *AMA Arch. Gen. Psychiat.,* 1959, **1,** 70–80.

Whatmore, G. B., & Ellis, R. M. Further neurophysiologic aspects of depressed states: An electromyographic study. *AMA Arch. Gen. Psychiat.,* 1962, **6,** 243–253.

Winter, C. A., & Flataker, L. Effect of blood plasma from psychotic patients upon performance of trained rats. *AMA Arch. Neurol. Psychiat.,* 1958, **80,** 411–419.

Witkin, H. A. Individual differences in ease of perception of embedded figures. *J. Pers.,* 1950, **19,** 1–15.

Witkin H. A. Psychological differentiation and forms of pathology. *J. Abnorm. Psychol.,* 1965, **70,** 317–336.

Witkin, H. A. et al. *Personality through perception: An experimental and clinical study.* New York: Harper, 1954.

Witkin, H. A. et al. *Psychological differentiation.* New York: Wiley, 1962.

Witkin, H. A., & Lewis, H. B. (Eds.) *Experimental studies of dreaming.* New York: Random House, 1967.

Wittenborn, J. R. Symptom patterns in a group of mental patients. *J. Consult. Psychol.,* 1950, **15,** 290–302.

Wolberg, L. R. Hypnotherapy. In S. Arieti (Ed.), *American handbook of psychiatry.* New York: Basic Books, 1959.

Yacorzynski, G. K. Organic mental disorders. In B. Wolman (Ed.), *Handbook of clinical psychology.* New York: McGraw-Hill, 1965.

Yarrow, M. R., Campbell, J. D., & Burton, R. V. Reliability of maternal retrospection: A preliminary report. *Family Process,* 1964, **3,** 207–218.

Yates, A. Abnormalities of psychomotor functions. In H. J. Eysenck (Ed.), *Handbook of abnormal psychology.* New York: Basic Books, 1961.

Zubin, J. The determination of response patterns in personality inventories. *J. Educ. Psychol.,* 1937, **28,** 401–413.

Zubin, J. Role of prognostic indicators in the evaluation of therapy. In J. Cole and R. Gerard (Eds.), *Psychopharmacology: Problems in evaluation.* Washington, D.C.: National Academy of Science—National Research Council, 1959.

Zubin, J. (Ed.) *Field studies in the mental disorders.* New York: Grune and Stratton, 1961.

Zubin, J., Eron, L. D., & Schumer, F. *An experimental approach to projective techniques.* New York: Wiley, 1965.

Zubin, J. et al. *Experimental abnormal psychology.* New York: Columbia University Bookstore, 1957, 1960.

Zuckerman, M., & Lubin, B. *Manual for the Multiple Affect Adjective Check List.* San Diego: Educational and Industrial Testing Service, 1966.

AUTHOR INDEX

SUBJECT INDEX